DATE

D1006929

Two presidents are better than one

Two
presidents
are better
than one

The case for a
bipartisan
executive branch

David Orentlicher

New York University Press
New York and London

New York University Press
New York and London
www.nyupress.org

References to Internet websites (URLs) were accurate at the time of writing.
Neither the author nor New York University Press is responsible for URLs
that may have expired or changed since the manuscript was prepared.

Library of Congress Cataloging-in-Publication Data
Orentlicher, David, 1955–
Two presidents are better than one : the case for a bipartisan executive branch /
David Orentlicher.
pages   cm
Includes bibliographical references and index.
ISBN 978-0-8147-8949-0 (cl : alk. paper)
ISBN 978-0-8147-2468-2 (e-book)
ISBN 978-0-8147-2445-3 (e-book)
1. Presidents—United States. 2. Executive departments—United States.
3. Political leadership—United States. 4. United States—Politics and
government—Decision making.   I. Title.
JK516.O75 2013
352.230973—dc23   2012039902

New York University Press books are printed on acid-free paper,
and their binding materials are chosen for strength and durability.
We strive to use environmentally responsible suppliers and materials
to the greatest extent possible in publishing our books.

Manufactured in the United States of America

10 9 8 7 6 5 4 3 2 1

To Judy, Cy, and Shayna
for their inspiration

Contents

Preface

This book is about the very high price the United States pays for its one-person presidency and how it can avoid those costs by adopting a two-person presidency.

When the framers of the Constitution decided to divide the legislative power between a House and Senate and rest an undivided executive power in a single president, they paved the way for the development of the "imperial presidency." Presidents have assumed far more power than was intended by the founding fathers and far more power than is good for the country.

The framers not only gave the United States a one-*person* presidency; they also gave it a one-*party* presidency. One party controls the immense power of the modern White House. This has fostered the high levels of partisan conflict that prevent Congress and the president from addressing pressing problems facing the country. A one-party presidency also prevents chief executives from recognizing the entire citizenry as their real constituency, leaving half or more of the public feeling unrepresented in the Oval Office.

I began my thinking for this book while immersed in partisan conflict during my six years as a member of the Indiana House of

Representatives. I quickly found that whether in Washington, DC, or Indiana, partisan conflict is not a phenomenon of the people we elect but of the political system that we elect them into. More specifically, I recognized that we will see high levels of partisan conflict at the national level as long as we have a one-person presidency. Every four years, we elect a president, and for the next four years, members of the party out of office try to block the president's initiatives. Indeed, the next presidential campaign begins within twenty-four hours of Election Day. If we want a more bipartisan ethic in Washington, we need to change the structure of the executive branch.

This is not surprising. James Madison rightly observed that the best way to encourage desirable political behavior is through appropriate design of the political system. Scholars can urge elected officers to govern in a bipartisan fashion, but appeals to virtue are far less successful than structural features that channel behavior in the right direction. Accordingly, if we are to lessen partisan conflict, we need to change the constitutional blueprint. Expanding representation in the White House beyond one political party can provide a much better incentive for cooperation across party lines.

A two-person presidency also could address the other problems that the one-person presidency has spawned. It would restore the balance of power between the executive and legislative branches, and by requiring a sharing of executive power across party lines, it would ensure a voice for the overwhelming majority of voters in the Oval Office.

A two-person executive may seem odd to Americans used to a one-person presidency. But plural executives are much more the norm in western Europe and other parts of the world. The United States would do well to learn from the experience of other countries with executive power that is divided and shared.

I owe a particular debt of gratitude to Judy Failer, who encouraged me to develop my thinking about a two-person presidency into a book and who provided superb feedback and insights from the beginning of the process through final publication.

I also am grateful for the commitment of Deborah Gershenowitz and her NYU Press colleagues to this project and their excellent editorial and publishing guidance. It was a pleasure to work with Deborah, Despina Papazoglou Gimbel, Constance Grady, Mary Beth Jarrad, Andrew Katz, Jodi Narde, Clara Platter, and Betsy Steve.

I have benefited considerably in the writing of this book from the thoughtful comments of Randall Bezanson, Subir Chakrabarti, Kathleen Clark, Dan Dalton, Talia Einhorn, Robert Elgie, Mark Graber, Deborah Hellman, Herbert Hovenkamp, Richard Izquierdo, Arend Lijphart, Gerard Magliocca, Scott Page, John Reitz, William Scheuerman, William Schneider, Ellen Waldman, and the anonymous peers who reviewed my manuscript.

I also have benefited from participants in faculty workshops at Indiana University Maurer School of Law, Indiana University Robert H. McKinney School of Law, University of Iowa College of Law, and S.J. Quinney College of Law at the University of Utah and from participants in sessions at annual meetings of the American Political Science Association, Law and Society Association, and Midwest Political Science Association.

I am grateful for the excellent research and editing assistance of Robin Bandy, John Bergstrom, Bianca Buechner, Courtney Campbell, Robert Courtney, Deborah Denslaw, Daniel Hageman, Miriam Murphy, Ryan Schwier, Jocelyn Sisson, Gregory Taylor, and Taylor Wright.

Financial support for this project was provided by summer research grants from Indiana University Robert H. McKinney School of Law.

1

Introduction

Weary after eight years of George W. Bush and Republican leadership, Americans voted in a big way for change in 2008. A strong economy had been shattered by the Great Recession, and U.S. troops had suffered thousands of casualties in two wars that yielded imperceptible gains for national security. The public believed it could restore peace and prosperity by sweeping out the GOP and bringing back the Democrats. Barack Obama won a resounding victory for the presidency, with two-thirds of the electoral vote, and Democrats gained dominant majorities in the House and Senate.

Two years later, with the economy still floundering and soldiers still dying, Americans again voted in a big way for change. Republicans picked up sixty-three seats in the U.S. House, regaining the majority. They also won six seats in the U.S. Senate, leaving Democrats with a narrow margin and an inability to overcome GOP-led filibusters. But turning to new leaders failed once again to solve the country's challenges. House Republicans proposed unpopular reforms such as their idea to privatize Medicare, many party leaders took a hard line on immigration and reproductive issues, and public enthusiasm dimmed quickly. In 2012, the public preferred the Democratic Party again, reelecting Obama with 62 percent of the electoral vote. In addition, Democrats increased their working majority in the Senate from six to ten seats and picked up ground in the House.

Americans think they can fix their problems by finding better elected officials to run the government. But America's problems lie not in the candidates the voters elect; rather, they lie in the political system into which candidates are elected.

Indeed, by all accounts, the system is broken. Once public officials arrive in Washington, they become more interested in winning partisan victories than promoting the public interest. According to Senate Minority Leader Mitch McConnell in November 2010, "the single most important thing" that he and his Republican colleagues could achieve was for "President Obama to be a one-term president."[1] Obama's predecessor, George W. Bush, faced similar hostility from Democratic legislators. When Bush tried to restructure Social Security during his second term, Capitol Hill Democrats decided that opposition would be their "highest priority." By choosing obstruction over negotiation, Democrats were able to block Bush's proposal for private Social Security accounts and to weaken him politically, but they also prevented any meaningful effort to secure the long-term solvency of the Social Security system.[2]

Instead of solving problems such as the struggling economy, global warming, and budget deficits, elected officials often make the problems worse. The debt ceiling crisis of 2011 is illustrative. When Democrats and Republicans could not settle on a long-term solution to close the nation's budget gap, the United States suffered the first lowering of its credit rating in the country's history.

Not surprisingly, the public is disgusted. Approval ratings for Congress reached an all-time low of 10 percent in February and August 2012, and they have generally fallen below 20 percent in Gallup polls since May 2011.

As these ratings suggest, observers lay most of the blame for political dysfunction with Congress. Partisan polarization has left legislators too keen to support a president from their party and too eager to obstruct a president from the other party. The moderate center that can cut bipartisan deals no longer exists. In this view, we can fix Washington if we reform Capitol Hill.

But focusing on Congress is like dealing with the symptoms rather than the causes of an illness. The problems with Congress are largely the result of a deeper problem with the U.S. political system—the decision by the founding fathers to place a single president atop the executive branch. When one person exercises the enormous power of the modern U.S. presidency, we should not be surprised that the system breaks down. A single president represents the views of just one political party. All citizens want to have a voice in their government, but only half the public enjoys meaningful input into the development of presidential policy. It is no wonder that the party out of power spends more of its time trying to regain the White House and less of its time trying to address the country's needs.

A one-person, very powerful presidency not only sparks partisan conflict; it also invites imperious behavior in the Oval Office. Modern presidents violate their constitutional limits by sending the military into battle without a congressional authorization of war and by giving short shrift to civil liberties. They also usurp legislative prerogatives with signing statements, executive orders, and the granting of waivers from statutory obligations. And presidents are quick to eliminate transparency in their activities. The Bush administration shaped energy policy behind closed doors with oil company executives, and the Obama administration shaped health care policy behind closed doors with health insurance and pharmaceutical executives.

While the framers gave the United States its single president, their decision was hardly preordained. When delegates discussed the structure of the presidency at the Constitutional Convention in June 1787, serious objections to a unitary executive were raised. Edmund Randolph warned, for example, that a one-person presidency would become the "foetus of monarchy."[3]

Controversy over the idea of a single president was predictable. Only recently had the framers freed themselves from the tyranny of King George III, and they were firmly committed to creating a new government that would not abuse its powers and oppress its citizens. It must have seemed preposterous to replace a hereditary monarch with an elected monarch.

Yet much as the founding fathers wanted to break with the past, they preserved many of its key elements. The U.S. president is a substitute for the British royal family, a constitutional monarch, if you will.[4] The Senate finds its origins in Britain's aristocratic House of Lords, and the House of Representatives emerged from the popular House of Commons. It is difficult for anyone, even visionary leaders, to abandon fundamental traditions, regardless of their imperfections.

To be sure, the framers invoked important arguments for a unitary executive. While Congress would deliberate, the president would act with decisiveness and dispatch. A single president would bring order and energy to the national government.[5]

With the passage of time, however, it has become clear that the founding fathers misjudged the consequences of their choice:

- They did not anticipate the extent to which executive power would expand and give us an "imperial presidency" that dominates the national government and that too often exercises its authority in ways that are detrimental to the country's interests.[6]
- They did not predict the role that political parties would come to play and how battles to capture the White House would greatly aggravate partisan conflict.
- They did not recognize that single presidents would represent party ideology much more than the overall public good.
- And they misjudged the advantages and disadvantages of single versus multiple decision makers.

Had the framers been able to predict the future, they would have been far less enamored with the idea of a unitary executive and far more receptive to the alternative proposals for a plural executive that they rejected. Like their counterparts in Europe, they might well have created an executive branch in which power is shared among multiple persons from multiple political parties.

If the presidency is to fulfill the founding fathers' vision and function more effectively, it needs to be reconceived. This need for constitutional change led me to the proposal for reform that I consider in this book—the replacement of the one-person, one-party presidency with a two-person, two-party presidency.

A coalition presidency carries the potential for many important benefits—a cabining of power in the executive branch, a dampening of partisan conflict in Washington, a White House more representative of the entire electorate, real opportunities for third-party candidates to win election, and wiser presidential decision making.

After more than two hundred years with the Constitution's one-person presidency, it may seem preposterous to suggest a plural executive. But a bipartisan presidency would be far more faithful to the framers' view of executive power. They wanted a president with limited authority who would serve as a coequal with Congress. They also believed that power should be contained by dividing it and requiring it to be shared. A two-person presidency relies on the framers' structural devices to promote their core values. And by correcting the dysfunction in Washington and making the executive branch operate more effectively, a two-person, coalition presidency can be justified even without reference to original intent.

The rest of this chapter provides a more developed summary of the book's argument.

For decades, the United States has struggled with two critical problems in its political system—an imperial presidency susceptible to the abuse of power and a partisan political atmosphere that can poison relations among members of Congress and between Congress and the president.

While these are longstanding problems, they have been especially troublesome in recent years, with George W. Bush violating basic civil liberties and human rights in the "war on terror" and Congress riven by partisan politics over legislative proposals to stimulate the economy, balance the budget, expand access to health care coverage, or respond to global warming.

The imperial presidency and partisan conflict are bipartisan problems, with culprits on both sides of the political aisle. Barack Obama may have addressed some of the excesses of his predecessor, but he too flouted the executive branch's constitutional limits, as when he contributed armed forces to the military operations against Libya without congressional authorization. Obama also took presidential obsession with secrecy to new heights. And members of Congress from both the Democratic and Republican Parties place partisan gain over the public good.

In trying to understand and address the imperial presidency and partisan conflict, scholars generally have proceeded on parallel tracks, inattentive to the ways in which the two problems are connected. But the connections are fundamental. Both problems reflect key miscalculations by the constitutional framers when they designed the executive and legislative branches. Both problems can be addressed by a common solution—the replacement of the one-person, one-party presidency with a two-person, two party presidency.

The imperial presidency

The drafters of the U.S. Constitution did not adequately protect against the imperial presidency because they did not anticipate the central role that the executive branch would come to play in shaping national policy. As the Federalist Papers indicate, the framers saw Congress as the potentially dominant institution. To ensure balance between the executive and legislative branches, the framers did two important things. They weakened the legislative power by dividing it between a House and a Senate, and they rested an undivided executive power with a single president. But presidential power has expanded over time to a degree unanticipated by the framers and has become much more susceptible to the kind of abuse that the framers feared and tried to guard against.[7]

In foreign affairs particularly, presidents play a far larger role in the determination of U.S. policy—and Congress plays a far smaller role—than intended by the framers. As illustrated most recently by the country's military intervention in Libya, presidents send troops into combat without congressional authorization. They also conclude agreements with foreign governments without Senate ratification or other congressional approval. In addition, with the huge growth of the regulatory state and its many federal departments and agencies, presidents have gained considerable and unanticipated domestic policy-making power.

The expansion of presidential policy making is problematic for two key reasons. First, it has skewed the balance of power between the legislative and executive branches in favor of the executive branch. In the effort to prevent a politically dominant Congress, the framers left the country instead with a politically dominant executive branch.

More importantly, presidential policy making has changed the nature of presidential power. The Constitution envisions a president with secondary responsibility for the *creation* of national policy and primary responsibility for the *execution* of national policy. However, the contemporary president enjoys primary responsibility for both the creation and execution of national policy. This assumption of policy-creating responsibility by the president allows national policy to be made in the absence of a robust debate among multiple decision makers. It may make sense to have a single person who can act decisively and with dispatch when the person is an executor of policy. But the founding fathers correctly reserved policy making for multiple-person bodies.

Dividing the power of the executive branch between presidential partners would respond to the expansion of presidential power. Just as dividing the legislative power weakened the legislative branch, dividing the executive power would weaken the executive branch. A bipartisan presidency would not undo the transfer of policy-making power to the executive branch, but it would decrease the ability of the executive branch to exercise its power unwisely or to usurp the power of the legislative branch. In addition, a two-person presidency would turn policy making in the executive branch into a deliberative process with multiple decision makers. The framers may have miscalculated how much presidential power would grow and the extent to which it would become a policy-making power, but we can correct for their miscalculation by revising the structure of the executive branch.

Partisan conflict

The problem of partisan conflict reflects a second miscalculation. Although the founding fathers recognized the threat to democracy and effective governance from factions such as political parties, the framers did not adequately protect against partisan conflict because they misjudged the ability of the constitutional structure to suppress factional activity. The Constitution's system of checks and balances simply has not served its purposes sufficiently. As scholars agree, political parties play a far larger role in our governmental system than originally envisioned. The framers incorrectly assumed that candidates would be chosen by a "politics of virtue" rather than a "politics of party."[8]

While there are salutary effects from the competition among parties, there also are serious ill effects. In particular, partisan conflict can too greatly impede the efforts of Congress to remedy national problems through legislative change. Party divisions have prevented Congress from addressing concerns about high budget deficits; they also have stalled efforts to alleviate the threat from global warming and to reform the immigration system. And partisan differences are becoming more intense—public polling data in the first three years of the Obama administration identified an electorate more polarized than in any other president's first three years in office going back to Dwight Eisenhower (for whom we have the earliest comparable data).[9]

While partisan conflict arises from a number of causes, a single-executive structure greatly exacerbates the problem. Under the current system, the Democratic and Republican Parties mount aggressive and expensive campaigns to capture the White House. Moreover, once an election is over, each party launches its effort to win the next presidential race. The party of the president lines up behind the president's initiatives to ensure a successful administration. The losing party tries to block the president's proposals so it can invoke a more persuasive argument for a change in party at the next presidential election.[10] If, on the other hand, each party knew it would elect a partner in a coalition presidency every four years, it would not stand to gain as much political advantage through partisan tactics. Instead, it would be freer to judge legislative proposals on their merits.

Or to put it another way, strong partisan conflict can be expected under a winner-take-all system for a presidency whose power has grown to the level of an imperial presidency. Indeed, the sharp increase in partisan behavior over the past several decades parallels the marked expansion of presidential power over the same time period. Currently, a candidate can win election with a small majority or even a minority of the popular vote. As a result, substantial numbers of voters feel that that their interests and concerns are not represented in a politically dominant White House. Instead of having a "government of the whole people by the whole people, equally represented," the United States has a "government of the whole people by a mere majority of the people, exclusively represented."[11]

With a two-person, coalition presidency, a much higher percentage of voters will have their preferred candidate serving and will be much more comfortable with the initiatives that emerge from the executive branch. A presidential partnership, with the two executives coming from different political parties, could promote the kind of political harmony that the framers thought desirable in the new nation. Instead of one major party being out of power and working to brake—and break—the president's administration, both major parties would have a stake in the success of the executive branch.

In short, as long as the United States has a one-person, one-party executive branch, we should expect highly partisan behavior in Washington. A two-person, coalition executive branch constitutes a reform of the constitutional structure that actually could foster a more bipartisan ethic.

Decision making in the executive branch

The framers might have adopted a two-person presidency but for a third miscalculation—the constitutional drafters overestimated the leadership qualities of a single executive. I have mentioned the framers' misguided preference for a single executive as a bulwark against a potentially dominant legislature. The framers also were incorrect in thinking that a single president would more effectively steer the national government.

To be sure, a single president is a key component of our constitutional structure, and Alexander Hamilton invoked important arguments against multiple executives in Federalist 70. In the Hamiltonian view, the executive branch needs to act with decisiveness and dispatch, and that requires a single officeholder. There may be drawbacks to granting so much power to one person, but, thought Hamilton and a majority of the other framers, the advantages outweigh the disadvantages.

However, the framers overestimated the value of a single president because they misjudged the differences between single decision makers and multiple decision makers. There is much truth to the maxim that two heads are better than one. Over the past two hundred years, our understanding of decision making has evolved. Studies by economists, psychologists, and other researchers demonstrate that shared decision making works well and indeed better than unilateral decision making. As the example of George W. Bush waging war against Iraq illustrates, a single decision maker can make very poor choices. Two presidents from different parties would bring the different perspectives and problem-solving skills that make for better decision making. And the benefits of multiple decision makers are especially important as the executive branch has assumed more policy-making responsibilities.

It is not only the case that two presidents would make better decisions for the country than a single president would. They also would make decisions that are viewed by the public as having greater legitimacy. A coalition presidency would ensure that most people feel they have a voice in executive branch decision making and therefore that their interests are adequately represented. Despite the common perception that contemporary presidents move to the middle to appeal to a broad range of voters, they generally hew to the partisan views that are representative of their political base.[12]

The representational benefit of a two-person presidency would have been especially valuable after the 2000 presidential campaign. Instead of George W. Bush taking office with half the country questioning the validity of his election and the Supreme Court compromising its credibility with the controversial decision in *Bush v. Gore*,[13] Bush and Al Gore would have assumed office together in a much more conciliatory atmosphere.

Society already has come to recognize the importance of shared decision making in other settings—husbands and wives for families and doctors and patients for medical care, for example. Similarly, the United States can improve the decision making of its national government if it changes from a single president to a coalition executive. To be sure, this is not to suggest that two presidents can or should have a marital- or medical-like relationship. Rather, the point is that decision making is improved by including more stakeholders in the decision-making process instead of assigning decision-making responsibility to a single person.

Elected officials realize the representational virtues of coalition governing. When faced with necessary but politically risky decisions, members of Congress and the president often turn to bipartisan decision making. Thus, for example, bipartisan commissions have been created to address high budget deficits, to propose reforms of the Social Security system, and to preserve the solvency of the Medicare program.[14]

Two presidents could provide more effective leadership than a single president not only when there is time for careful study and deliberation but also in times of crisis. As the internment of Japanese Americans during World War II and the torture of suspected terrorists after 9/11 indicate, it is all too easy for a president to act in authoritarian and unconstitutional ways during an emergency. The founding fathers thought that Congress and the courts would check presidential exercises of power, but these external checks have rarely been able to avoid the abuse of executive power. Having a two-person, bipartisan presidency could provide the kind of internal check on the executive branch that is necessary precisely in emergencies, when other checks are not effective. And two-person decision making can accommodate the need for rapid decision making. Presidents always confer with trusted advisers before making even the most urgent decisions.

But would two presidents bicker too much and become paralyzed by their inability to share power? While the framers were concerned about dissension and rivalry between multiple executives, it is more likely that two presidents would develop a meaningful willingness to cooperate with each other. That is the lesson of the Swiss model for the executive branch. In Switzerland, the Federal Council comprises seven department heads who possess equal decision-making authority. Decisions are made by consensus, with resort to a majority vote only in exceptional cases.[15] For more than fifty years, the seven councilors have come from the major political parties (currently five) that represent roughly 80 percent of the country's voters, and the councilors work cooperatively. Similarly, when presidents and prime ministers from different parties shared the executive power in French "cohabitation" governments for much of the time between 1986 and 2002, their level of cooperation resulted in governments that were popular with the public. And of course, in all parliamentary systems, the cabinet ministers participate in the decision making of the executive branch.

Even if the Swiss, French, or other plural-executive experiences would not transfer readily to the different political culture of the United States, there are many other reasons to be confident about the functioning of a bipartisan presidency. Consider in this regard the productive working relationships that can develop between senior U.S. senators from the Democratic and Republican Parties, as happened with Senators Orrin Hatch (R-UT) and Ted Kennedy (D-MA).

There are important reasons why we can expect collegial, rather than unfriendly, working relationships between two presidents. In particular, the presidents would not have incentives to develop a relationship of conflict. Elected officials may be highly partisan, but they are partisan for a purpose. Drawing sharp distinctions with candidates or officeholders of the opposing party can help politicians gain power.[16] In addition, in typical power-sharing settings, one person can hope to establish a dominant position by outmaneuvering the other person. In the coalition presidency that I discuss, neither president could hope to prevail over the other president. During their terms, they would share power equally, and reelection also would come with half of the executive power.

Not only would the two presidents lack an incentive to engage in conflict; they also would have an important incentive to work cooperatively. Having reached the pinnacle of political life, their focus would turn to making important contributions and establishing a meaningful and enduring legacy. George W. Bush's decision in 2003 to invade Iraq and overthrow Saddam Hussein is illustrative. While there were a number of reasons for his decision, it appears that he was influenced by the potential for introducing democratic governance to the Arab Middle East and providing a model that could spread to neighboring countries. The possibility of transforming a major region of the world overcame his opposition during the presidential campaign to policies of "nation building."

Similarly, when Barack Obama pressed his health care legislation in 2009 and 2010, he was driven by the desire to accomplish a goal that had been pursued by many Democratic and Republican presidents from Franklin Delano Roosevelt to Bill Clinton. Even though his advisers warned him that the pursuit of health care reform was unwise when the public wanted its president to devote his energies to the economy, Obama wanted to do something more than secure his reelection. He wanted to secure his legacy, and "for greatness he needed health care."[17]

If the two members of a coalition presidency spent their terms locking horns, they would not be able to implement key proposals that could enhance their reputations and burnish their legacies. Accordingly, they likely would come to accommodations that would allow them to implement meaningful policy changes.

My predictions about the behavior of presidential pairs may be based on educated guesses, but they also are well supported by principles of game theory. Game theory can identify the kinds of relationships that are likely to encourage cooperative strategies. And a coalition presidency would incorporate the key elements of cooperative relationships. Thus, for example, when individuals have an ongoing relationship, they are much more likely to choose cooperation than if they have a one-shot relationship with another person. Other factors that promote cooperation are frequent interactions and regular communication between the individuals in the relationship, factors that would be features of a relationship between two executives. Cooperative strategies also are more likely in two-person relationships, where noncooperation is obvious, than in many-person relationships, where some participants can hope to exploit the cooperation of others and become free riders.[18]

Most importantly, the coalition presidents would be in a symmetrical relationship with respect to the amount of power that they exercise. As I have indicated, the willingness of presidential partners to work cooperatively depends in large part on the fact that each of them would possess exactly half of the executive power. No maneuvering could change that symmetry and give one or the other of the two presidents the upper hand in the relationship. This feature of a coalition presidency is a key consideration in applying principles of game theory. If the potential benefits from not cooperating become too large, then we can expect people to act in a noncooperative fashion. But in the bipartisan executive, nothing would be gained by obstruction rather than collaboration, and we could expect each presidential partner to cooperate out of self-interest.[19]

The inclination of people to adopt cooperative strategies in long-term relationships extends even to individuals who come into the relationship from highly antagonistic positions—as one might expect with presidents from different political parties. An important illustration comes from the example of trench warfare in Europe during World War I at the Western Front of battle. When small units faced each other for extended periods of time, the British or French foot soldiers often would develop cooperative strategies with their German counterparts. Each side realized that noncooperation would result in both sides being bloodied, while cooperation would minimize casualties on each side of the battle line.[20]

That elected officials with strong philosophical differences would work cooperatively may seem surprising. But it is important to recognize that the ideological views of candidates and elected officials are as much means as they are ends. While candidates and officials may choose their positions out of core beliefs (ideological views as ends), they more often stake out positions because they view the positions as useful for getting elected (ideological views as means). Thus, it is common to see candidates change their positions dramatically when doing so is politically expedient. Recall in this regard how Mitt Romney moved from his moderate positions as Massachusetts governor to much more conservative positions as a presidential candidate in 2008 and 2012.

Presidents and the savior phenomenon

If shared decision making is better than individual decision making and the framers suffered mightily under the dominion of a single ruler, we would do well to wonder whether the usual arguments for a one-person presidency fully explain its use. Might there be additional reasons for the adoption and retention of a form of leadership that has not worked well and that has been rejected by the many countries with a parliamentary system?[21]

Much of the enthusiasm for a single president may reflect a tendency for the public to develop exaggerated expectations as to what its leaders can accomplish. For many people, there seems to be an important psychological drive for an all-powerful savior who can solve serious problems and deliver individuals from their travails. Thus, just as the framers turned to a president despite their experience with a king, so did the Israelites ask for a king despite their enslavement by the Egyptian pharaohs and despite the warnings they received about the royal abuse of power. More recently, corporate boards have taken the view that a poorly performing company can be saved by hiring a star CEO, despite empirical evidence to the contrary. Candidates and presidents appear to recognize the desire for a savior and appeal to it in the way they speak about the presidential role and the results they promise to achieve.[22]

The savior status of presidents is damaging not only because it rests on unrealistic expectations. In addition, it discourages the pursuit of meaningful reform.[23] In particular, the savior phenomenon encourages voters to believe that they can solve the dysfunction in Washington simply by changing their elected officials rather than by making the changes in the political system that really could correct the dysfunction.

In sum, there is much to be said for a two-person, coalition executive. It can address two serious concerns about the current operation of our national government—it can provide a check against the excessive expansion of executive branch authority, and it can remove incentives for strongly partisan behavior and replace them with incentives for a more bipartisan ethic. In addition, a coalition presidency can address these serious concerns while fostering the interest in an executive branch that provides both effective leadership and broad public representation. Thus, this book considers the possibility of a presidency of two persons, with no political party supplying more than one of the two presidents.

The nature of a bipartisan executive

What would a two-person, bipartisan presidency look like? The executive power would be shared by the two presidents such that they would enjoy joint and equal authority. Both presidents would have to agree on any decision, whether it entailed the signing of legislation passed by Congress, the issuance of an executive order, or the nomination of a cabinet member or judge. In all likelihood, the two presidents would choose to divide primary responsibilities for different areas of authority. For example, one might oversee health care policy, while the other might direct energy policy. Nevertheless, when a decision needed to be made, the concurrence of both presidents would be required.

Joint decision making would make for more representative decision making. Instead of a Democratic president pressing the agenda of the Democratic Party or a Republican president championing the platform of the Republican Party, there would be presidential partners advocating policies that reflect the preferences of the full range of voters.

A two-person presidency and constitutional values

This book does not suggest that people have misunderstood the text of the Constitution or the intent of the framers with regard to the structure of the presidency. Rather, it argues that the founding fathers were too rooted in the thinking of their day and the traditions of their British heritage. When countries were ruled by kings, and families were governed by husbands, one would expect the constitutional framers to take for granted the need for a single president. The founding fathers also assumed the rightness of Britain's winner-take-all system for elections.[24] However, it has become clear that a one-person, one-party presidency leaves us too vulnerable to the problems of the imperial presidency and of factional activity from political parties. It also has become clear that the framers overestimated the benefits of a single president.

Although a two-person, bipartisan presidency may ignore the express intent of the framers about the structure of the executive branch, it would be more faithful than a single president to the framers' overall vision of the national government. The framers did not anticipate the emergence of a powerful, policy-making president, nor did they foresee its impact on the constitutional balance between the executive and legislative branches. They also did not predict the enormous role of political parties and their distortion of the political process. A two-person presidency can do much to address these problems so the national government better realizes the founding fathers' vision. And it can do so via the kind of structural approach that typifies the U.S. constitutional system. Just as the framers protected against the accumulation of power and factional conflict by dividing power and requiring it to be shared, so would a coalition presidency work by dividing the executive power and requiring it to be shared.

My claim that a two-person presidency would be more faithful to the framers' vision gains support from an important theory for the imperial presidency. As Woodrow Wilson wrote, principles of representation can justify viewing the president—the one official elected by the entire country—as the central institution in the national government. But as Wilson recognized, ceding a dominant role to the president requires a break from the framers' conception of separate and equal powers checking and balancing each other.[25]

One need not subscribe to original intent to find virtue in a two-person presidency. It also would be more faithful to basic democratic principles. Sanford Levinson and other scholars have discussed the many ways in which the Constitution has spawned an undemocratic political system.[26] Currently, the United States suffers from a too-powerful president who represents half or less of the public. With a bipartisan presidency that gives most of the people a voice in the shaping of presidential policy, the executive branch would become a much more democratic institution.

A two-party presidency and third-party or independent candidates

There are other advantages of a two-person, coalition presidency. In particular, it would help counteract the unhealthy "duopoly" that the Democratic and Republican Parties enjoy in U.S. politics. Currently, third-party or independent candidates have little chance of winning the presidency. With a two-person presidency, third-party and independent candidates would have a much better chance at success. In 2000, for example, many Democratic voters preferred Ralph Nader but believed that a vote for Nader would simply ensure the election of George W. Bush. With a two-person presidency, those Democrats could have voted for Nader with the assurance that either Nader or Al Gore would become one of the two presidents. Similarly, in 1980, many voters preferred John Anderson to Jimmy Carter or Ronald Reagan. Although opinion polls indicated that Anderson had nearly as much support as did Carter, he ended up with only 7 percent of the vote. A coalition presidency could convert third-party and independent candidates from being at best spoilers who can determine which of the major party candidates wins election to candidates who can win in their own right.[27]

A feasible approach to governance?

While a two-person presidency would be novel for the United States, single executives are by no means used universally. Indeed, a collegial or collective executive cabinet is one of the hallmarks of parliamentary systems. The prime minister or premier may have a preeminent position, but decision making is, to a high degree, a joint endeavor of the cabinet ministers. Thus, for example, major policy decisions by the executive branch in parliamentary systems are taken up for a vote by the full cabinet. In contrast, cabinet secretaries in a presidential system serve only as advisers, and presidents may take action on major policies alone or even against the advice of their cabinets.[28]

The two-person presidency that I consider has an important advantage over the shared decision making in a parliamentary system. Parliamentary coalitions can be unstable from partisan maneuvering designed to gain majority control of the government, especially since new elections can be called at any time. In a two-person executive, the presidents would recognize that they could not gain dominant power by obstructive behavior, either during the current four-year term or after the next presidential election. They could achieve their goals only through cooperation with their presidential colleague.

Even in the United States, the executive branch has deviated in practice from a pure model of single-person control to include elements of a plural executive. Congress has established boards or commissions such as the Federal Reserve and the Securities Exchange Commission that are independent of presidential control, and a number of federal statutes vest authority for their execution with cabinet secretaries rather than with the president.[29]

A two-person, coalition presidency would require a constitutional amendment, but we can expect a good deal of interest in the possibility. For both institutional and personal reasons, members of Congress should like the idea. Weakening the executive power by dividing it would level the balance of power between the executive and legislative branches. In addition, members of Congress find the partisan atmosphere unpleasant to the extent that prominent legislators such as Senators Evan Bayh (D-IN) and Olympia Snowe (R-ME) choose to leave office rather than continue working in Washington. Defusing partisan conflict would make for a more rewarding experience for senators and representatives.

To the extent that members of Congress aspire to the presidency, the calculus is more complicated. But they might well prefer a system in which their chances of becoming president double even though they would have to share power. In addition, the reduction in partisan conflict facing the executive branch might more than compensate for the need of one president to cooperate with the other president. It would be easier to work with a presidential partner of another party inclined to be collegial rather than legislators of another party inclined to be uncompromising.

The public also might like the idea of a two-person presidency since that would accommodate the desire of the public for a more bipartisan ethic in Washington, DC. Partisan conflict has bred greater and greater cynicism among voters about their government.

Most importantly, other proposals to address the imperial presidency and partisan conflict will not resolve those problems. A two-person presidency may seem radical, but dysfunction in Washington has gotten to the point that radical reform is needed. Moreover, a change to a two-person presidency would not be written in stone. In the end, I may be wrong about the advantages of a coalition presidency, but its potential for substantial benefit gives good reason for a trial run to see whether the functioning of the national government improves. If not, then it would be a simple matter to restore the one-person executive.

And even if a two-person presidency would not be adopted, there is much to gain by its consideration. Other authors have discussed the problems of presidential power and partisan conflict, but no one has analyzed the extent to which they reflect the one-person, one-party presidency. This book breaks new ground in illuminating the very high costs the United States pays for the current structure of its executive branch. Considering the alternative of a two-person executive will bring greater understanding to critical problems in the U.S. political system and the remedies that might be implemented for those problems. Indeed, it is through thinking about goals that may be infeasible that we often identify policies that are feasible and that move us down the path to finding a full solution to our challenges.[30]

This book continues in chapter 2 with a discussion of how a two-person presidency would operate and why it would improve the judicial nomination process, negotiations with foreign countries, and other features of our political system. Chapter 3 documents the rise of the imperial presidency and explains how two presidents could correct for the excesses of executive power. Chapter 4 reviews the problem of partisan conflict and discusses how it could be defused by a coalition presidency. Chapter 5 presents the view that two presidents would make for better decision making, and chapter 6 shows how a bipartisan executive would provide the public with broader representation in Washington. Chapter 7 provides reasons why the prospects for adopting a two-person presidency are greater than one might expect, and chapter 8 concludes with some final reflections.

2

A two-person, bipartisan executive

If the United States adopted a two-person, bipartisan executive, how would the two presidents be nominated and elected, and how would they share presidential responsibilities and White House office space? Who would be in charge in the event of an emergency? This chapter answers these and other questions about the structure of a two-person presidency.

Electing a two-person, bipartisan executive

Under a two-person presidency, there would be a doubling in the number of presidents, but most of the current features of the presidency would be retained. Voters would elect two presidents from two different political parties every four years, and each of the presidents would serve a four-year term. Thus, the two presidents would serve concurrent rather than partially overlapping terms.

The two presidents could be allowed to serve only two four-year terms, as is now the case for the president. But it makes more sense to eliminate presidential term limits. Because a two-person executive responds to the problem of the imperial presidency, it diminishes the need for other safeguards against the expansion of executive power. I elaborate on this point later in the chapter.

Presidential candidates would be nominated by their respective parties, through the existing primary, caucus, and national convention system. Each presidential candidate would run with a vice presidential candidate, so voters also would elect two vice presidents. This would provide for succession in the event of presidential disability, death, or impeachment. (Note an important benefit of a two-person presidency for vice presidents who take office upon a vacancy in the White House. While the new presidents still would assume their executive responsibilities without Oval Office experience, their transition would be eased by their partnership with an incumbent president.[1])

Voters would cast a single ballot, and the top two vote getters would be elected to the presidency. Ordinarily, the top two vote getters would come from the Democratic and Republican Parties, but there may be occasions in which a third-party or independent candidate would run second. Indeed, as I discuss in chapter 6, a two-person presidency would make election of a third-party candidate much more likely than under the current one-person presidency.[2]

The Electoral College could be retained, or the two presidents could be chosen directly by popular vote. If the Electoral College were retained, it might be important for all states to follow the lead of Maine and Nebraska and allocate their votes on a more proportional basis than do the forty-eight states that employ a winner-take-all approach.[3] Thus, for example, Florida's electoral votes in a pure proportional system would have been divided evenly between George W. Bush and Al Gore in 2000 rather than awarded in full to Bush. If the states retained their winner-take-all method of allocating electoral votes, it might be difficult to sort out the voters' preferences between the second- and third-place candidates in the event of a strong third-party candidacy. In 1860, for example, Stephen Douglas came in second in popular vote (29.5 percent) but only fourth in electoral votes (4 percent), while John Breckinridge came in second in electoral votes (24 percent) but third in popular vote (18 percent).[4] Third-party candidates with strong regional strength but weak national support fare much better in the Electoral College than do third-party candidates who can appeal to voters throughout the country but not enough to win a plurality of the vote in any one state.

The election of a two-person executive would represent a slight variation on the original constitutional provisions for election. Until the Twelfth Amendment was adopted in 1804, members of the Electoral College cast two ballots, with the top vote getter becoming president, and the second vote getter becoming vice president. Thus, under the original Constitution, presidents and vice presidents could come from different parties and indeed did so in 1796, when the Federalist John Adams was elected president and the Democratic-Republican Thomas Jefferson was elected vice president. (The Twelfth Amendment was adopted not because it allowed for presidents and vice presidents from different political parties but because of a tie between Thomas Jefferson and Aaron Burr in the 1800 electoral vote.[5])

While I have described a two-person presidency in which both presidents would be elected at the same time, would it make more sense to have them serve overlapping terms, so there could be more continuity from administration to administration? Instead of electing two presidents every four years, the United States could elect one president every two years for a four-year term.

Overlapping terms would be less desirable than concurrent terms. If only one of the presidents was elected at a time, we would see a lot of strategic voting that could undermine some of the key purposes for a two-person presidency. Assume, for example, that the Democratic president is in the middle of a four-year term, and the Republican president decides to retire. Democratic voters could try to elect a particularly moderate Republican president or a third-party candidate in an effort to limit the influence of the Republican Party. Electing the presidents to overlapping terms would prevent the two-person presidency from ensuring an equal sharing of power across party lines.

Sharing the executive power

The executive power would be shared by the two presidents such that they would enjoy joint and equal authority. Both presidents would have to agree on any executive decision. If a bill passed Congress, each would have to sign it before it would become law, and they would have to agree before issuing any signing statement with their understanding of the law's meaning. Because both presidents would have to agree on the enactment of legislation, either president acting alone would have authority to veto a bill. The two presidents also would have to agree on executive orders, the text of the State of the Union message, or military decisions as commanders in chief.

If a judicial seat became vacant, the two presidents would have to agree on a single nominee before submitting the name to the Senate for confirmation. Similarly, both presidents would have to agree on members of their cabinet. (Thus, there would be a single officeholder for each position in the cabinet, as well as for other executive branch positions).

In all likelihood, the two presidents would choose to assume primary responsibility for different areas of authority. For example, one might oversee health care policy, while the other might direct energy policy. One might supervise relations with European countries, while the other might manage relations with Asian countries. The exact division of responsibility would vary from one administration to another, depending on the preferences of each pair of presidents. Regardless of the division of responsibility, when a decision needed to be made, the concurrence of both presidents would be required.

Why require equal decision-making authority? Why not divide decision-making authority in accordance with the division of supervisory responsibility? As I discuss in chapter 4, the ability of a two-person presidency to overcome partisan conflict and encourage cooperative behavior by the presidential partners depends in large part on the fact that each of them would possess exactly half of the executive power. If there were an imbalance in power between the two presidents, the relationship could easily devolve into the dissension that the framers worried would occur with multiple executives.

Complications might arise from the sharing of responsibility for legislative proposals. The White House's legislative initiatives would not represent legally binding actions of the executive branch and therefore could be presented individually by either of the presidents. Or either of the two presidents could work with legislative colleagues from his or her party to shape a partisan proposal in Congress. Thus, for example, in a McCain-Obama presidency, we might have seen two different proposals emerge from the Oval Office to reform the health care system.

However, there is good reason to expect that presidential pairs would issue joint legislative proposals. Because they would have to agree on so many executive decisions, it would be important for them to develop a relationship of collegiality and trust. If one or both started working in partisan fashion, it would be difficult to sustain the kind of cooperation needed to make the executive branch function effectively. And as I discuss in chapter 4, a cooperative relationship would be desired by the two presidents so they could generate a record of accomplishment.[6]

Logistics of a two-person presidency

As I also discuss in chapter 4, principles of game theory tell us that cooperative relationships are more likely when the participants in the relationship communicate regularly and frequently. The many responsibilities of the presidency automatically will encourage regular and frequent communication between the two presidents. In addition, it would be important to reconfigure the White House to further encourage good communication. In particular, the two presidents and their staffs should work in adjoining offices. While this would mean that some of the staff would have offices outside the White House (as is the case already for many members of the presidential staff), the White House is large enough to accommodate two presidents and a significant number of their senior staff. Each president also should have personal quarters in the White House. Again, there is sufficient space in the current White House for two families, but some of the rooms that are currently used as guest quarters would have to be converted to presidential space.

Provision would have to be made for presidential conferral in the event of an unexpected attack by a terrorist group or another country. If the two presidents were in different locations, they would have to be able to speak with each other. This should not raise any new problems. Already, presidents need to confer with military officials from different locations in the event of an attack on the United States. Recall, for example, that George W. Bush was visiting with students in a Florida classroom when al-Qaeda operatives hijacked domestic airplanes and flew them into the World Trade Center and the Pentagon on September 11, 2001. Instead of creating a link between the military command and one president, communications specialists would create a link between the military command and two presidents.

In later chapters, I discuss how dividing responsibility between two presidents would respond to the problems of executive power, partisan conflict, and inadequate representation for the public in the Oval Office. Here, I discuss one aspect of the partisan conflict problem and identify some other important benefits from a two-person executive branch.

Impact on the judicial appointment process

After Democrats blocked the nomination of Judge Robert Bork to the U.S. Supreme Court in 1987 by Republican Ronald Reagan, the judicial appointment process became increasingly partisan for both Supreme Court justices and lower federal court judges.[7] When power is divided between a Democratic president and a Republican Senate or a Republican president and a Democratic Senate, many nominees are denied a hearing before the Senate Judiciary Committee, or the committee votes against sending nominations to the floor for a vote. Moreover, even when a judge or justice is approved by the Senate, the process may stretch out over months or years. Because of the partisan barriers to appointment, many potential nominees are never sent to the Senate by the president for approval.

Statistics from the administration of Bill Clinton are illustrative. In his first two years of office, Democrats controlled a majority of seats in the Senate, and the Judiciary Committee held hearings on more than 90 percent of Clinton's nominees. Republicans regained control of the Senate in November 1994, and the Judiciary Committee held hearings on 74 percent, 79 percent, and 47 percent of Clinton nominees over the subsequent two-year segments of Clinton's eight years in office.[8]

One-party control of the national government does not necessarily solve the problem. When either Democrats or Republicans occupy the White House and hold a majority in the Senate, the filibuster still allows a minority of senators (forty-one or more) to block an appointment. Individual senators also can put a hold on a nominee. Thus, even with a strong majority of Democrats in the Senate during his first two years in the White House (fifty-nine to sixty Democrats), Barack Obama came out of those two years with many more judicial vacancies than when he took office. The number of open seats rose from fifty-five to ninety-seven, leaving nearly one out of eight federal judgeships unfilled. Moreover, Obama had the lowest percentage of nominees approved for a first two years in office—58 percent—of any president in U.S. history.[9]

Consider some recent examples of well-qualified nominees failing to gain Senate approval:

After more than a year of delay and a Republican filibuster against his nomination in May 2011, Goodwin Liu withdrew his name from consideration for an appointment to the U.S. Court of Appeals for the Ninth Circuit. Liu had been a Rhodes Scholar, was a graduate of Yale Law School, and had served as a law clerk to Supreme Court Justice Ruth Bader Ginsburg. He was a widely respected professor of law at University of California–Berkeley, and his nomination by Barack Obama was supported by a number of prominent conservative lawyers. The American Bar Association gave Liu its highest rating for a nominee. However, he was viewed as too liberal by Republican senators. He also had provoked opposition for his own vocal criticism in 2006 of the nomination of Associate Justice Samuel Alito to the Supreme Court.[10]

After more than two years of delay and a Democratic filibuster against his nomination in 2003, Miguel Estrada withdrew his name from consideration for an appointment to the U.S. Court of Appeals for the D.C. Circuit. Estrada served as an editor on the *Harvard Law Review* while in law school, clerked for Supreme Court Justice Anthony Kennedy, and was an assistant to the solicitor general during the George H. W. Bush administration. His nomination by George W. Bush provoked controversy both because of his strong conservative views and because he appeared to be less than forthcoming in his responses to questions or requests for information from Democratic members of the Senate.[11]

With a two-person presidency, judicial nominees would have to earn the support of Democratic and Republican presidents, and this means that nominees would need to have staked out moderate positions on key policy matters (or not taken public positions at all on controversial issues). A Republican president would not agree to nominate a strongly liberal Democrat, and a Democratic president would not agree to nominate a strongly conservative Republican. With moderate nominees coming to the Senate with bipartisan support in the Oval Office, there would be little reason for senators on either side of the aisle to oppose any of the nominations. Judicial openings could be filled quickly, and the long backlogs of vacant positions would disappear.

If a two-person presidency would promote more moderate judges and justices, what would that mean for the role of the judiciary in deciding cases? Courts often are viewed as engines of social reform. If justices no longer had strong political views, would the Supreme Court change from a leader of social change into a follower of social change that is championed by the president or Congress?

As Gerald Rosenberg has observed, the Supreme Court actually plays a surprisingly limited role in implementing social reform. There are important structural constraints on the effectiveness of the courts. As Alexander Hamilton wrote in Federalist 78, the judicial branch is the "weakest" branch because it controls neither the "sword or the purse" and must rely instead on the other branches of government to carry out its decisions. With these and other constraints (e.g., the political pressures that the president and Congress can exert on courts), judicially driven social reform generally requires that political, social, and economic changes already have begun. It also requires substantial support for reform from the president and Congress.[12]

Thus, for example, the Supreme Court's 1954 school desegregation decision in *Brown v. Board of Education* did not result in any real integration of southern schools for a decade. National, state, and local political leaders, as well as the public, did not provide support for—and indeed often opposed—the integration of schools. Ten years after *Brown*, a number of factors allowed the decision to have an impact in the South. Congress passed the Civil Rights Act of 1964 and the Elementary and Secondary Education Act of 1965, the U.S. Department of Health, Education, and Welfare exercised its authority under the two acts to shape school policies, and public sentiment had shifted. As a result, the decision in *Brown* and subsequent judicial decisions were able to desegregate southern public schools.[13]

The lesson from *Brown* and other key cases is that courts can play an important role in social reform, but they cannot do so when they try to implement policies that go against the grain of existing social norms. Rather, they must work in tandem with prevailing political and social currents. Supreme Court justices generally recognize this reality. While they felt comfortable issuing their opinion in *Brown* by a unanimous vote that included conservatives Felix Frankfurter and Sherman Minton, the justices declined to override bans on interracial marriage two years later in *Naim v. Naim*. Instead, they waited until the *Loving* case in 1967, when public sentiment was more receptive to a decision on behalf of mixed-race couples.[14]

Even what is perhaps the Court's most controversial modern opinion, *Roe v. Wade*, came at a point when public support for a right to abortion was strong, with 80 percent of Americans reporting that they supported a right in some or all circumstances, and a decision in favor of abortion rights could attract broad support among the justices. In *Roe*, the Court recognized a constitutional right to abortion by a vote of 7–2, with conservatives Warren Burger, Lewis Powell, and Potter Stewart in the majority.[15]

When the Court fails to reflect public sentiment, it can trigger a backlash. The *Kelo* eminent domain case provides a useful illustration. In that case, the Court upheld the ability of governments to exercise their power of eminent domain and seize the property of homeowners for privately operated economic development. Public anger erupted quickly, and it led states across the country to pass statutes curtailing the eminent domain power. Within five years of the *Kelo* decision, forty-three states had revised their eminent domain statutes to make them more restrictive.[16]

In short, filling the Supreme Court with moderate justices probably would not have a significant effect on the likelihood that the Court would champion social reform. However, it would eliminate the political maneuvering that has made for a drawn-out and highly partisan judicial selection process.

Matching presidential abilities with presidential responsibilities

A two-person presidency also would help alleviate the huge burden that presidents assume when trying to oversee the many issues that need their attention.[17] In just his first eighteen months in the Oval Office, Barack Obama had to manage a struggling economy, wars in Iraq and Afghanistan, Iran's nuclear threat, continuing conflict between Israel and the Palestinians, a massive oil spill in the Gulf of Mexico, the passage of health care legislation, bills to reform the financial system and respond to global climate change, two Supreme Court nominations, and much more. It is impossible to give adequate attention to so many issues at one time; a second president would double the number of issues that can receive close attention from the top.

Another key benefit from a division of responsibility would be better alignment between presidential responsibilities on one hand and presidential interests and abilities on the other hand. A president trying to manage policy for the economy, energy, health care, immigration, taxes, and relations with European countries, Asian countries, and African countries is not likely to possess a passion or talent for all of those issues. Issues may be neglected by the White House not because they are unimportant but because the president does not bring a strong personal interest to the matter. With two presidents, there would be a much better chance that a particular issue will be overseen by a leader with a real interest in, and understanding of, the issue.[18]

Most importantly, two presidents from different parties would bring different perspectives about the role of government and the kinds of policies that the federal government should adopt. A Democratic president would promote principles of governmental regulation, a Republican president would promote free-market principles, and the two together could reach a balance between the two perspectives that often elude presidents from one party. To put it another way, the executive branch is more likely to identify policies that grow the economy or improve education when it works from a broader range of perspectives.[19]

Examples in the corporate world illustrate the value of executive partners who bring different strengths to their roles. A pair of corporate officers with complementary talents can provide a broader range of skills than can a single CEO. Thus, Microsoft flourished under the shared leadership of Bill Gates and Steve Ballmer, Hewlett-Packard (now HP) prospered under the shared leadership of Bill Hewlett and David Packard, and Goldman Sachs has generally thrived for decades under a series of executive pairs.[20] Of course, leadership teams do not always succeed in the corporate world. Co-executives may fight for control rather than cooperate. In chapter 5, I discuss the reasons why presidential partners would be more likely to cooperate than to develop a relationship of conflict.

Negotiations with foreign governments

A two-person presidency also could improve negotiations with foreign chiefs of state. To be sure, one might wonder whether presidential pairs would be handicapped when dealing with other governments. It is important for the national government to speak with a single voice in its international relations. Would two presidents be able to present a strong front in negotiations with leaders of other nations?

Most likely, a two-person executive would be more effective than a single president in relationships with foreign governments. Currently, when a president takes an aggressive stance toward another country, the other government can stall talks in the hope that the next election will yield a more favorable partner. When Barack Obama pressured Israel to make concessions to the Palestinians in 2009–2010, he may only have encouraged Prime Minister Benjamin Netanyahu to delay the peace process until 2013, when a Republican might become president and take strongly supportive positions of Israel. And in light of George W. Bush's support for Israel during his eight-year administration, this would have been a sensible strategy for Netanyahu. With a two-person presidency, a foreign leader would see little benefit in deferring deliberations until the next presidential election.

A two-person executive also could facilitate treaty negotiations between the United States and other countries. When a Democratic president discusses the terms of potential agreements, a foreign government might wonder whether Republicans in the Senate would block ratification of the treaty. After Obama negotiated a new pact with Russia in 2010 to reduce each side's nuclear arsenal, he struggled to secure Senate approval with a Democratic majority of fifty-nine seats. Following the 2010 elections, the forty-seven Republican senators were in a much better position to muster the forty-one votes needed to mount a filibuster and prevent ratification of other treaties. With a two-person executive, on the other hand, the foreign government would negotiate with the leaders of both major parties and therefore could be more confident that any agreement would come to fruition.

A bipartisan presidency would improve negotiations with a foreign country in other ways. Research comparing two-person teams with single negotiators has found that the negotiations yield better outcomes for both sides when at least one side is represented by a team. Teams are more likely to identify common interests, advantageous compromises, and ultimately win-win options that can lead to an agreement rather than a breakdown of talks. Interestingly, two-person teams of nonfriends outperform two-person teams of friends, a finding that bodes well for an executive branch composed of presidents from different political parties.[21]

Term limits

Because of concerns with the potential for abuse of power, presidential systems of government typically limit their chief executives to holding one or two terms in office. The United States did not impose term limits initially, but after Franklin Delano Roosevelt was elected to four consecutive terms and began the real consolidation of executive power that launched the imperial presidency, the Twenty-Second Amendment established the current two-term limit. In contrast, parliamentary systems allow their prime ministers to run for reelection as often as they want.[22]

There are real disadvantages to term limits for the presidency. Realizing that there is no long term over which to shape public policy, the term-limited executive may press for change too quickly and adopt ill-advised proposals in the rush to implement a vision.[23]

The haste with which a president may act can be exacerbated by two other considerations. First, reelection comes with lame-duck status and often requires presidents to rely primarily on their first terms to achieve their goals. Second, presidents commonly are accompanied into office by significant majorities for their party in Congress, majorities that often are eroded or lost at the next midterm election. While term limits alone reduce the president's time line from an indefinite period to eight years, these other factors can further reduce the president's time line to two years.

It is quite plausible to think that in Barack Obama's rush to pass as much legislation as he could in his first two years, he made policy choices that reflected unwise priorities. Arguably, he spent too much time on such issues as health care and the environment and not enough time promoting economic recovery. Thus, more than two years into his administration, unemployment remained stubbornly above 9 percent, and his approval rating dropped below 40 percent. If presidents could shape their administrations with a long-term horizon, they could be more patient with their policy initiatives and act more wisely. In short, term limits may protect against presidential excess, but they hamper presidential planning.

With a two-person presidency, the United States no longer would have to choose between restraining executive power and allowing presidents more time in office to pursue their policy goals. Because a presidential partner would provide a strong internal check on the activity of the executive branch, term limits should no longer be needed to provide an external check. Term limits could be eliminated, presidents could govern with the assurance that they could develop their policy proposals over a longer-term horizon, and the public could be confident that reelecting a long-serving president would not invite authoritarian government.

Eliminating term limits also would promote a productive relationship between the two presidents. As I discuss in chapter 4, principles of game theory tell us that individuals are more likely to cooperate when they are engaged in a relationship with an indefinite time horizon than when they face a finite time horizon.

Effects on voter participation

One might worry that a bipartisan executive would diminish voter participation in the electoral process. In the absence of a strong third-party candidate, the November election would become a mere formality in the way general elections currently are formalities in legislative districts dominated by one party. Since the Democratic and Republican nominees usually would become the two presidents, there would be little reason to vote for president in November. Or to put it another way, one would expect the nomination process for presidential elections to become much more important than the general election. Since voter participation in primary elections is lower than voter participation in general elections, a coalition presidency might diminish voter participation overall.

Moreover, while sharp partisan conflict has its drawbacks, it does seem to promote voter engagement. The greater the apparent differences between candidates, the greater the reason for voters to care who wins. Thus, for example, as support for presidential candidates has become more polarized in recent years, public participation also has increased. People are more likely to follow the election in the news, to engage in a campaign-related activity such as displaying a yard sign or contributing to a candidate, or to vote. Indeed, voter turnout in November 2008 was the highest since the voting age was lowered from twenty-one to eighteen in 1972.[24] If a coalition executive defuses partisan conflict, voter interest might diminish.

Nevertheless, there are good reasons to think that a two-person presidency would enhance, rather than diminish, voter participation. First, because a bipartisan executive makes third-party or independent candidacies more viable, November general elections might retain their significance. People would turn out to decide which of the three or more candidates would become the two presidents. And strong third-party or independent candidates could become a more common phenomenon. Because the major-party nominees usually would win election as the two presidents, major-party candidates might be even more inclined to appeal to party regulars rather than to the general electorate. There would be less to gain by articulating more moderate positions and more to gain by staking out positions more faithful to the party's core principles. Third-party and independent candidates could exploit the polarization of major-party nominees by positioning themselves in the middle of the political spectrum and appealing to the substantial numbers of American voters who do not affiliate with a major political party.[25] With a strong alternative candidate, November turnouts should remain high.

What if strong third-party or independent candidates are uncommon, and November elections become mere formalities? Under this scenario, voter participation still might increase overall. We might see voter turnout increase more in the primaries than it would diminish in the general election. Indeed, there could be a real surge in primary voting. A change to a bipartisan executive would quickly change the dynamics of party politics. If presidential elections were settled at the nominating process, people would have a much greater incentive to participate in the party primaries than they do today. Voters who currently are not affiliated with either major party might choose to do so, to ensure that they have a say in deciding who becomes president. If that were to happen, primary election turnouts could rise substantially.

And there is considerable room for primary voting to rise. Primary turnout in 2008 came in below 30 percent in many states and below 40 percent in most states, even though neither the Democratic nor the Republican Party had an incumbent seeking reelection, and both parties saw vigorously contested nominations. In more typical years such as 2004, with an incumbent running for renomination by one of the major parties, primary turnouts often fall below 10 or 20 percent in different states. If primary voting rose from 10 or 20 percent to 50 percent, it would more than compensate for any decline in general election turnout.[26]

In short, it is uncertain whether voter turnout would increase or decrease. But all of the reasons to think voter turnout would increase should provide sufficient assurance for consideration of a two-person presidency.

In addition to the potential for enhancing voter participation in primaries, a two-person presidency could have an important effect on the kinds of candidates who would be successful running for their parties' nominations. An increased primary turnout would come from people who are not core party activists and whose positions would be less extreme than those of the typical primary voter today. As the primary voting pools became more moderate, the major-party candidates would have a strong incentive to moderate their positions. That way they could attract more of the newly affiliated voters at primary time. Thus, rather than generating more extreme candidates, a bipartisan executive easily could generate candidates who appeal to a broader base of support.

In addition to the potential benefits discussed in this chapter, a two-person presidency would address a number of critical and fundamental problems with our current political system. The next chapter considers the problem of excessive executive power—the problem of the imperial presidency.

3

The problem of the
imperial presidency

When the constitutional drafters considered the possibility of excessive power in one of the branches of the national government, they worried not about the executive branch but about the legislative branch. As James Madison wrote about the legislature in Federalist 48, "it is against the enterprising ambition of this department that the people ought to indulge all their jealousy and exhaust all their precautions."[1]

Madison identified multiple concerns with the legislative power: Because the Constitution grants Congress powers that are more extensive and less bounded by precise limits than those of the executive or judicial branches, Congress is in a better position to exceed its authority and invade the prerogatives of other branches. In addition, only the legislative branch has the power to levy taxes, leaving officials in the other parts of government dependent on Congress for their compensation. The leverage this creates facilitates encroachments on the executive and judicial branches by the legislature.[2]

Alexander Hamilton amplified Madison's concerns. In Federalist 71, he discussed the "tendency of the legislative authority to absorb every other." Because legislators in a representative assembly are inclined to think that they are "the people themselves," they "often appear disposed to exert an imperious control over the other departments; and as they commonly have the people on their side, they always act with such momentum as to make it very difficult for the other members of the government to maintain the balance of the Constitution."

The framers' concern with legislative authority may seem odd after their revolt against the tyranny of King George III. In the Declaration of Independence, they documented no fewer than twenty-seven grievances about the royal abuse of power.

But the Constitution was written after a decade of experience with state constitutions that had severely restricted executive authority and greatly expanded legislative authority. The original thirteen states had denied their governors the traditional prerogatives of kings, including the power to appoint government officials or to veto legislation. The states also created councils that were elected by the legislatures and that shared the executive duties with governors. Pennsylvania had no governor and relied instead on a twelve-member executive council. Governance by very powerful state legislatures turned out to yield its own form of tyranny, a democratic despotism characterized by unjust laws, constantly changing laws that bred confusion and instability, and legislative interference with judicial decisions. Legislatures, it was thought, were compromising property rights by the excessive printing of money and the cancellation of debts.[3]

While the experience with state governments exposed the problems with unrestrained legislative bodies, the experience with national government under the Articles of Confederation demonstrated the need for a strong executive authority. Under the Articles, there was no real executive, only a series of congressional committees. In addition, the states retained much of their sovereignty, forming an association more like the European Union than the United States of America that emerged under the Constitution. The "absence of a powerful executive hampered the war effort, limited the ability of the national government to respond to internal rebellions, and put the American people at a disadvantage in commercial disputes with foreign nations."[4]

The framers compensated for the potential for legislative tyranny by weakening the legislative branch. As indicated in Federalist 51, the legislative power would be divided between a House and Senate. In addition, the two chambers would be organized differently, with distinct compositions and separate responsibilities, so as to keep them as disconnected from each other as possible.[5] And indeed, the two branches of Congress have evolved over time with different ways of operating and a good deal of independence from each other.

At the same time that the framers divided legislative power to prevent a dominant Congress, they tried to prevent a weak executive by granting the president substantial powers that were undivided. While presidents would share many of their powers with Congress, they would wield the executive branch's share of the power as a unitary executive. Presidents alone would negotiate treaties, serve as commander in chief of the military, grant pardons, and nominate judges and senior executive branch officials. In addition, they were given a power to veto legislation passed by Congress.[6]

In the view of the framers (though not the Antifederalists, who worried greatly about the presidency evolving into a monarchy),[7] the Constitution would right the imbalance between the legislative and executive authorities that existed under state constitutions and the Articles of Confederation. With the passage of time, however, it has become clear that the framers greatly misjudged the balance of power between the executive and legislative branches. While there is disagreement on some of the details, scholars generally agree that presidential power has substantially exceeded the intent of the framers.[8]

The executive branch's reach has exceeded the expectations of the framers in both domestic and foreign affairs, with presidents assuming far more policy-making authority than anticipated in 1787. The founding fathers did not envision an executive branch with control over the vast regulatory state and sprawling bureaucracy that has sprung up since the New Deal, nor did they envision that presidents would exercise the kind of dominance in foreign relations that they in fact exercise today. To be sure, presidential power was more constrained during much of the 19th Century. Many presidents between Andrew Jackson and Abraham Lincoln were weak and ineffective. Congress did not appropriate funds for White House staff until 1857, and the attorney general served as a part-time official until 1855.[9] But the 20th Century saw the emergence of an imperial presidency.

The expansion of presidential power

The founding fathers expected the executive power to be contained by the checks and balances of their constitutional system. By assigning some powers only to the legislative and judicial branches, requiring presidents to share key powers with Congress, and subjecting executive branch actions to legislative overrides and judicial scrutiny, the framers thought that Congress and the courts would prevent presidents from expanding their authority.

However, instead of opposing the expansion of executive power, the legislative and judicial branches have acquiesced in, and even aided, the growth of presidential power. Congress has been especially willing to foster the development of the imperial presidency by delegating much of its legislative power to the executive branch.

Congressional transfer of domestic policy power

The creation of the modern administrative state has involved a remarkable transfer of domestic legislative power by Congress to the executive branch. When the Department of Housing and Urban Development, the Environmental Protection Agency (EPA), or other agencies write their rules and regulations, they essentially engage in the writing of laws. They are supposed to be engaged only in the implementation of laws that Congress writes, but congressional direction often is so vague as to provide "little guidance for the task." Executive offices may once have acted as "transmission belts" that merely carried out legislative directives, but today they very much "*make* law."[10]

Consider the distinction between two existing statutory provisions. In one, Congress has prohibited the possession of machine guns. In the other, Congress has directed the EPA to set air-quality standards for air pollutants, with the only instructions being to set those standards that are required to protect the public health. A U.S. Attorney enforcing the machine-gun statute must simply determine whether a suspect actually had possession of a firearm that meets the statute's definition of a machine gun. There is no need to make law but only to implement a law that Congress wrote. In contrast, the EPA is unable to enforce the federal requirement to maintain air quality until the agency first determines how much of the different pollutants should be allowed in the air. Once it makes its determinations, EPA then must work with state environmental protection agencies to develop "implementation plans" in each state for the new air-pollutant standards. The implementation plans establish "enforceable emission limitations and other control measures . . . (including economic incentives such as fees, marketable permits, and auctions of emissions rights), as well as schedules and timetables for compliance."[11]

Thus, it is EPA rather than Congress that ultimately decides how much of a pollutant a factory should be able to emit. It is EPA that decides whether to impose a cap on emissions by the factory or to use financial incentives to get the factory to reduce its emissions. In addition, EPA sets the date by which its rules will take effect. After all of this (and more) is done, the agency can file enforcement actions in response to violations of the Clean Air Act.[12]

A recent example illustrates the broad discretion of executive agencies such as the EPA. In December 2009, the agency exercised its authority under the Clean Air Act to regulate emissions of carbon dioxide and five other greenhouse gases from motor vehicles. As part of its new regulatory regime and in conjunction with the Department of Transportation, the EPA proposed more demanding fuel-efficiency standards for cars and light trucks—Chrysler, Ford, GM, and other manufacturers would have to achieve a fleet average of 35.5 mpg by 2016, an increase from the previous requirement of 27.5 mpg.

After considering public comments about the proposal, the EPA announced the new standards as final rules in April 2010.[13] EPA and the Department of Transportation—not Congress—decided how fuel efficient cars must become.

Other statutes grant similar levels of discretion to executive branch agencies to determine the scope of federal law. When the Occupational Safety and Health Administration issues regulations to protect workplace safety, it may set standards that are "reasonably necessary . . . to provide safe or healthful employment." It also may regulate employee exposure to toxic materials in a way that "most adequately assures . . . that no employee will suffer material impairment of health."[14]

At one time, delegation of lawmaking power to the executive branch did not necessarily result in a meaningful expansion of presidential power. While Congress gave executive agencies broad authority to make law, the rule-making process often was driven more by the views of the civil service bureaucracy or the advocacy of the industries being regulated than by the views of the current president.[15]

However, recent presidents have increased their control over executive rule making to ensure that federal policy reflects presidential preferences. Ronald Reagan used his appointment power to staff agencies with officials who were distinguished by their personal loyalty and ideological commitment. He also expanded Office of Management and Budget (OMB) review of proposed rules to assess the rules' "regulatory impact." OMB review might delay implementation of a rule, cause it to be modified, or even result in its withdrawal by the agency. George H. W. Bush created the President's Council on Competitiveness to oversee rule making. Chaired by Vice President Dan Quayle, the council diluted or killed regulations applying to commercial aircraft noise, pollution from municipal incinerators, disclosure requirements for pension plans, and accessibility to housing for the disabled.[16]

Bill Clinton further expanded presidential control over administrative action. He brought independent agencies such as the Federal Trade Commission partially into the OMB review process, though with substantially less oversight than with executive branch agencies. For example, while independent agencies were not required to submit proposed individual rules for review, they were required to share their plans for regulatory action with other agencies, OMB, and Vice President Al Gore. If concerns arose regarding the consistency of the regulatory plans with other agency action or presidential priorities, Gore could request further consideration of the plan by the independent agency.[17]

Clinton also announced a more explicit policy of presidential authority to override executive agency decisions, even when Congress had rested decision-making authority in the office of the agency director. And Clinton's successors maintained this policy. Thus, for example, in September 2011, Barack Obama blocked a proposed rule by the EPA that would have significantly reduced emissions of chemicals that cause smog. In the next two months, Obama took other steps to exercise control over agency decision making. He delayed two other major clean-air regulations, authorized a significant expansion in offshore drilling for oil and gas, and postponed a decision on a controversial pipeline to transport Canadian shale oil to refineries in Oklahoma and Texas. In a ten-year period covering the administration of George W. Bush and the first two years of the Obama administration, White House review led to changes in 84 percent of EPA rules and 65 percent of rules from other agencies.[18]

Reagan, Clinton, and other recent presidents also assumed a more prominent personal role in the initiation of the rule-making process, making it clearer than their predecessors that they would be using executive agencies more aggressively to advance their political agendas. In 2011, for example, Obama's White House staff negotiated a sharp increase in fuel-economy standards for automobile manufacturers. As mentioned earlier, new standards were implemented in 2010. The next year, discussions that included administration representatives, auto companies, environmental groups, and public-health organizations resulted in an agreement to raise the standards even further, from 35.5 mpg in 2016 to 54.5 mpg in 2025. Once agreement was reached, EPA and the Department of Transportation were able to issue proposed rules for public comment.[19]

The White House has other ways to exploit the broad delegations of legislative authority. Rather than relying on the cumbersome rule-making process to exercise their statutory power, presidents can issue an executive order or similar directive to quickly turn their ideas into law. In addition, when presidents have failed to move parts of their policy agenda through Congress or when they knew that Congress would not enact their proposals, they have resorted to executive orders.

Thus, for example, when Congress did not pass a patients' bill of rights, Clinton implemented one through a pair of memoranda to executive branch agencies responsible for regulating health insurance plans offered to federal employees or to workers in the private sector. And when Congress was unwilling to fund loan guarantees to Mexico at a time of economic crisis for the country, Clinton authorized $20 billion in guarantees from his broad Exchange Stabilization Fund authority. Similarly, when Congress was poised to impose sweeping sanctions against South Africa in 1985, Reagan preempted legislative action by imposing his preferred milder sanctions through an executive order.[20]

To be sure, executive orders have their drawbacks. Because later presidents can revoke their predecessors' orders, the directives are less durable than joint legislative-executive action or administrative agency rule making. Barack Obama overrode George W. Bush's limitations on federal funding for stem cell research, and William Taft rescinded a number of Theodore Roosevelt's orders to conserve public lands as national parks or wildlife preserves. Jimmy Carter revised Richard Nixon's policy for the security classification of government information, and Ronald Reagan then revised Carter's policy.

Nevertheless, executive orders can be long-lived, as with the Peace Corps, which resulted from an executive order by John Kennedy in 1961. And they often are used for a president's most important policy initiatives, especially when managing wars and other national security matters, but also for domestic policy concerns such as civil rights. Abraham Lincoln used an executive order to suspend habeas corpus during the Civil War, Franklin Roosevelt used an executive order to intern Japanese Americans during World War II, and Harry Truman used an executive order to desegregate the military.[21]

In short, presidents from both parties have employed a number of practices to increase the extent to which executive branch policies reflect presidential rather than congressional philosophy. This has ensured that the transfer of lawmaking power from Congress has entailed not only a diminution of legislative power but also an increase in presidential power.[22]

The transfer of power to the executive branch has provoked criticism from some scholars, who view it as a violation of the Constitution's assignment of lawmaking power to the legislative branch. Nevertheless, the Supreme Court has accepted the delegations, reasoning that "in our increasingly complex society, replete with ever changing and more technical problems, Congress simply cannot do its job absent an ability to delegate power under broad general directives." (While the Court has cited considerations of efficiency, we also should worry that Congress may yield its authority to escape responsibility for controversial decisions. The public may applaud when Congress passes a law to clean up the environment, but people may become less enthusiastic when the EPA issues rules that exact a price for environmental protection.)[23]

Even though the transfer of authority has survived constitutional challenge, we cannot conclude that the transfer fulfills the Constitution's vision for the allocation of power between Congress and the president. Indeed, the main point of this section stands—the executive branch's extensive lawmaking power represents a substantial change from the balance of power that was envisioned by the founding fathers.[24]

And one need not be committed to original intent to be troubled by the transfer of authority. There were very good reasons for the framers' desire that lawmaking be a shared enterprise between Congress and the president, with primary responsibility rested in Congress. The sharing of responsibility prevents either branch from assuming too much power over the lawmaking process. An overweening Congress can be checked by the president, and a presumptuous president can be contained by Congress. In addition, by reserving the principal lawmaking role for the legislative branch, the framers sought to ensure that policy making would emerge from a robust debate among multiple decision makers who bring diverse perspectives to the table. Executive branch policy making is controlled by a single president with a single political perspective.

Presidential assumption of domestic policy power

In addition to exploiting congressional delegations of power, presidents have taken the initiative to expand their domestic authority in other ways. Executive orders are typically justified as authorized by statute, but presidents also may invoke the Constitution to take action that could properly be viewed as legislative in nature. For example, when Theodore Roosevelt and other presidents have used executive orders to reserve federal lands for national parks, they arguably were exercising their executive power to manage property owned by the federal government. But one also could argue that they were usurping the authority of Congress to determine the national government's policies for conservation.[25]

Presidents have other ways to substitute their own authority for legislative authority. For example, they may decline to enforce a federal statute, either by approving requests for waivers from statutory requirements or by exercising their discretion to refrain from prosecuting violations. In 2012, Barack Obama announced that he would not deport more than eight hundred thousand young immigrants who were in the United States illegally. Other presidents have been slow to crack down on anticompetitive behavior by large corporations.[26]

In another controversial approach, presidents have tried to increase their policy-making power through "signing statements" when approving new laws. Signing statements mostly are used to assert presidential authority on matters of foreign policy, but they also are used for statutes addressing domestic policy. The statements often provide the president's understanding of the legislation and therefore can play an important role in statutory interpretation.[27] However, presidents have used signing statements to effectively rewrite legislation after it has been passed by the House and Senate.

For example, George W. Bush issued signing statements rejecting provisions to establish affirmative action programs, to require disclosure of information to Congress, and to limit the president's discretion when making appointments to legislatively created commissions. For an earlier example involving international relations, Congress passed the Immigration Reform and Control Act of 1986 and created a pathway to citizenship for undocumented immigrants who had maintained a "continuous unlawful residence" in the United States since January 1, 1982. In creating the pathway, Congress decided that "brief, casual, and innocent" absences from the United States would not jeopardize an immigrant's eligibility for legal status. After approving the bill, Ronald Reagan issued a signing statement adding a requirement that any brief, casual, and innocent absences be authorized in advance by the Immigration and Naturalization Service.[28]

Presidents have used signing statements to expand not only their statutory authority but also their constitutional authority. After Congress passed legislation banning the torture of prisoners (the Detainee Treatment Act of 2005), George W. Bush issued a signing statement indicating that he reserved the right to authorize torture under his commander in chief power.[29]

Other practices by presidents have been questioned as well. Scholars have attacked efforts by the executive branch to maintain the secrecy of governmental information, as when presidents or other officials have asserted executive privilege or the need to protect national security. Recall, for example, Vice President Dick Cheney's refusal to disclose the names of oil industry executives with whom he discussed national energy policy.

Barack Obama acknowledged the problems with prior administration practices when he issued two memoranda the day after his inauguration directing executive branch agencies to observe a policy of greater transparency. But he was criticized for failing to live up to his promises. During the debate over health care legislation in 2009, Obama was slow to disclose meetings at the White House with health industry executives, and to avoid the new administration's disclosure requirements, officials often met with lobbyists at coffee shops rather than in the White House. After the massive oil spill from the BP well in the Gulf of Mexico in 2010, underwater video of the spill was withheld from the public by both BP and the Obama administration for three weeks, until congressional pressure finally led to its disclosure.[30]

This discussion of executive branch secrecy responds to an argument made by Alexander Hamilton in Federalist 70 for a single executive. According to Hamilton, it is important to have a one-person presidency to promote the government's interest in secrecy. However, experience has shown that a unitary executive results in too much secrecy. In addition to the examples already mentioned, the Reagan administration executed secret arms deals with Iran in the 1980s to raise funds for the Contras in their efforts to overthrow the government of Nicaragua. The transfers of weapons to Iran and funds to the Contras violated limitations imposed by federal legislation regarding international arms sales and U.S. intervention in Nicaragua.[31]

In some cases, the presidential exercise of power has crossed all constitutional barriers, as happened with Richard Nixon during the Watergate crisis. Watergate began on a night in June 1972 when police arrested agents for Nixon's reelection campaign. The agents had broken into Democratic National Committee headquarters at the Watergate office building in Washington, DC. Ultimately, Nixon was impeached and forced to resign because of a series of grave abuses of executive power. For a number of years, he had used the Internal Revenue Service, the Federal Bureau of Investigation, the Central Intelligence Agency, and other federal offices to undermine political opponents. Among the abuses perpetrated were an enemies list of people subject to illegal surveillance and leaks of information designed to discredit them. Nixon also used his presidential power to obstruct the investigation of the Watergate break-in. For example, he fired Justice Department officials who were investigating his administration (including those sacked in the infamous "Saturday Night Massacre").[32]

But even when presidents remain within the boundaries of the law, the growth of presidential power has entailed a substantial shift in domestic authority that undoes the balance of power envisioned by the constitutional framers.

Erosion of the unitary executive

To be sure, concerns about the balance of domestic power between the executive and legislative branches flow in both directions. While I have sketched a balance increasingly skewed in favor of the executive branch, scholars have engaged in lively debate on the question whether Congress has eroded the authority of the president and failed to recognize that the Constitution provides for a "unitary" executive who must exercise all of the executive branch's power. In this view, Congress acts unconstitutionally when it deprives presidents of some of their authority to direct the activity of the executive branch.[33]

And according to the unitary executive argument, Congress has redistributed the executive power frequently. It has created independent commissions and boards such as the Securities and Exchange Commission (SEC) and the Federal Reserve's Board of Governors to implement federal statutes. In addition, in an act that that led to the impeachment of Bill Clinton and that has since lapsed, Congress authorized the appointment of special counsels to investigate criminal allegations against high-ranking federal officials. Like the commissions and boards, the special counsels exercised their executive authority independently.

The loss of presidential control is apparent in a few ways. With the commissions or boards, presidents appoint the commissioners or board members, but once the officials are confirmed by the Senate and take office, they serve fixed terms that protect them from removal by the president who appointed them or the president's successor, who might want to appoint different officers. In addition, when the officials exercise their legislatively granted authority, the president may not modify or override the decisions. If presidents disagree with an enforcement action by the SEC or an interest-rate hike by the Federal Reserve, they can express their displeasure, and they might be able to influence future actions by their statements, but they cannot require a change in the decisions.

In the case of the special counsels, the attorney general recommended the appointments, but a panel of three federal judges actually made the appointments, and the counsels operated independently of the Justice Department or any other executive branch oversight.[34]

Most scholars do not think that the creation of independent commissions, boards, or counsels entails an unconstitutional diminution of presidential power, and in any event, presidents are able to exercise a good deal of control over even independent agencies through their control of the appointment process for agency officials.

But even to the extent that there are constraints on presidential power, they simply limit the extent to which lawmaking power has been transferred by Congress to the executive branch. There still has been a considerable transfer of power overall. In other words, while the president may not have full control of the entire executive power, the substantial growth of the executive power leaves the president with much more power than anticipated by the framers (just as 75 or 85 percent of one thousand is greater than 100 percent of five hundred).[35]

For the purposes of this book, the debate over the erosion of the unitary executive is important in another way. With the creation of independent commissions and boards and the dispersal of executive power among different officials, the executive branch has evolved from a unitary executive model to something that looks more like a plural executive. In chapter 7, I discuss the likelihood of this country adopting a two-person presidency. While it might seem that a two-person presidency entails a dramatic break from a one-person presidency, the fact that the U.S. government already has moved some distance from the unitary executive to a plural executive makes it easier to imagine the further move to a two-person presidency.

The expansion of presidential power over foreign affairs

The executive branch may have expanded its power substantially over domestic policy, but it has assumed even more power over foreign affairs. While presidents need to work with Congress to pass reforms for health care, Social Security, or other domestic matters, they frequently press their international initiatives unilaterally, with little congressional input.

As other scholars have noted, one would not predict the degree of presidential control over foreign affairs by reading the Constitution. When the Constitution assigns powers relating to foreign policy, it mostly assigns them to Congress. Thus, under Article I, Congress has the power to regulate commerce with other countries, to determine when foreign citizens can become U.S. citizens, to make violations of international law violations of federal law, to declare war, and to raise and support military forces. The power to regulate commerce was particularly important. The framers expected that "commercial rela-tions would constitute a major portion of America's overall relations with the world."[36]

The president, on the other hand, has a small set of powers, and most of them are to be shared with Congress. According to Article II, the president is commander in chief of the military forces, negotiates treaties with Senate advice and consent, and appoints ambassadors with Senate advice and consent. (The president also receives ambas-sadors from other countries, but that authority falls under Section 3 of Article II, which lists presidential duties rather than powers.[37]) Over time, however, by both presidential assumption and congressio-nal transfer, the president has come to play a dominant role in for-eign relations.

Presidential assumption of foreign policy power

Although constitutional text and original intent assign a primary role for Congress in shaping foreign policy that the president implements (as one would expect from a presidential power to execute the law), the president has assumed a primary role in shaping foreign policy.

Consider in this regard the evolution in understanding of the president's role as the "sole organ" of the country in foreign relations. While originally used to describe the president's responsibility to *communicate* the country's policies to foreign governments, the sole organ principle has come to describe the president's role in *deciding* the country's policies in foreign affairs, most notably in the opinion of Justice George Sutherland in the *Curtiss-Wright* case.[38]

Or consider the emergence of a presidential power to recognize foreign governments. Presidents have taken a shared power to appoint ambassadors and a unilateral, essentially ceremonial, duty to receive ambassadors from other countries and turned them into a unilateral power to recognize foreign governments. Presidents also reach agree-ments with other countries without congressional participation, they unilaterally terminate treaties, and they decide on their own about restrictions on the rights of U.S. citizens to travel abroad.[39]

It is not surprising that presidents have more aggressively expanded their authority in foreign policy than on matters of domestic policy. When contemplating unilateral action, they must consider the potential that their action will provoke opposition by Congress. Because domestic policies are more likely to offend the interests of legislators' constituents, presidents have to be more constrained in the domestic sphere. In addition, because of the implications for the country's international standing, Congress may be reluctant to undercut a president's foreign policy once it has been implemented.[40]

Some scholars mount an argument for broad presidential authority under a theory of inherent executive power in foreign affairs, an argument that finds support from the writings of Alexander Hamilton and theorists such as William Blackstone, John Locke, and Baron de Montesquieu, who influenced the framers and reflected the traditions of their time. In this view, the framers understood the Article II "executive power" to include substantial authority to make foreign policy.

But the inherent executive power argument exaggerates the support from Blackstone, Locke, and Montesquieu and goes against the great weight of other evidence, as indicated not only by the constitutional text but also by the Federalist Papers, the records of the Constitutional Convention, the debates in the states over ratification, the writings of James Madison, and Justice Robert Jackson's important opinion about the balance of foreign policy power in the *Steel Seizure* case.[41]

Consider, for example, the perspective of James Wilson, who made the motion for a single executive at the Constitutional Convention in June 1787 and was a leading advocate for its adoption. When discussing his motion, Wilson observed that the "only powers he conceived strictly Executive were those of executing the laws." Or recall the point in Federalist 48 that the executive power is less extensive, more susceptible to precise limits, and restrained within a narrower compass than is the legislative power. And when Alexander Hamilton discussed the powers of the president in Federalist 69, he gave no hint of any inherent executive power. Rather, he described the executive power as being comparable to that of a state's governor, but for the president's shared authority with the Senate to make treaties.[42]

The framers meant to break with the executive traditions of their time, not to preserve them. And in any event, even under a theory of inherent executive power, it is difficult to justify the extent to which presidents have exercised their authority on matters of foreign policy.

Constitutional experts have expressed particular concern about the expansion of presidential power with regard to wartime activities. Despite the provision in Article I of the Constitution that Congress shall have the power to declare war, Harry Truman took the United States into the Korean War without congressional authorization. Similarly, when Bill Clinton unilaterally sent U.S. troops or air power for smaller-scale operations in Afghanistan, Iraq, Somalia, and Sudan, he violated the Constitution's division of war-making power. Indeed, when Clinton approved the military's 1999 bombings of Serbian military targets to halt the slaughter of ethnic Albanians in Kosovo, he not only did so without prior congressional authorization; he also continued the air strikes even after the House of Representatives failed to approve them in a 213–213 vote. More recently, Barack Obama launched military action against Libya without congressional authorization.[43]

The framers deliberately chose to divide the war-making power between Congress and the president as part of its effort to avoid the kinds of abuses of power that occurred with rulers who possessed the authority of a king. The president was to be the commander in chief of the armed forces on the battlefield, but it was for Congress to decide in the first place whether to commit U.S. forces to battle. By giving Congress the authority to decide when to commence hostilities against another country, the framers sought to make it difficult for the country to go to war. The framers recognized that executives are more prone than legislators to wage war. Moreover, legislatures move more slowly than executives. As George Mason put it, the Constitution should be about clogging rather than facilitating war.[44]

To be sure, the framers wanted to reserve for the president the ability to repel a military attack on the United States. Hence, when choosing the specific language for Congress's war power, the framers chose to make it a power to "declare" war rather than "make" war. But in the absence of an enemy's attack, the president must wait for congressional permission to launch military operations. As John Hart Ely wrote, the original understanding of the Constitution often is obscure, but not in the case of the power to initiate a war. The historical evidence establishes, observed Ely, that "all wars, big or small, . . . had to be legislatively authorized."[45] Nevertheless, presidential encroachment on the legislative war power has been common.

Also very troubling are the examples of presidential action that go beyond the constitutional authority of either the executive or legislative branch. Launching military operations without a congressional declaration of war may violate the Constitution's allocation of powers, but the waging of war is permissible under our Constitution when initiated by a congressional declaration. Sometimes, however, presidents do things that the national government may not lawfully do, regardless of the procedures employed.

In the aftermath of the September 11, 2001, attacks by al-Qaeda on the United States, the executive branch was unusually aggressive in pushing the president's authority beyond all constitutional limits. An important insider's perspective is provided by Jack Goldsmith, who headed the Justice Department's Office of Legal Counsel during the George W. Bush administration until he resigned after nine and a half months. As Goldsmith observed, the Bush administration promoted an unusually expansive view of executive power, which led it to embrace highly troublesome and unconstitutional policies. When Bush authorized the torture of enemy combatants, he was authorizing action that no government official had the power to authorize.[46]

Other presidents also have crossed constitutional limits in wartime. Roosevelt wrongly approved the internment of American citizens of Japanese descent during World War II, and Lincoln "imprisoned thousands of southern sympathizers and war agitators without any charge or due process."[47]

In short, presidents often have acted on their own to greatly expand the executive branch's foreign policy power. As discussed in the next section, presidents also have seen that power enlarged by Congress.

Congressional transfer of foreign policy power

Just as Congress has increased presidential control of *domestic* affairs by a transfer of legislative authority to the executive branch, so has Congress increased presidential control of *foreign* affairs by a transfer of legislative authority to the executive branch. And just as the Supreme Court has permitted Congress to delegate its domestic legislative authority to the president, so it has permitted Congress to delegate to the president its authority over foreign relations. The transfer of authority began in the late 19th Century, but it was carefully limited until the New Deal. As with the delegation of domestic authority, the delegation of foreign authority accelerated during the administration of Franklin Delano Roosevelt, and it has resulted since then in quite a substantial transfer of power.[48]

Congress has especially ceded its authority to participate in the reaching of accords with other countries. The Constitution's only mechanism for such agreements is set out in Article II, which states that treaties are to be negotiated by the president and ratified by the Senate. Important examples of treaties include the Treaty of Ghent, which ended the War of 1812 between the United States and Great Britain, and the North Atlantic Treaty in 1949, which created NATO. In the 19th Century, presidents and Congresses began to depart from the constitutional model for treaties, with each acting unilaterally at times and at other times setting foreign policy through the joint participation of the president, the House, and the Senate. Since World War II, Congress and presidents have favored the option of presidentially negotiated agreements that are subsequently passed by both the House and the Senate. Major trade agreements such as the North American Free Trade Agreement (NAFTA) followed this path.[49]

While presidential-congressional agreement ensures legislative approval of the actual terms of accords with other countries, Congress also has given presidents broad powers to enter into executive agreements with foreign governments without requiring legislative approval of the terms of the pacts. In these "ex-ante congressional-executive agreements," Congress authorizes the president to undertake negotiations with governments of foreign countries on military cooperation, drug interdiction, economic trade, or other policy matters, and leaves the United States bound by the commitments made by the president.

At one time, Congress authorized ex-ante congressional-executive agreements rarely and subjected the president to strict constraints. Now these agreements have become the avenue for the great majority of all legal commitments by the United States to foreign countries, and presidents are given broad leeway in negotiating their terms. Under a series of acts, for example, the president is authorized to provide military assistance to other countries if the president finds that the assistance will "strengthen the security interests of the United States and promote world peace." The president also may make loans "on such terms and conditions as he may determine, in order to promote the economic development" of other countries. Once Congress has granted such authority, its approval is not needed for the agreements to take effect. In sensitive areas such as military sales, Congress may require notice before an agreement is concluded, so it can exercise its option to block the sale. But to do so, the House and Senate both would have to pass a joint resolution or legislative proposal rejecting the sale, and the resolution or bill would be subject to a presidential veto.[50]

Note how the degree of discretion for the president to conclude executive agreements with other countries parallels the degree of discretion granted domestic agencies in the executive branch to implement federal statutes. Military assistance can be provided to other countries as a president deems necessary to protect the security interests of the United States, and the EPA can set air-quality standards as needed to protect the public health of the United States.

There also is overlap between the delegation of domestic policy power and the delegation of foreign policy power in the reasons for the congressional transfers of authority. As discussed, considerations of efficiency can justify the transfer of domestic legislative power to the executive branch. In an increasingly complex society, it does not seem feasible for Congress to decide the details of all of the federal government's policies. Similarly, it may be more feasible for the executive branch than Congress to take action with respect to international affairs. For some foreign policy matters, the executive branch will have better access to key information and therefore will be better equipped than Congress to make decisions.[51] Or some matters may demand that action be taken more quickly than is possible for a large, deliberative body.

But there also may be foreign policy issues for which Congress is tempted to abdicate its decision-making responsibilities. Making the wrong call on a matter of foreign policy can impose very high costs on a member of Congress. Senators and representatives do not want to face charges by an opponent that they compromised national security or placed American troops in danger. Just as leaving domestic policy decisions to the president allows members of Congress to pass the buck for potentially controversial decisions, so does leaving foreign policy decisions to the president.[52]

In sum, consideration of the balance of power between the president and Congress on both domestic and foreign affairs makes clear that the executive branch exercises far more policy-making power than anticipated by the framers and has become the stronger rather than the weaker branch when compared to Congress. The framers were simply incorrect in Federalists 48, 51, and 71 when they worried about the dominance of the legislative branch and felt they had to divide the legislative power between the Senate and House to maintain balance between Congress and the president. Indeed, since the dissolution of the Soviet Union, the president of the United States may be the most powerful public official in world history, at least when it comes to shaping policy on international affairs.[53]

The failure of Congress or the courts to check the president

Despite decades of concern about the expansion of executive power and the potential for abuse of that power, neither Congress nor the Supreme Court has fulfilled its constitutional role and checked the expansion.[54] Indeed, in the transfer of legislative power to the executive branch, Congress has fostered the growth of presidential control over both domestic and foreign policy.

Other examples of congressional abdication abound. In the face of presidential assertions of power to conduct military operations, Congress often has ducked its constitutional responsibilities and failed to act. When Barack Obama decided in 2009 to escalate the military's role in Afghanistan, for example, Congress remained on the sidelines.

Similarly, Congress assumed a mostly passive role when George W. Bush and Obama made other military decisions after the September 11, 2001, attacks on the United States. A week after 9/11, Congress passed its Authorization for the Use of Military Force, in which it gave the president authority to "to use all necessary and appropriate force" against "those nations, organizations, or persons" that the president determines were involved in the 9/11 attacks "in order to prevent any future acts of international terrorism against the United States." In contrast to what one might expect in a declaration of war, Congress gave the president broad discretion to decide whom we should fight, where we should fight, and for how long we should fight. There has not been the jockeying for control—the countering of ambition against ambition—that the framers envisioned between the executive and legislative branches. Rather, Congress has deferred to presidential decision making in the war on terror and supported without much question the presidents' requests for military appropriations. Of course, the president is the commander in chief and enjoys constitutional authority to determine military strategy once a war is declared. However, Congress's power to declare war should result in something more precise than an open-ended authorization to pursue an undefined group of targets.[55]

When Congress has tried to check presidential action, it has not been very effective. To prevent unilateral commitments of military forces by the president, Congress passed the War Powers Resolution in 1973, essentially codifying its constitutional authority to declare war. However, the resolution has been rejected by every president since its passage, and it was violated most recently by Obama's use of the military in Libya. Congress also has struggled when it tried to address domestic abuse of executive power. In the wake of the Watergate crisis, Congress enacted the independent counsel provisions of the Ethics in Government Act of 1978. While the provisions were upheld against constitutional attack by the Supreme Court, many investigations and prosecutions by the independent counsel were highly controversial—most notably the Kenneth Starr–led investigation that led to the impeachment of Bill Clinton—and Congress allowed the provisions to expire. Or consider the weak efforts by Congress to cabin the presidential power to issue executive orders. Between 1973 and 1997, Congress considered legislation to limit executive orders only three times, and none of the bills emerged from committee.[56]

The judiciary also has facilitated the development of the imperial presidency. At one time, the Supreme Court applied a "nondelegation doctrine" to limit congressional transfer of lawmaking power to the executive branch, but no statute has been invalidated on nondelegation grounds since 1935.[57]

When individuals have objected to a presidential foreign policy decision, the Supreme Court and circuit courts of appeal frequently have failed to act by invoking procedural doctrines that prevent a case from being heard. During the Vietnam War, the Supreme Court often declined to hear challenges to the constitutionality of the war by denying petitions for reconsideration of lower court decisions (petitions for certiorari). In other cases involving the Vietnam War or other military actions, the Supreme Court and the courts of appeal have held that the plaintiffs objecting to presidential action lacked "standing" to do so, have found that the challenges were brought prematurely and were not yet "ripe" for adjudication, or have remained uninvolved by deciding that the matter was a "political question" that must be resolved through the political process. When Jimmy Carter decided to recognize mainland China instead of Taiwan as the government of China, the Supreme Court declined to hear a challenge to Carter's unilateral termination of a mutual defense treaty with Taiwan. A majority of justices saw the case as involving a political question or as not yet ripe for adjudication.[58]

At other times, courts have affirmed presidential assertions of extraconstitutional authority. In *United States v. Curtiss-Wright Corp.*, the Supreme Court recognized an inherent authority for the president to be the sole representative of the United States in its relations with foreign nations. Shortly thereafter, the Court upheld presidential power to recognize foreign governments and to enter into agreements with foreign countries even when there was no prior congressional authorization or subsequent congressional approval.[59]

To be sure, the Supreme Court sometimes has stepped in when the president has engaged in action that went beyond the executive branch's authority or beyond any national government authority. Thus, for example, the Court rejected Harry Truman's seizure of steel mills because of a labor strike during the Korean War. In addition, the Court has intervened to ensure that suspected members or supporters of al-Qaeda be treated fairly when imprisoned by the United States. However, the Court also has failed to block egregious presidential action that exceeds the power of the national government, as when it upheld the internment of Americans of Japanese descent during World War II.[60]

Moreover, even when the Court does override executive action, its rulings may have little consequence. Although the Court invoked constitutional restraints on executive branch treatment of al-Qaeda suspects and other "enemy combatants," the decisions appear not to have changed executive branch behavior. Indeed after 2008, by which time the Supreme Court had issued three decisions in which it rejected assertions of executive authority, the executive branch had become less likely to release prisoners held at its detention facility in Guantanamo Bay, Cuba, and more likely to detain prisoners at its facility in Bagram, Afghanistan. Moreover, in its decisions, the Court has declined to reach the merits of detention policy and so failed to give guidance on when it is permissible to detain an enemy combatant.[61]

Problems with the expansion of presidential power

The broad expansion of presidential policy-making authority is problematic for two important reasons. First, it has skewed the balance of power between the legislative and executive branches in favor of the executive branch. Second, it allows for policy making in the absence of a deliberative process among individuals who bring diverse perspectives to their decision making.

Undermining the balance of power

As discussed earlier, the framers of the Constitution worried about the potential for the abuse of power by the legislative branch. But in their efforts to prevent a politically dominant Congress, the framers left the country instead with a politically dominant executive branch. The constitutional plan for coequal branches of government may have worked reasonably well for the first 150 years, but since the 1930s, it has collapsed.

For many scholars, this is a sufficient argument to condemn the imperial presidency. The separation of powers is a core feature of the constitutional system in the United States. If there are developments that compromise the framers' goal of a balance of powers in the national government, then steps should be taken to restore the intended balance. Whether one believes in the Constitution's allocation of governmental power from principles of original intent or because balance is needed to prevent the aggrandizement and abuse of power, the status quo is not acceptable. Imperial presidents have too many opportunities to take action detrimental to the public interest.

Might one instead argue that the expansion of presidential power is actually a good thing? Perhaps the framers misjudged the roles of the president and Congress and failed to appreciate how the demands of governance would change over time. The United States is a far larger, far more globally interdependent country than it was in 1787. In the view of some scholars, an imperial president is exactly what the United States needs for the 21st Century.

Indeed, it is argued, the growth of presidential power reflects the necessities of the modern American state. In an increasingly complex economy, a legislative body simply lacks the capacity to regulate directly all of the different industries that need governmental oversight. In this view, Congress cannot write specific rules for banks, insurers, airlines, railroads, automobile makers, mining companies, gas and oil drillers, and pharmaceutical, food, or cigarette manufacturers, nor can it adopt comprehensive rules that govern the issuance of securities or the extension of credit. There are too many enterprises to be regulated and too many rules to be written for Congress to retain full responsibility for policy making.

Moreover, legislative bodies lack the kind of expertise that is required to oversee the many kinds of economic activity that take place in the United States. A few members of Congress may be specialists in health care, energy generation, environmental protection, or banking, but they do not have the time to study the issues within their field of expertise when the issues come before the House or the Senate. And no member brings a deep understanding on all of the matters that Congress addresses.[62]

It is not only the case that we live in an increasingly complex society. As William Scheuerman has argued, we also leave in an era of "social acceleration" in which the economy operates at a much faster pace, technological innovation occurs more rapidly, and social organization is more frequently reordered. A slow-acting, deliberative legislature cannot keep up and adapt the law quickly enough to societal change. Alexander Hamilton's "energetic" executive who can act with dispatch, on the other hand, is much better suited for policy making in the modern, high-speed environment. From the perspective of a complex, swiftly moving, and rapidly evolving society, it does not seem so surprising that Congress has delegated much of its policy-making authority to the executive branch.[63]

But must Congress yield as much discretion as it does to the executive branch?

In fact, Congress sometimes does retain much more control over the details of lawmaking than it does at other times. Congress may have given the EPA wide discretion to set air-quality standards for factory emissions or fuel-efficiency requirements for motor vehicles, but Congress has not given the Department of the Treasury the same authority when it comes to writing the tax code. It was Congress that decided to recognize a reduction in tax liability for payments of interest on home mortgages, it was Congress that decided to grant a deduction from income rather than a credit against taxes due, and it was Congress that decided that the deduction applies to a person's principal residence and one other residence. And Congress sometimes writes its environmental laws with greater specificity.[64]

If Congress could have retained more of its legislative power, we might better understand the delegation of power in terms of the extent to which there are political benefits or risks for legislators in retaining control of policy. In many cases, delegation allows Congress to avoid politically controversial decisions. Senators and representatives can take credit for passing legislation to protect the environment, children, or workers but leave it to the executive branch to fashion the regulations that inevitably will anger some people for being too onerous or other people for being too lax.[65]

Writing tax codes also can elicit public discontent, but there are important political benefits to retaining tight control over tax policy. The ability to grant tax breaks for interest groups that represent politically powerful constituencies can assure important support for members of Congress when they run for reelection or higher office. Thus, the tax code abounds with deductions or credits for corporations, homeowners, and others who play decisive roles in the electoral process because of their financial resources or their votes.[66]

Whatever the respective roles of legislative capacity and legislative abdication to explain the transfer of power to the executive branch, we should be concerned. Even if it is true that Congress had no choice but to foster the expansion of presidential policy-making power, the framers were right to worry about governmental power that is not subject to meaningful checks and balances. Power really does corrupt. The harm to the public from the abuse of power can be serious, as when soldiers die during the waging of an unnecessary war or when governmental agencies are used by a president to harass those who are critical of the administration's policies. Delegation of legislative power to the executive branch may have been necessary, but that does not justify a delegation without sufficient safeguards to cabin the exercise of the transferred power.

What about the safeguards that Congress employs to check its delegations of power? Congress has not given the president a blank check; rather, it has employed a number of strategies for containing executive power. It has oversight committees, for example, and it can use its budget-authorizing power to discourage inappropriate regulatory actions by the executive branch. These safeguards are important, but oversight that occurs from a distance and often after the fact (as when Congress convenes hearings to investigate a mine disaster or a meltdown in the financial markets) is less effective than retaining direct responsibility for the actions.

In addition, the Supreme Court took away a key form of legislative oversight when it held the "legislative veto" unconstitutional in the *Chadha* case. Before *INS v. Chadha*, Congress included legislative veto provisions in many of its statutes. The legislative veto allowed both houses of Congress, one house alone, a committee of either house, or even a single legislator to override an action taken by the executive branch to implement a statute. Absent a legislative veto, Congress can override executive interpretation of a statute only by amending the statute and securing the president's agreement for the amendment.[67]

But even if Congress had adequate tools to police the president, congressional oversight would be weakened too much by an additional defect—the influence of partisan considerations. On one hand, oversight can be excessive when power is divided along party lines between the executive and legislative branches. A Republican majority in Congress may use its oversight authority to harass a Democratic president, while a Democratic majority in Congress may use the oversight power to harass a Republican president. One-party control of the White House and Capitol Hill may correct for the problem of excessive oversight, but it overcompensates by leaving members of the congressional majority insufficiently willing to challenge their party colleague in the Oval Office.

In short, we should worry about the expansion of executive power and the inability of Congress to contain presidential exercise of that power.

Unilateral policy making

The growth of executive power is problematic not only because it upsets the balance of power between Congress and the president.

More importantly, the broad expansion of presidential policy making has changed the nature of the presidential role in a way that compromises the effectiveness of the national government. The Constitution envisions a president with secondary responsibility for the creation of national policy and primary responsibility for the execution of national policy. However, the contemporary president enjoys primary responsibility for both the creation and execution of national policy. As a result, there is a mismatch between the design of the executive branch and the responsibilities of the executive branch. The assumption of policy-making responsibility by the president allows national policy to be made in the absence of a deliberative process involving multiple decision makers.

Of course, it makes sense to have a single person who can act decisively and with dispatch when the person is an executor of policy made by others. But the founding fathers correctly reserved policy making for multiple-person bodies that can develop the country's positions through a robust and unrushed debate among diverse perspectives. As Woodrow Wilson wrote, the "whole purpose of democracy is that we may hold counsel with one another, so as not to depend upon the understanding of one man." And as I discuss in chapter 5, studies by economists, psychologists, and other researchers have shown that multiple decision makers are better decision makers than single decision makers. The assumption of policy-making responsibility by the president has resulted in a less effective decision-making process for the national government.[68]

To be sure, there are times when the desire to provide for adequate deliberation conflicts with the need for expeditious action. Rapidly evolving events occur that were not expected by the legislature and therefore not anticipated in existing law. When a quick response by the government is needed, a unitary executive can act with the dispatch that is beyond the capability of a legislative body.[69] And by using the power to issue executive orders, presidents often have moved quickly.

But we do not have to choose between good decision making and expeditious decision making. A 535-person Congress may move slowly, but small groups do not. As discussed in the next section and in chapter 5, a two-person presidency offers the promise of better decision making without having to sacrifice timeliness in making the decisions.

Moreover, even with a single president, the executive branch generally does not act with decisiveness and dispatch when exercising its policy-making responsibilities. The wheels of the administrative agency regulatory process turn slowly, and it can take years or even decades for new rules to be issued. When the Obama administration took office in January 2009, it recognized the need to overhaul the Minerals Management Service's regulation of deep-water drilling for oil and gas. However, the Secretary of the Interior did not implement the needed changes at Minerals Management until it was forced to do so in April 2010 by the major oil spill from a BP well in the Gulf of Mexico.[70]

Other rules take even longer. In 1982, the EPA began a required review of its air-quality standards for the "particulate matter" that causes smog. Fifteen years passed before a final rule was issued. It took EPA more than twenty years to issue limits on the emissions of mercury, arsenic, and other toxins from power plants that burn coal or oil. In general, administrative agencies issue only a fraction of the rules that Congress has mandated them to write.[71]

Even with respect to foreign affairs, which may unfold in especially unpredictable and fast-paced fashion, it is not clear that the argument in favor of dispatch is persuasive. As William Scheuerman has observed, "history is filled with the annals of expeditious but irresponsible and adventuresome rulers." A quick decision can turn out badly and cause much harm, while a slower decision can ensure time for a correct analysis of the situation.[72]

Indeed, it can take a fair amount of time to understand what is going on with, and how best to respond to, unanticipated and rapidly evolving developments. During the 2008 presidential campaign, for example, when armed conflict erupted between Russia and Georgia, Republican nominee John McCain reacted quickly on the basis of incomplete information and aimed all of his criticism at Russia. As more facts came out, it became clear that both countries acted badly. Or consider the problems that the Obama administration encountered when officials hastily characterized the chain of events that led to the September 2012 killing of Christopher Stevens, the

U.S. ambassador to Libya. In early comments, the administration described the attack as a spontaneous outgrowth of anti-American protests provoked by a video offensive to Muslims. As more information became available, the administration recognized that the assassination reflected a planned terrorist operation.[73] Taking some time before responding to unexpected events makes it more likely that the response will be appropriate.

In short, policy making in the executive branch generally does not benefit from the ability of a single president to act decisively and with dispatch, but it does suffer from the absence of a deliberative process among multiple decision makers.[74]

What about the fact that presidents do not make decisions by themselves? Do they not always consult with advisers and receive input from many experts? As discussed in the next section and in chapter 5, a single decision maker with multiple advisers does not make for the kind of deliberative process that results from multiple decision makers with diverse perspectives. Presidential decision making results in policy making without the robustness of debate that promotes good policy making.

The promise of a two-person presidency

As discussed, the executive branch has exercised power far beyond the intentions of the constitutional framers. History has shown that the external checks and balances of Congress and the Supreme Court have not worked as intended. Congress has fostered the imperial presidency by transferring some of its own power to the executive branch, failing to oppose presidential exercises of excessive power, or acting ineffectively when it has tried to check the president. The Supreme Court too has aided the expansion of presidential power, sometimes by approving it, other times by refusing to consider challenges to executive action.

If the constitutional structure has yielded an executive branch that has gained too much policy-making power, we need to revise the basic structure to compensate for the misallocation of power. Dividing the authority of the executive branch between two presidents would provide a well-tailored response to the problem.

Dividing the executive power

While a two-person presidency would not undo much of the transfer of policy-making power to the executive branch during the past seventy-five years, it would decrease the ability of the executive branch to exercise its power or to usurp the power of the legislative branch. In addition, a two-person presidency would turn policy making in the executive branch into a deliberative process with multiple decision makers.

First, a two-person presidency would restore the framers' intended balance of power between the president and Congress, and it would do so with the kind of structural mechanism for containing power that the framers favored.

Specifically, a bipartisan executive would remain faithful to the constitutional design of limiting power by dividing it and requiring it to be shared. Just as the framers purposely weakened the legislative power by dividing it between a House and a Senate, so can we purposely weaken the executive power by dividing it between two presidents. Just as the need to reach a consensus between the House and the Senate slows the pace of legislative activity, so would the need to reach a consensus between the two presidents slow the pace of executive activity. A bipartisan presidency ought to produce fewer legislative proposals, fewer executive orders, less rule making, and fewer military operations. The framers caused an imbalance in executive-legislative power with their division of only the legislative power; a two-person presidency can restore balance with its division of the executive power.

But might less executive activity be undesirable? What about the good regulations, executive orders, and military operations that have come from the White House?

Answering these questions takes us to the second key advantage of a two-person presidency—it addresses the problem of *unilateral* policy making in the executive branch. Presidents consult with advisers before taking action, but they alone have authority to decide, and their advisers tend to reinforce, rather than challenge, their thinking. Poor judgment may not be corrected. With presidential pairs, policy making would emerge from a deliberative process between two, equal decision makers. And because the two presidents would represent different political parties, they would bring different governing philosophies to their deliberations. As I discuss in chapter 5, two persons with different perspectives make better decisions than do single decision makers, even when single decision makers operate with the advice of others. Hence, while presidential pairs might be less active than single executives, their actions would be better for the country.

In addition, a two-person presidency could actually make it easier for the White House to promote its initiatives. As I discuss in chapter 4, the sharing of power across party lines would dampen partisan conflict and diminish the level of obstruction that presidents face from Congress. For many proposals, two presidents could find a clearer path to adoption than would a single president.

There are other advantages from a two-person presidency. For example, it would not suffer from the debilities that occur when large groups try to make collective decisions. While I elaborate on this point in chapter 5, it is worth some discussion here too. Supporters of expansive presidential authority point to the ineffectual decision making of Congress. As the proponents of executive power observe, very large legislative groups can bog down quickly from partisan disputes or the individual pursuit of personal interest by members of the group. The July–August 2011 effort to raise the U.S. debt ceiling is illustrative. Barack Obama and House Speaker John Boehner seemed poised at a number of points in the process to agree on a major deficit-cutting deal, but each time, the "Tea Party" wing of the Republican House caucus nixed Boehner's concessions and demanded stricter fiscal terms. Because of the inability of Congress to respond decisively and with dispatch, it is argued, we really do need the president to take charge of important decisions, especially when the country faces an economic or national security crisis.[75]

But the fact that one president can be a superior decision maker to a 535-person Congress does not mean that one president would be a superior decision maker to a two-person presidency. In fact, while large groups become unwieldy in their decision making, small groups do not. Small groups make better decisions than do either large groups or individual decision makers. And people in small groups can come to a consensus when people in large groups cannot. Thus, while Boehner was frustrated in rallying the support of his 239 House Republican colleagues, he was much better able to come to terms with Obama alone.[76]

In addition to restoring balance between the executive and legislative branches and ensuring that policy making in the executive branch occurs through a deliberative process, there is another important benefit from a two-person presidency. It does not try to settle the debate as to exactly where the line should be drawn between executive and legislative authority. As the case law and the academic debate illustrate, there is much uncertainty on that question. According to Justice Robert Jackson's highly influential opinion in the *Steel Seizure* case, for example, "there is a zone of twilight in which [the president] and Congress may have concurrent authority, or in which its distribution is uncertain."[77]

The framers left some flexibility in the allocation of power, expecting the president and Congress to sort things out. Rather than engaging in a fruitless effort to define clear boundaries, we can follow the model of the framers. They used their structural provisions—the division and sharing of authority—to foster an appropriate balance of power between the executive and legislative branches. A two-person presidency can expand the division and sharing of power to ensure the more balanced playing field that the framers intended.

In addition, a two-person, bipartisan executive would generate the kind of competition for power that Madison envisioned. While Congress has not challenged presidential assertions of power but instead has fostered them, a second president would play the checking and balancing role intended by the Constitution's separation of powers.

Adopting a bipartisan executive not only can help protect against presidential encroachment on congressional power; it also would make it much more difficult for presidents to engage in action that the Constitution forbids for any branch of the national government.

It is difficult to imagine Democratic nominee Hubert Humphrey having agreed with Richard Nixon to use the CIA, FBI, and IRS against political enemies or to imagine joint appointees of Humphrey and Nixon cooperating with presidential orders to misuse the powers of the CIA, FBI, and IRS. Similarly, it is difficult to imagine legal memos approving torture having emerged from a Justice Department overseen by a joint appointee of George W. Bush and Democratic nominee Al Gore.

Shared decision making in medicine demonstrates nicely how a second decision maker can check the excesses of a single decision maker. Historically, physicians made treatment decisions unilaterally, often without even disclosing important information to patients about the need for the treatment or the patient's condition. In one illustrative study, 88 percent of physicians reported a standard practice of not disclosing the diagnosis when they discovered that their patients had cancer. But unilateral decision making by physicians is susceptible to abuse. In particular, during the debate over health care reform in 2009 and 2010, policy makers focused on the extent to which health care costs are driven up because physicians have financial incentives to perform too many surgeries or other procedures. Under the predominant "fee-for-service" method of compensation, a physician earns more by doing more, regardless of whether a procedure is desirable. As a result, procedures often are provided when the patient would be better off without the treatment. Researchers have found that involving patients in the decision-making process supplies an effective constraint on the tendency for physicians to overuse surgery and other medical treatments. When patients are involved in deciding about their medical care, they are less likely to choose treatments that are more aggressive, more expensive, and not likely to result in any improvement in their condition.[78] Just as a patient can check the excesses of physician decision making, a second president can check the excesses of executive decision making.

Indeed, it is not clear that the framers would have chosen a single president had they been able to anticipate the extent to which presidential power would grow. Their unhappy experiences with King George III left them very familiar with the potential for abuse of executive power, and they relied on electoral accountability and their system of checks and balances to contain the president. However, they misjudged how presidential power would evolve over time. With a greater capacity to predict the future, they would have been much more receptive to the option of a plural executive that they considered and rejected.[79]

Changing the relationship between the executive and legislative branches

If a two-person presidency would reduce the policy-making activity of the executive branch, there would be a noticeable shift from presidents to Congresses in terms of where policy initiatives originate. Nevertheless, we still would see an active and engaged executive branch. Presidents are eager to leave a legacy, and that would encourage two presidents to work cooperatively on major policy initiatives. I discuss this point in more detail in chapter 5.

But is it really a good idea to change the balance of power between the executive and legislative branches in favor of the legislative branch? Given the level of dysfunction on Capitol Hill and of public dissatisfaction with Congress, why shrink the White House's policy-making role?

Much of the dissatisfaction with Congress reflects the increasingly partisan nature of Washington politics. As I discuss in chapter 4, a coalition presidency is designed to address not only the expansion of executive power but also the excesses of partisan conflict. Currently with an imperial presidency, one political party secures a tremendous amount of power after a presidential election. Accordingly, legislators from the president's party have strong incentives to support Oval Office policies so their party can retain the executive power, and members from the other party have strong incentives to oppose Oval Office policies so their party can retake the executive power. If members of Congress were to deal with a bipartisan White House that had diminished power, they would have much less reason to draw battle lines in terms of partisan considerations.

While I have argued that a bipartisan presidency would result in a better balance of power between the executive and legislative branches, there also is the possibility that any rebalancing would be undone by an increased use of the presidential veto. Since enactment of a bill would require agreement by both of the presidents, each one would possess the power to veto legislation. Bills passed by a Democratic Congress always would come before a Republican president, and bills passed by a Republican Congress always would come before a Democratic president. Might the presidential veto compromise the goal of leveling the balance of power between the executive and legislative branches by weakening the legislative power?

During particular election cycles, there likely would be a diminution in congressional activity from a two-person presidency, in addition to the diminution in presidential activity. Overall, however, the impact is unpredictable. Whether Congress would be more or less active would depend on partisan control of the legislative branch. If Democrats controlled Congress, and a one-person presidency would yield a Democratic president, then adding a Republican president would make it more difficult for Congress to enact its preferred laws. An Obama-McCain presidency would have given less support than did President Obama to the legislative agenda of the Democrats in Congress in 2009–2010. However, if a one-person presidency would yield a Republican president to work with a Democratic Congress, then adding a Democratic president should make it easier for Congress to enact its preferred laws. If the House and Senate were divided by party, then adding a second president should not affect the ability of Congress to enact its preferred laws. Before any bill was passed out of Congress, it would have to satisfy the concerns of both Democrats and Republicans, whether there were one or two presidents.

The relationship between the national and state governments

In addition to changes within the national government, we might wonder whether a two-person presidency would result in a change in the balance of power between the national and state governments. If a two-person presidency would diminish the activity of the president and Congress, would state governments assume a greater role in the country's making of policy?

It is difficult to know how a two-person presidency would affect the national-state balance. If a coalition presidency sufficiently damp-ened partisan conflict and resulted in more cooperation across party lines, then its overall effect on the activity of the national government might result in an increase or no change rather than a decrease.

The inadequacy of other proposed solutions

Other scholars have discussed the problem of excessive executive power and have suggested a number of solutions, but none of them is up to the task of containing the imperial presidency. For example, Arthur Schlesinger, Jr., considered structural changes such as requir-ing the president to consult with a Council of State or switching to a parliamentary system. He concluded that such changes would cause more problems than they would solve and therefore argued against tinkering with the constitutional machinery. In his view, the impe-rial presidency results not from a defective constitutional system but from the defective use of a good constitutional system. The Consti-tution's primary recourse for presidential excesses is its principle of accountability. Accordingly, the public and Congress must take their political responsibilities more seriously and exercise their ample abili-ties to check excessive exercises of presidential power.[80]

Jack Goldsmith has taken a similar view. In his reflections on the exercise of executive power in the George W. Bush administra-tion, Goldsmith wrote that "our constitutional democracy will not be preserved by better laws and institutional structures, but rather . . . by leaders . . . who have checks and balances stitched into their breasts." Frederick A. O. Schwarz, Jr., and Aziz Huq also have called on Congress to exercise its constitutional authority and responsibility more effectively, and Peter Shane has discussed ways in which presi-dents could temper the executive branch's assumption of power and members of Congress could play their checking and balancing role more effectively.[81]

Schlesinger, Goldsmith, Schwarz and Huq, and Shane are correct about the availability of tools for Congress and the public to hold the president in check and about the duty of presidents to adhere to their constitutional obligations. If presidents, members of Congress, and voters exercised their political responsibilities more appropriately, executive power would be reined in. But as all five of those observers recognized, presidents, members of Congress, and the public have defaulted on their responsibilities. Moreover, Congress has not only failed to contain presidential power; it has done much to increase it. It is unlikely that moral suasion will change the way that elected officials or the public respond to the imperial presidency. James Madison was right when he concluded that we must rely on structural mechanisms rather than the virtue of elected officials or voters to protect against the abuse of governmental power. But because the Madisonian structure has not worked as intended, better structural devices must be found to cabin executive power.

Indeed, it may be that the failure of Congress to check the executive branch was inevitable. As a number of scholars have observed, Madison misgauged the extent to which members of Congress would champion the interests of the legislative branch. The desire to aggrandize legislative power does not motivate members of Congress as much as do their other interests. Thus, as we have seen, Congress has actually diluted legislative power when it has delegated policy-making authority to the executive branch.

There are multiple factors at work. For example, the individual interests of members often diverge from those of Congress as an institution. Representatives and senators want to be reelected, and the need to promote the interests of their constituents may lead them to support greater presidential power. A member of Congress from a district or state that is home to military contractors and hawkish voters may want to give the president greater freedom to initiate military operations. Even though the legislator could try to retain the legislature's prerogative to declare war and author bills or resolutions to initiate military operations, the representative or senator would recognize that presidents are more prone than Congresses to send the military into battle. Members of Congress can improve their chances for reelection in another way by ceding policy-making authority to the president. They can duck responsibility for tough decisions and let the president take the political heat if things go wrong.[82]

In addition to being driven by personal interests, representatives and senators are responsive to the interests of their political party, and those interests often diverge from the interests of Congress as an institution. Indeed, the relationship between the executive and legislative branches is defined more by partisan considerations than by institutional interests. For example, Congress is less willing to delegate power to the executive branch if the two branches are divided by party. When Congress does delegate power in times of divided control, it is more likely to transfer legislative authority to independent commissions rather than to administrative agencies that would operate under greater presidential control. Or if Congress chooses to delegate power to administrative agencies overseen by a president from across the aisle, it attaches more procedural constraints to, and greater congressional oversight on, the exercise of the power. Similarly, congressional oversight of the presidential exercise of the war powers is greater when the executive and legislative branches are divided by party.[83]

In short, while Madison was correct to worry that elected officials would seek to aggrandize their power, he was incorrect in thinking that the interests of elected officials automatically would line up with the interests of their institutions. Members of Congress may increase their own power by increasing the power of Congress overall, but they also might increase their power more efficiently in other ways. An increase in institutional power has to be shared with other members of Congress, while other avenues to power can be limited to party colleagues or to themselves as individuals.

For the president, on the other hand, the interests of the person and the interests of the institution align much more closely. When the power of the executive branch increases, the power of the president increases by the same amount.[84]

Thus, Madison got it right with respect to the executive branch but wrong with respect to the legislative branch. Presidents will seek to increase their own power and rebuff efforts by Congress to encroach on their power. For example, presidents have initiated military operations without congressional authorization, and after Congress pushed back by passing the War Powers Resolution, every president has taken the position that the resolution is not binding on the executive branch. Presidents Clinton and Obama followed their words with consistent action. Both failed to comply with the resolution when they committed troops to Somalia and Libya, respectively. In contrast, members of Congress do not play their Madisonian role as intended. They not only have failed to resist many encroachments on the legislative power; they also have voluntarily transferred much of their power to the executive branch.

As discussed, the Supreme Court also has not exercised its checking responsibilities adequately. And as with Congress, it is not surprising. There are key reasons limiting the likelihood of the judiciary playing an effective policing role. The Court cannot enforce its rulings but generally must rely on the executive branch to do so. Presidents can undermine judicial authority by dragging their feet on compliance, and the justices will be reluctant to appear ineffectual. In addition, presidents can use their appointment power to select justices who are sympathetic to the exercise of executive power. Indeed, Justices Samuel Alito, Elena Kagan, and John Roberts all had defended the strong assertion of presidential authority before they were nominated to the Supreme Court.[85]

If relying on the existing constitutional structure will not respond to the imperial presidency, what changes might be implemented that will serve the intended role of the separation of powers? Some scholars would modify the constitutional structure to augment legislative power.[86] But even with that augmentation, it is difficult to envision a sufficiently aggressive legislative branch. Congress has shown too little inclination to police the executive branch.

Indeed, the willingness of Congress to yield power to the executive branch tells us that as a general matter, we will not solve the imperial presidency problem by strengthening the legislative branch. Congress already has defied the Constitution's allocation of power by transferring much of the legislative share to the president. If Congress were given greater power, it would give up more power to the executive branch.

Rather than relying on ineffective external checks, it makes much more sense to employ a strong internal check on presidential power.

If presidential power cannot be contained from outside, it should be contained from within the executive branch.

Neil Katyal shares this book's preference for internal checks on the executive branch, and he makes several important recommendations. Still, it is difficult to see how his prescriptions would be sufficient to cabin presidential power. For example, he discusses how overlapping jurisdictions among executive branch agencies can both slow the exercise of presidential power and, by providing a president with more diverse perspectives, improve the quality of presidential decision making. Thus, he recommends legislation to mandate consultation among different agencies before presidential action. This would be valuable. However, as Katyal acknowledges, it is very difficult to police consultation mandates, and the Supreme Court has decided that it lacks authority to enforce them. Moreover, consultation does not address the problem of policy making by a single decision maker rather than multiple decision makers. Katyal also would take steps to insulate executive branch employees from political control, but he recognizes that in the end, their decisions would not bind the president. It likely would not take long for agency officials to understand how far they can go before triggering the president's rejection of their ideas.[87]

William Marshall and Christopher Berry and Jacob Gersen also recommend an internal check on presidential power with their proposals for dividing the executive power. They look for guidance to state governments, which typically split executive authority among multiple elected officials, including governors, attorneys general, secretaries of state, and treasurers. Following the lead of the states, Marshall and Berry and Gersen would divide the federal executive power among multiple elected officials, with voters choosing the U.S. attorney general, secretary of state, and other cabinet officers.[88]

Proposals for an "unbundled executive" are correct in trying to limit executive power by dividing it, and they offer more promise than other ideas. As proponents observe, state governments have functioned well with an unbundling of the executive power. And unbundling would improve accountability. Some people may like a president's foreign policy initiatives but dislike the domestic policy decisions. With a single executive, these individuals can either signal their foreign policy approval or their domestic policy disapproval at the next election, but they cannot do both. If different executives assume responsibility for foreign and domestic policy, then the public can cast both a "foreign policy vote" and a "domestic policy vote."[89]

However, an unbundled executive would not address the problem of policy making by one person with one perspective rather than through deliberation among a diverse group of decision makers. An unbundled executive would yield multiple decision makers, but they all would be single decision makers within their own departments.

In short, while a two-person presidency may seem like too radical a solution to the problem of the imperial presidency, less radical solutions are not up to the challenge. The alternative to a bipartisan presidency is to preserve the imperial presidency.

Do we really need reform?

While most scholars call for a revitalization of the existing constitutional structure or propose reforms of the constitutional structure to contain the imperial presidency, Eric Posner and Adrian Vermeule argue that the search for the right legal constraints on the executive branch is misguided. Even though Congress and the courts have not exercised effective oversight of the executive branch, the president does face meaningful constraints that serve the checking and balancing role that the legislative and judicial branches were supposed to serve. Politics and public opinion have stepped in to fill the checking function that was abandoned by Congress and the courts. In this view, "the system of elections, the party system, and American political culture constrain the executive far more than do legal rules created by Congress or the courts." Presidents need to maintain their credibility with the public to achieve their policy goals, and their desire to preserve public trust may place a "far greater check on the president's actions than do the reactions of the other branches."[90] In short, political constraints prevent the presidency from becoming too imperial.

Indeed, write Posner and Vermeule, the fear of presidential tyranny is a "bogeyman of liberal legal and political theory that rests on little or no evidence." We do not have a problem with the abuse of executive power, and efforts to constrain the executive branch any further would incur too high a cost in terms of political gridlock. Political accountability—the framers' "primary control on the government" —has been a sufficient check and balance such that the "auxiliary precautions" of the separation of powers have not proved necessary.[91]

The argument by Posner and Vermeule reflects disagreement about the existence or nature of the imperial presidency. If one believes that presidential power has expanded too far and is already subject to abuse, then history tells us that political constraints have not worked adequately. Like many other scholars and political observers, I believe that Richard Nixon abused governmental power in activities that culminated in the Watergate scandal, that George W. Bush abused governmental power when he authorized "enhanced interrogation" methods that amounted to torture, and that Bill Clinton and Barack Obama abused governmental power when they launched military operations without congressional authorization. Posner and Vermeule observe that the United States has never suffered from the kind of dictatorial government that would demonstrate the need for stricter legal constraints on the executive branch,[92] but setting a threshold for concern at the level of dictatorial government allows presidents too many opportunities to misuse their powers.

Posner and Vermeule also believe that the United States has benefited from strong assertions of presidential power, as during the administrations of Abraham Lincoln and Franklin Delano Roosevelt. However, the two scholars overestimate the benefits of strong, single presidents. In chapter 5, I discuss how decision making by two presidents with different political perspectives makes for better decision making than when a single person with one perspective sits in the Oval Office.

There is an additional problem with the view of Posner and Vermeule. A reliance on politics and public opinion to cabin the executive branch gives short shrift to another key feature of the constitutional design—the fact that we have a constitutional democracy. Because majorities can exploit their power unfairly, the Constitution provides for fundamental rights that bind even a majority. In situations in which presidents wish to abuse their power and violate the rights of minorities, politics and public opinion will only reinforce the abuse rather than prevent or override it. Indeed, Posner and Vermeule recognize this problem in their discussion of counterterrorism tactics by the military and the CIA. As they observe, "majorities passionately [believe] that the U.S. government should use any and all means to counter terrorist threats."[93] The courts are supposed to provide a check on presidents who exploit majority sentiments, but as discussed, judges have not done so sufficiently.

Even taking Posner and Vermeule on their own terms suggests that they underestimate the value of the separation of powers. If political constraints are the coin of the realm, there still is an important role for the separation of powers. Jide Nzelibe and Matthew Stephenson have shown how the sharing of power between the president and Congress can reinforce political accountability by giving the public more reliable information on which to base their votes. In doing so, Nzelibe and Stephenson respond to a common concern of scholars and courts about the ways in which the separation of powers can compromise accountability. Legislators might delegate authority for controversial decisions to the executive branch, letting the administrative agencies and the president take any political heat, while they continue to influence agency decision making behind the scenes. Or Congress might provide incentives for states to implement public policies that could provoke a public backlash, with state officials suffering the electoral blame.[94] According to the standard analysis, dividing and sharing power interferes with principles of accountability.

But the separation of powers actually can make it easier for voters to assign accountability correctly. Ordinarily, a voter struggles with the problem of how to react when a president chooses a policy that diverges from the voter's preferred policy. The president might have better information than the voter, but the president also might be biased by the self-serving goals of an influential interest group. In order to discourage the president from acting out of bias, the voter will be more likely to blame the president if the president's policy choice appears to have failed than to credit the president if the president's policy choice turns out to have succeeded. The separation of powers reduces the need for the voter to blame the president for a failed policy choice. If the president has persuaded Congress to support the policy choice, then the voter does not need to discount the president's choice because of the potential for bias. It is less likely that an interest group can capture both the president and Congress than to capture the president alone.[95]

The analysis of Nzelibe and Stephenson tells us that the key question is not whether to have a separation of powers but how best to structure the sharing of power among the branches of government. Their analysis also suggests that a two-person presidency would do a better job than Congress of reinforcing political constraints on the exercise of executive power. When Congress is controlled by the president's party, the agreement of the president and Congress on policy matters provides less reassurance to voters about presidential bias than when Congress is controlled by the opposition party. Members of the president's party may support the president's policy decisions purely out of party loyalty, or interest groups that might influence the president's decision making probably can also influence members of the president's party in Congress. In a bipartisan presidency, on the other hand, there will be two presidents who are responsive to different political parties and different interest groups. Hence, the public always will have reassurance from agreement between the two presidents that they need not worry so much about the propriety of the decision-making process.

In short, we really do need reform of the constitutional structure. Political accountability is important, but many expansions of presidential power go unchecked, and presidential decision making suffers from its unilateral nature. The framers may have misjudged the effectiveness of their constitutional design in containing executive power, but they were correct in their view about the value of dividing the national government's powers to protect against their abuse. By dividing the executive power and requiring that it be shared, we can ensure that the separation of powers serves its intended role.

As I have indicated, it is not only important to have shared executive power; it also is important to have power shared across party lines. In the next section, I elaborate on the value of bipartisan control of the executive power.

Dividing the executive power along partisan lines

Simply dividing the executive power can provide an important check on the exercise of executive power. Dividing it along partisan lines will make the check especially effective. Edmund Burke and other political theorists have recognized that partisan differences play an important role in limiting the abuse of power in the national government. Members of one party serve as watchdogs over members of other parties, exposing the abuses and failings of each other. When Democrats hold power in the executive branch, Republican officeholders and candidates are quick to take them to task when there is evidence of misconduct or misjudgment. Similarly, when Republicans are in power, Democrats are quick to point out problems in governance. Partisan differences thus provide an important supplement to the checks and balances of the separation of powers.[96]

But with a one-person presidency, the party out of power often will not be in a position to *prevent* misconduct. Instead, it may only be able to ensure that the party in power is held accountable after the fact for its misconduct or misjudgments. With a coalition executive, on the other hand, one president will not be able to act without the agreement of a presidential partner from another party. The need for advance approval will provide a critical check on the potential for the misuse of presidential power.

Daryl Levinson and Richard Pildes also have recognized that separation-of-powers concerns must be analyzed in conjunction with consideration of the relationship between political parties. As they observe, when one party controls both Congress and the White House and there is unified government, competition between the executive and legislative branches weakens, undermining the Madisonian vision of checks and balances. In contrast, when different parties control Congress and the White House, creating divided government in Washington, there is strong competition between the two branches. Thus, Levinson and Pildes recommend reforms that would encourage voters to split control of the executive and legislative branches between the Democratic and Republican Parties. They also suggest reforms that would bolster the influence of the minority party. Many of these proposed reforms would be quite valuable. For example, greater use of supermajority requirements like the Senate filibuster would allow the minority more leverage in Congress and allow it to protect against overreaching by the majority party. Other constitutional democracies such as Germany have supermajority voting requirements for the approval of appointments to their countries' supreme courts.[97]

While Levinson and Pildes and I agree about the importance of having the national government's power shared across party lines, I do not think their proposed reforms go far enough. To the extent that their reforms would only encourage rather than require shared power, the proposals likely would fall short. To change the behavior of elected officials, it is necessary to implement reforms that will ensure that the sharing actually occurs. In addition, without an equal sharing of power, partisan conflict will remain high, as each party fights for control.

Why would my proposal not generate excessive partisan conflict and gridlock? I respond to this concern in chapters 4 and 5. There I argue that partisan conflict becomes a problem when the minority party chooses obstruction purely for electoral benefit. It is the constant maneuvering for political control that pushes partisan conflict beyond healthy competition to counterproductive gridlock. If, on the other hand, the different parties understand that they always will share the executive power equally, the electoral benefits of partisan conflict diminish, and we can expect a much better balance between the benefits and disadvantages of partisan differences. We can expect partisan behavior that is "responsible" and that promotes, rather than prevents, effective governance.[98]

For strong partisans who believe that they are "on the side of the angels,"[99] it may seem preposterous to make room for a standard-bearer of another political party. But they should consider whether they prefer a president from the other party serving alone or whether they would prefer that the other party's presidents always have to serve alongside presidents from their own party. Democrats would have been much happier with a George W. Bush–Al Gore administration than having Bush serve alone, and Republicans would have been much happier with a Barack Obama–John McCain administration than having Obama serve alone.

This book takes the view that there are important truths on both sides of the political spectrum. This book also takes the view that there are serious excesses on both sides of the political spectrum. Because a one-person presidency often neglects the other side's truths while failing to contain the excesses of its own side, a different structure to the executive branch is needed to realize more of the truths and fewer of the excesses. A two-person presidency would give due weight to political perspectives on both sides of the aisle. Thus, a two-person presidency should prevent national policy from being too skewed in favor of either liberal or conservative, regulatory or deregulatory, positions. In many ways, then, this book is about the search for a better balance in the behavior of the national government. In chapter 4, I discuss how a two-person presidency can defuse partisan conflict by bringing a better balance to the interaction of elected officials from different political parties.

4

The problem of partisan conflict

As discussed in chapter 3, the U.S. constitutional structure has not been able to cabin the power of the presidency. Although the framers worried about the balance of power between the executive and legislative branches, and designed a system to ensure an appropriate balance, they did not leave the United States with the intended balance. The decision to adopt a one-*person* presidency has contributed to the development of an imperial presidency.

This chapter considers the failure of the framers to adequately protect against partisan conflict. Here too the framers anticipated the problem, and here too they misjudged the future. Politics in Washington are highly partisan, and often have been bitterly divisive. The separation of powers was supposed to suppress factional strife, but it has not done so. While multiple factors contribute to the problem of partisan conflict, the fact that the United States has a one-*party* presidency is a very important part of the equation.

Like the founding fathers, observers today object to strong partisan conflict. Newspaper editors, political commentators, voters, elected officials, and candidates regularly call for a more bipartisan ethic in Washington, DC. During his first presidential campaign, Barack Obama not only promised a postpartisan Washington; he made that pledge a centerpiece of his platform. And in his efforts to enact major health care reform, Obama repeatedly emphasized his preference for a bill that had support from both sides of the aisles.

Too often, it is thought, conflicts between Democrats and Republicans stymie efforts to pass important legislation. Thus, for example, Congress has struggled to address climate change or immigration reform, and in August 2011, the U.S. credit rating was lowered for the first time when Congress and the president failed to agree on a long-term fix for the country's budget deficits.[1]

Many of the framers of the Constitution hoped for a nonpartisan ethic in Washington. In 18th Century America, political thinkers universally condemned political parties as examples of "factions" that pursued narrow self-interests and threatened the ability of government to promote the broad public interest. Alexander Hamilton believed that party differences could be eliminated through the emergence of a national unity party that embodied the common interest. For James Madison, John Adams, and other founding fathers, parties were seen as the inevitable result of a free society and to be dealt with by governmental structures that would diminish their influence.[2]

Despite the framers' hopes, Washington is rife with partisan conflict, and calls for change have failed. If appeals to elected officials for a more bipartisan ethic in Washington are not working, how might we better respond to the problem? This book takes a page from Federalist 51. Madison recognized that people are not angels and that therefore government must be structured to block the harmful impulses of public officials and their constituents.[3] Similarly, we should look to structural change to deal with the undesirable effects of partisan conflict. A two-person, coalition presidency provides a promising structural change.

The rise in partisanship

Scholars have documented a striking increase in partisan behavior in Congress over the past several decades. The degree of partisan divide is not unprecedented—while Congress has not been as divided as it is today in more than a century, high levels of partisan conflict were seen during much of the country's first one hundred years, and particularly during the Gilded Age at the end of the 19th Century. Still, partisan conflict has risen substantially in recent years to exceptionally high levels. When compared with their predecessors of thirty years ago, today's members of Congress are much more polarized on ideological grounds and much more likely to vote along party lines. Moderates in both parties have been replaced by more conservative or more liberal legislators.[4]

Theory would suggest less polarization between Democrats and Republicans. Indeed, one might expect each of the national political parties to exhibit a fair amount of diversity in terms of ideology. Some people might join the Republican Party because of fiscal conservatism, others to promote a strong military, and others to make abortion illegal. Republicans from Arizona will have different concerns than Republicans in North Dakota. And ideologies should cross party lines. Fiscally conservative voters may generally identify with the Republican Party, but the socially liberal ones may feel more at home in the Democratic Party.[5]

In the middle of the 20th Century, political parties were much closer to the ideologically diverse institutions that theorists describe. The Democratic Party once had conservative southerners to go with its liberal base, while the Republican Party once had liberal northerners to join with its conservative base. When Democratic presidents Harry Truman and John Kennedy tried to expand access to health care or enact other social reforms, they were stymied not just by Republicans but by a coalition of conservative Republicans and conservative Democrats.[6]

Because of the ideological diversity within the major parties, presidents could try to cultivate the support of a bipartisan coalition. Many Republicans had accepted the social welfare programs of the New Deal, and Democrats tended to back foreign policies designed to contain communism. Even as late as 1980, as the parties were becoming more divided in their political philosophies, Ronald Reagan was able to cobble together a coalition of traditional Republican voters plus the "Reagan Democrats," white, socially conservative, blue-collar workers.[7]

Today, however, the Democratic and Republican Parties each have developed a more coherent ideological identity and have become more polarized from each other. Thus, for example, conservative Democratic members of Congress have largely been replaced in the South by conservative Republican members of Congress. At the same time, liberal Republican members of Congress in the Northeast have been replaced by liberal Democrats or conservative Republicans. Nationally, one could divide the Senate by party or in terms of ideology, and the results would be the same. The most conservative Democratic senators are more liberal than the most liberal Republican senators.[8]

Thus, party-line voting in Congress is much more common than in the recent past. In 1969, members of Congress voted with the majority of their party a little more than 60 percent of the time; in 2009, they did so nearly 90 percent of the time. Indeed, party affiliation has become the predominant driver of political behavior in Washington —the best predictor of how a member of Congress will vote is the member's party identification.[9]

As Congress has become more polarized by party, legislators have found that their personal fortunes are tied more closely to public perceptions of their party than to public perceptions of Congress as an institution. And probably the most important determinant of their party's stature is the level of public satisfaction with the president. Democrats did very well in the 2006 and 2008 congressional elections because of the public's dissatisfaction with George W. Bush and the Republican Party. Conversely, Republicans did very well in the 2010 congressional elections because of the public's dissatisfaction with Barack Obama and the Democratic Party.[10]

The increase in partisan behavior has been apparent in other ways as well:

- The filibuster is now used routinely by the minority party in the Senate to block legislation favored by the majority party.

- It takes much longer for presidents to gain confirmation by the Senate for their nominees to the executive or judicial branch, and presidents have increasingly bypassed the Senate for executive branch officers by making appointments when the Senate is in recess or by creating senior advisory positions that do not require confirmation.
- Republicans led the charge to impeach Bill Clinton in 1998 on grounds that were highly controversial as a basis for impeachment.
- The Democratic leadership in Congress approached its relationship with George W. Bush as one of opposition rather than partnership, and prominent Republican senators in 2009 acknowledged that their opposition to health care reform reflected in part a desire to "break" the Obama administration.[11]

Consider also the contrast between Republican support for Social Security legislation during the Great Depression and Republican support for economic-recovery legislation during the Great Recession that began in 2007. Nearly two-thirds of Republican senators and almost 80 percent of Republican representatives voted for FDR's Social Security program in 1935. Obama's economic-recovery bill received virtually no support from across the aisle in February 2009. Not one of the 178 Republican representatives and only three of the forty-one Republican senators voted for the stimulus package. Similarly, when the House passed health care legislation in November 2009, only one Republican voted in favor of the bill. No Republicans supported the Senate bill in December 2009. After the Democrats lost Ted Kennedy's Senate seat in a special election and their ability to override a filibuster, the House took up the Senate bill rather than form a conference committee to reconcile the House and Senate bills. When the House voted on the Senate bill, not one Republican voted in support.[12]

Of course, the increased polarization among members of Congress coincides with an increase in polarization among voters. Public opinion about Obama was more polarized during his first three years than it was for every president from Dwight Eisenhower to George W.

Bush. Democratic members of Congress were hung in effigy, shouted down, and confronted by a mob mentality in August 2009 as they tried to discuss proposals to reform the U.S. health care system. And the Tea Party that led the charge against health care reform and other initiatives of the Obama administration is composed largely of very conservative Republican voters.[13]

Reasons for the increase in partisan behavior

Why are politics so polarized again? It appears that partisan conflict over time reflects some factors that are recurring and other influences that are peculiar to their eras. In the early years of the country, elected officials were intensely divided over competing conceptions of the new nation. On the Federalist side, Alexander Hamilton as secretary of the treasury championed policies designed to promote industrialization and trade with Britain. Financiers, manufacturers, and merchants stood to benefit most. On the Democratic-Republican side, James Madison and Thomas Jefferson preferred an agrarian republic of independent farmers who would market their harvests to the entire world. The Federalists favored social hierarchies, the Democratic-Republicans a more egalitarian society. The Federalists believed that democracy and freedom were dangerous in the hands of ordinary citizens; the Democratic-Republicans worried that the new country would adopt its own aristocracy in place of the British one it had escaped.

The Federalists and Democratic-Republicans also split over relations with Britain and France. When those two countries went to war with each other in 1793, the Federalists wanted to align with Britain, the Democratic-Republicans with France. The Federalists saw a French Revolution spiraling out of control into anarchy, the Democratic-Republicans saw a genuine birth of democratic governance.

When George Washington stepped down as president after two terms, the election of 1796 featured fierce party competition that only intensified during the administration of John Adams. Congress passed the Alien and Sedition Acts, which Adams employed primarily to suppress the Democratic-Republican press. Party relationships were bitter to the point that, as Thomas Jefferson observed, "men who have been intimate all their lives, cross the streets to avoid meeting, and turn their heads another way," lest they have to acknowledge each other.[14]

The divide over slavery in the years leading up to the Civil War and the Reconstruction era following the war provoked new partisan battles over the ethos of the United States.

As for contemporary partisan conflict, political scientists have identified a number of explanations for the sharp increase in recent decades. For example, the realignment of party politics in the South has played an important role. In the view of some scholars, this has been the key factor in explaining the rise in partisan conflict.

For much of the 20th Century, Democrats enjoyed a one-party monopoly in the South through the manipulation of state statutory and constitutional law. This resulted in a national party that combined conservatives from the South and moderates or liberals from other parts of the country. The Republican Party, on the other hand, represented an alliance of conservatives from the Midwest and rural communities elsewhere and moderates or liberals from the Northeast and the West Coast. Because of the ideological differences within each party, legislative coalitions typically formed across party lines.

But progress in civil rights and the economy fostered greater ideological homogeneity in the two parties. With the passage of voting-rights legislation in 1965 and the mobilization of black voters, the Democratic Party in the South saw an infusion of more liberal members. As the southern Democratic Party became more liberal, many of its conservative voters became more comfortable with the Republican Party. Economic growth also was important. As the South experienced its evolution from an agricultural to a modern economy after World War II, wealthier, more conservative whites migrated to the Republican Party, while lower-income, more liberal whites retained their Democratic affiliation. These changes resulted not only in a liberal-conservative divide between Democrats and Republicans in the South but also greater ideological polarization between the two parties nationally.[15]

While the South saw the emergence of a stronger, more conservative Republican Party, the North was becoming more Democratic and more liberal. In addition to the influence from the southern realignment, key demographic shifts played a critical role. Since the 1970s, congressional districts in northern states have become more urban and less affluent, with higher percentages of nonwhite constituents. As a result, more districts are politically liberal and more likely to elect liberal Democrats.[16]

The regional changes have been fueled by important national trends —increases in income inequality, a greater influx of immigrants, and heightened residential segregation by economic and racial class. Some scholars argue that the increases in income inequality and immigration are the primary reasons for the increase in polarization.[17]

With the rise in income inequality, the population's views on income redistribution have become more distinct, and the policy preferences of the political parties have mirrored the polarization in views. As the wealthy became more opposed to redistributive policies, so did the Republican Party. Indeed, Republicans not only have blocked policies to reduce income inequality; they have championed policies that aggravate the inequalities. Despite the common perception that differences on social issues such as abortion drive the divisions between Democrats and Republicans, it turns out that differences in income are much more important.[18]

Immigration has exacerbated income inequality and party polarization because recent immigrants make up a disproportionate percentage of the indigent, and that discourages social welfare policies that might narrow the gap between rich and poor. Recent immigrants are not a popular social class. In addition, to the extent that immigrants are here illegally and are unable to vote, they cannot exercise political power in support of public policies that would benefit them.[19]

Why has income inequality inexorably increased during the past several decades? Can Democrats not enact policies to narrow the economic gap between rich and poor? It is difficult for Democrats to do so. Even when they have held the presidency and majorities in Congress, they have struggled to enact redistributive policies that could reduce the degree of income inequality. Minority political parties can use the filibuster and other procedural tactics to block change.

Of course, Democratic minorities can block Republican policies that would aggravate income inequality, but some Democrats have supported tax cuts that have resulted in a less progressive tax system.[20]

Moreover, the status quo results in greater income inequality. Policies that ameliorate income inequality often provide benefits that are not indexed for inflation. Unless Congress acts, for example, the federal minimum wage remains flat in nominal dollars and therefore loses value in real dollars. Or unless state legislatures act, welfare benefits decline in real dollars. As a result, the income gap between rich and poor automatically has increased over time. Similarly, if income-tax rates are not adjusted when people at the top of the economic ladder earn a rising share of national income, the wealthy retain an increasing share of the country's wealth.[21]

Income inequalities have been an important source of political polarization in the past as well. Indeed until now, the peak in congressional polarization occurred after Reconstruction, in the Gilded Age of the late 1800s when America's industrialization led to great concentrations of power and wealth among corporate titans, while workers frequently lived on the edge of poverty. In 1890, the richest 1 percent of Americans "owned more property than the remaining 99 percent."[22]

The idea that economic inequalities would polarize the electorate and Congress is not surprising. In Federalist 10, when Madison discussed the inevitability of factions, he identified inequalities in wealth as the key source of factional behavior. As Madison wrote, "The most common and durable source of factions has been the various and unequal distribution of property. Those who hold and those who are without property have ever formed distinct interests in society."

There are other factors that may have contributed to party polarization in the United States. The strategies of party leadership probably played a role in stimulating greater partisanship. When Newt Gingrich planted the seeds for his Republican Revolution in 1994, he settled on a confrontational approach of noncooperation and non-accommodation with the Democrats and a sharpening of ideological differences. Similarly, when Democrats won strong majorities in Congress and the presidency in 2008, Senate Minority Leader Mitch

McConnell chose a strategy of noncooperation to regain seats in the 2010 election.[23]

The emergence of an imperial presidency likely has done much to amplify the polarization of the public and Congress. Chapter 3 discussed the significance of expansive executive authority as a problem in its own right, but that expansion is important here as well. While the presidency has always been a prominent public position, over time it has assumed particular importance, both in the United States and in the world. As the United States became the preeminent world power, economically and militarily, and the president assumed ever greater responsibility for setting domestic and foreign policy, the electoral stakes rose greatly. To hold the presidency is to wield a very high level of power, perhaps a level unprecedented in world history. Accordingly, one would expect the battle for the presidency to become increasingly intense. Indeed, presidential power and partisan conflict both have increased dramatically since World War II.

The prominence of the U.S. presidency is reflected in the time and money devoted by candidates for the Oval Office. In 1976, the presidential campaign was a two-year effort. Now presidential campaigns are virtually a four-year effort, and spending has risen dramatically. When Jimmy Carter captured the Democratic nomination in 1976, he raised just under $14 million. In earning the 2008 Democratic nomination, Barack Obama collected $414 million, an eightfold increase after adjusting for inflation.[24]

Parties compete fiercely for the presidency not only during the campaign but also through the legislative process. Congressional members of the party out of power are inclined to block the president's agenda in the hope that by discrediting the president, their party can regain the presidency and capture more legislative seats at upcoming elections. Congressional members of the president's party, on the other hand, are inclined to support the president's agenda in order to enhance the president's and their own standing.[25]

In fact, the link between presidential politics and partisan conflict has a long pedigree in the United States. Political parties first appeared in Congress when legislators aligned themselves either in support of or in opposition to the executive policies of George

Washington and Treasury Secretary Alexander Hamilton. Similarly, parties first mobilized nationally around presidential elections, starting with the 1796 contest between the Federalist John Adams and the Democratic-Republican Thomas Jefferson. After John Quincy Adams prevailed over Andrew Jackson in 1824 in the second straight election with only the Democratic-Republican Party fielding candidates for the presidency, politicians created a new two-party system in order to compete for the White House in 1828. Thus were born the Jacksonian Democrats and the National Republicans, who later became the Whigs, and by 1840, a Democratic–Whig divide was established.[26]

While the Democrat–Whig competition later evolved into a Democratic–Republican competition, national party politics continued to reflect the presidentially driven, two-party alignment that took hold in 1840. Thus, for example, the Democratic and Republican Parties today are most active and effective at raising money, rallying activists and getting their voters to the polls for presidential elections. Indeed, the national political committees act primarily as agents for the presidential nominees to wage their campaigns for the White House.[27]

It is not surprising that battles over presidential power would exacerbate partisan conflict in the United States. In a comparison of presidential and parliamentary government, Arend Lijphart observed that the concentration of executive power in one party and one person in presidential government makes for especially majoritarian government and can prevent the kind of cooperative efforts that occur in parliamentary systems, where executive power is distributed on a collegial and shared basis.[28]

Moreover, as Juan Linz has noted, the fixed-term nature of presidential government further aggravates partisan conflict. In parliamentary government, elections can be called earlier than the scheduled end of the term, and opposition parties can hope to gain more power in a relatively short period of time. In the United States, on the other hand, the losing party must wait a minimum of four years without any access to executive power, raising the stakes of presidential elections even higher and further polarizing party relationships.[29]

The founding fathers recognized these disadvantages of one-person government. Hence, when they designed the other elements of their new national government, the framers ensured that power would be divided and shared by multiple persons rather than assigned to a single elected official. However, they wrongly concluded that the government would function more effectively with a single executive.

To be sure, there are ways in which a one-person presidency can reduce rather than exacerbate party polarization. Presidents may campaign as the standard-bearer of their party, but they assume office as an elected official who represents the entire citizenry. Accordingly, at one time, presidents often appealed to the public generally rather than only to their partisan supporters when advocating major domestic or foreign policies.[30] But contemporary presidents are much more likely to represent the ideology of their political base than the views of the public generally.

Also, in the past, the adoption of a presidential system of government may have discouraged polarization among political parties in the United States, and that probably helped compensate for the anticollegial nature of the executive branch. In parliamentary systems, the party controlling the executive branch can retain its hold on power only with the support of the party's legislative officials, so party cohesion becomes critical.[31] In presidential systems, presidents do not serve at the pleasure of the legislature, so party discipline is not as important. Hence, members of the legislature are freer to work with their colleagues on the other side of the aisle. A minority party might not have much influence on policy coming out of the White House, but it could have considerable influence over policy coming out of Capitol Hill. Thus, coalitions in Congress in the past often crossed party lines. However, as U.S. political parties have become more internally cohesive and polarized from each other, collegial relations between Democrats and Republicans have declined in Congress and reinforced the partisan-heightening nature of the one-person presidency.

In sum, the increase in partisan polarization likely reflects multiple factors, and there is good reason to assign an important role to the rise of the imperial presidency.

The antipathy of the framers toward political parties

As mentioned earlier, the framers worried about partisan conflict. Thus, they thought it important to prevent parties from assuming a significant role in the political process, just as they viewed it critical to suppress the influence of other factions in the political process. Accordingly, sums up Richard Hofstadter, the framers wrote a "Constitution against parties."[32]

This rejection of a role for political parties stands in stark contrast to the political systems of other countries, which more readily have embraced a role for parties as intermediaries between the voters and their elected representatives. Under article 21 of the German constitution, for example, "political parties shall participate in forming the political will of the people."[33]

The opposition to political parties by the framers also stands in stark contrast to the views of many scholars, who see much virtue in the role that political parties play. It is commonly argued by political scientists that "parties are essential to both the creation and the furthering of democratic values." Parties provide a vehicle for representing the interests of different ethnic and racial groups, they provide a link between officeholders in state and federal government, and they bring the benefits of competition to the political sphere. Parties also create the organizational structures that are needed for effective governance once their candidates are elected. Parties develop policy proposals that public officials can try to enact, they train individuals to serve as political leaders, and they connect their members in the legislatures through caucuses that can act collectively.[34]

Given these benefits, it is easy to imagine the framers having embraced political parties in the way others have. Indeed, the founding fathers might have seen parties as useful to their constitutional structure. They worried deeply about preserving liberty and devised an elaborate structure of checks and balances to cabin governmental power. The framers might have looked to political parties as institutions that could provide a check on the exercise of power.

But they instead viewed parties as "sores on the body politic." Like other factions, parties would pursue their narrow self-interests at the expense of the common good. Political leaders such as John Adams and William Paterson were quick to quote from Jonathan Swift, who had written that "Party is the madness of many, for the gain of the few." According to George Washington, who attacked parties in his farewell address at the end of his presidency, "the spirit of party . . . agitates the Community with ill-founded jealousies and false alarms; kindles the animosity of one part against another, foments occasionally riot and insurrection."[35]

Federalist 10 captures well the common view in late 18th Century America that parties and other factions were detrimental to the public good:

> The instability, injustice, and confusion introduced into the public councils [by factional conflict], have, in truth, been the mortal diseases under which popular governments have everywhere perished. . . . Complaints are everywhere heard . . . that our governments are too unstable, *that the public good is disregarded in the conflicts of rival parties.* . . .
>
> . . . A zeal for different opinions . . . ha[s], in turn, divided mankind into parties, inflamed them with mutual animosity, and rendered them much more disposed to vex and oppress each other than to co-operate for their common good. (Emphases added)[36]

Note too that the unfavorable view of parties was not limited to the Federalists. Anti-Federalists too disdained political parties. They not only shared the Federalist view of parties as dangerous factions. They also feared the potential for exploitation of party power by the upper socioeconomic classes, whose "superior capacity and opportunity for [party] organization" would allow them to exercise disproportionate influence in the election of members of Congress.[37]

Much of the antipathy to political parties can be explained by the understanding that the framers had developed about political party influence from the British experience during the 17th and early 18th Centuries. England experienced a convulsive period of political history during that time, rife with violence, rebellion, and treason. Government was unstable, prone to religious bigotry and the suppression of liberty, and ready to punish its challengers with exile and death. And the excesses of this unhappy period were viewed to be the consequence of party division.[38]

The framers also could rely on their experience with parties in colonial America. In Federalist 50, James Madison cited the damaging example of political parties in Pennsylvania, which contrasted with the positively viewed political system in Virginia, where political parties had not formed.[39] Moreover, at the time of the founding, no political theorist had developed a theory of the role of the party in the state. The founders understood that parties would exist, but not in a permanent, institutionalized form.

The failure of the constitutional design to contain partisan conflict

As Federalists 10 and 51 indicate, the Constitution employed two solutions to the problem of political parties and other factions. Federalist 10 discussed how the nature of a national government could tamp factional conflict. Narrow factions thrive most in small, homogeneous constituencies in which it is more feasible for a parochial interest to represent majority sentiment. In large, heterogeneous constituencies, on the other hand, narrow factions find it difficult to attract broad support for their views. Large republics such as the United States generate a great variety of interests and factions, and that would prevent a single faction from substituting its preferences for the common good.

Federalist 51 supplied a remedy for situations in which factions overcame the obstacles of large, heterogeneous constituencies and were able to gain political power. By dividing the national government's power among three branches and pitting the interest of one branch against the interests of the other branches, the antisocial efforts of factions in one branch of government could be checked by the other branches of the national government.[40]

The solutions to factional conflict discussed in Federalists 10 and 51 failed because the founding fathers did not anticipate the role that political parties would come to play in unifying different members of Congress or in unifying members of Congress with the president. Indeed, the framers' very system of winner-take-all elections became the culprit. Even though the United States has a great variety of political parties, the absence of a proportional system of representation has resulted in the dominance of the Democratic and Republican Parties. Each of the two major parties has evolved into a faction that can gain control of the government and impose its ideology on others.[41]

In sum, although the framers misjudged the degree to which political parties would exercise influence, they did try to limit the impact of parties and other interest groups. However, their separation of powers and other structural mechanisms have not been successful at containing partisan conflict. Hence, it is desirable to modify the constitutional structure so it better serves its role in restraining the self-serving efforts of factions. As discussed later in this chapter, a two-person, coalition presidency can serve that role very well.

Partisan conflict is a real problem

Some scholars recognize the rise in partisan behavior but argue that it does not in fact cause gridlock or diminish the likelihood that Congress and the president will enact important legislation. David Mayhew, a leading proponent of this view, has studied the legislative record between 1946 and 2002 and concluded that Congress and the president are as likely to enact significant legislation when they are divided by party affiliation as when they are united by party affiliation. Thus, for example, a Democratic Congress and a Republican Richard Nixon passed the Tax Reform Act of 1969, the Clean Air Act of 1970, and the Occupational Safety and Health Act of 1970. Similarly, a Republican Congress and a Democratic Bill Clinton enacted welfare reform, telecommunications reform, and a line-item veto in 1996.[42] Partisan conflict, in this view, is more bark than bite.

Other scholars have challenged this take on partisan conflict. In explaining the apparent absence of a difference between unified and divided government, Keith Krehbiel has cited the supermajoritarian nature of our political system: Because forty-one senators can filibuster bills preferred by a majority of the Senate, it can take sixty senators rather than a simple majority of fifty-one to pass legislation. Even with unified government, the minority party is typically in a position to prevent passage of legislation that it opposes.[43] In other words, partisan conflict can overcome even undivided government.

Moreover, with more refined analyses, studies have found important differences between unified and divided government. By narrowing the definition of significant legislation, for example, researchers have found that unified governments pass more important legislation than do divided governments. Sean Kelly believes that legislation should be deemed important only if viewed as significant at both the time of passage and in later years. Mayhew counted legislation that was deemed important at the time of passage even when it did not stand the test of time as being important. Under Kelly's definition, unified governments are more productive than divided governments.

Other scholars have considered not only how much legislation gets passed but also how much legislation gets blocked. The impact of political conflict may show up not in the amount of legislation passed but in the *percentage* of legislation that passes. With this refinement, Sarah Binder has found that partisan polarization really does matter. As the number of moderates in Congress shrinks, the likelihood of gridlock increases.[44]

Partisan divide not only affects whether legislation will pass but also what kind of legislation will pass. Divided government leads to higher budget deficits and greater protectionism in trade policy.[45]

Finally, scholars have recognized that other factors influence the legislative process. Congress may pass more bills during some of its terms because the public mood favors an active government, and it may pass fewer bills when the public prefers quiet government. The level of legislative activity also will be affected by whether the Democratic and Republican Parties are split internally by factions. By controlling the analysis for these other influences, the impact of divided government becomes clearer.[46]

Or consider some other pieces of data. "Presidential vetoes all but disappear during periods of unified government." And congressional oversight of the presidential exercise of the war powers is greater when the executive and legislative branches are divided by party. When presidents face a Congress controlled by the opposition party, they are less likely to send military forces into battle abroad, and they are likely to take a longer time to deploy American troops once the possibility of using military force arises.[47] In sum, partisan conflict does have real consequences, and it can lead to gridlock within Congress or between Congress and the president.

Could one argue that partisan conflict provides an important counterweight to the imperial presidency and that the imperial presidency provides an important counterweight to partisan conflict? If executive authority and partisan conflict have exceeded the framers' expectations, why worry if each contains the other? Barack Obama may have enjoyed the power of an imperial president, but Republicans were able to block his initiatives once they regained the majority in the House of Representatives and a large enough minority to mount a filibuster in the Senate. As Daryl Levinson and Richard Pildes have observed, the checks and balances in the national government are provided today not by the different branches of government butting heads but by the different political parties doing so.[48] Perhaps the rise in partisan polarization is exactly what we need in an era of an imperial presidency.

Similarly, perhaps we need an imperial presidency in an era of sharp partisan divides. Just as partisan conflict can limit presidential power, so can presidential power limit the effects of partisan conflict. If partisan behavior leads the opposition party to obstruct the president, it may be useful to augment executive power so the president is in a better position from which to resist the other party's intransigence.[49]

There are several problems with this argument. First, partisan conflict is not only a matter of the relationship between the president and Congress. It also poisons relations among members of Congress. Even if very high levels of partisan conflict can play a useful role in executive-legislative relationships, they do not serve a useful purpose within the legislative branch. In addition, while partisan conflict may be able to cabin executive power in the domestic sphere, it has not resulted in sufficient constraints on the president's foreign affair powers. Republicans were quick to block Obama's proposals to limit greenhouse gases, to reform the immigration laws, or to reduce budget deficits, but they did not interfere with his escalation of the Afghan War or his military offensive in Libya. Republican cooperation was particularly striking with the Libyan offensive. Even though Obama sent troops to battle without a declaration of war by Congress and even though he did not comply with the requirements of the War Powers Resolution after committing U.S. troops to battle, Republican protest was mild at best.

Importantly, partisan conflict contains the president only when the executive and legislative branches are divided by party. When a president's party enjoys majority control in the House and Senate, executive-legislative relations are characterized by collaboration rather than conflict. Thus, during his first two years in office, Obama could rely on the House and Senate to promote his initiatives to stimulate the economy, to increase access to health care coverage, and to reform the financial services industry. With undivided government, congressional cooperation can exacerbate the problem of presidential power.

Finally, just as partisan conflict is not a satisfactory response to the imperial presidency, so is the imperial presidency not an appropriate response to partisan conflict. If presidents find it unduly difficult to work with Congress because of excessive partisanship, then we should fix the problem of partisan conflict, not let the president simply bypass Congress.

In other words, we should not rely on one defect in the political system to compensate for another defect. It would be far better to fix both defects—just as it would be far better to fix a defective accelerator and defective brakes rather than letting the two defects compensate for each other. Otherwise, we only encourage a reinforcing spiral of expanding presidential power and intensifying partisan conflict—as presidents try to overcome partisan opposition by acting unilaterally, members of the opposition party increase their obstruction, and presidents may respond in kind with even more unilateral action.

A two-person executive and partisan conflict

There is good reason to think that a two-person, coalition presidency can preserve the benefits of partisan activity while reducing the harmful effects. Political parties still would compete in elections for Congress, the state legislatures, and other state and local offices, and they still would compete to see their ideas adopted by government. This competition would foster the development of innovative policies. Party competition also would provide an incentive for public officials to remain responsive to the preferences of their constituents. The desire to be reelected is an important stimulus for people holding office, and elected officials are more likely to face a serious challenge by a candidate from a different party than from their own party.

At the same time as a two-person presidency would preserve the benefits of partisan activity, it could discourage the excesses of partisan competition. With each party having representation in the executive branch, a two-person presidency would diminish the incentive for members of Congress to obstruct the executive branch for purely partisan purposes. There no longer would be a minority party that could increase its chances of regaining the presidency by undermining the current president, and there no longer would be a majority party that could increase its chances of retaining the presidency by supporting the current president. Obstruction for obstruction's sake and support for support's sake no longer would have purchase.

Or to put it another way, there would not be a minority party that would have much to gain by "breaking" the presidency. Rather, both of the major parties generally would be represented by a president trying to advance a common agenda with a presidential partner from the other party. Accordingly, both parties' members of Congress would be more inclined to work cooperatively with the executive branch's initiatives and therefore with their congressional colleagues from the other side of the aisle.

Consider, for example, how things might have played out differently in February 2009, when Barack Obama proposed an economic stimulus package that ultimately was transformed into the American Recovery and Reinvestment Act of 2009. As mentioned earlier, no

Republican representative and only three Republican senators voted for the legislation. If the bill had taken the form of a joint proposal by co-presidents Obama and John McCain, then Republican legislators would not have seen opposition as their best strategy for realizing political advantage. Because a McCain-Obama bill would have been a bipartisan proposal, both parties would have received credit for its success, and members of Congress from both parties would have benefited from supporting the bill.

The actual bill, on the other hand, was a Democratic proposal, and Republicans recognized that Democrats would have received all the credit for its success. Thus, Republicans had nothing to gain by supporting it, while they might have had something to gain by opposing it, if it proved to be an unpopular law. Indeed, when the economy sputtered in 2011, Republicans persuaded many voters that the legislation drove up the nation's budget deficit without generating an economic recovery or even reducing the rate of unemployment.[50]

It is not only the case that political calculations would lead to more of a bipartisan ethic in Congress under a coalition presidency. Democratic and Republican legislators also would cooperate more to the extent that their votes were based on a bill's merits. Republicans opposed Obama's economic stimulus proposal in part because it was driven more by Democratic Party principles than by Republican Party principles. A McCain-Obama proposal, on the other hand, would have reflected key Republican principles as much as key Democratic principles. Accordingly, it would have fared much better than the actual Obama proposal among Republican senators and representatives.

Voter sentiment would reinforce the more cooperative inclinations of members of Congress under a bipartisan executive branch. As discussed in chapter 6, a two-person presidency would generate greater public support for Oval Office policies because most voters would feel that they have a voice in the deliberations of the executive branch. Accordingly, parties would have less to gain through obstruction of presidential proposals. Currently, the party out of power can exploit voter discontent with the White House by opposing presidential initiatives. But if voters are satisfied with the executive branch, then neither party has anything to gain by blocking Oval Office policies.

Indeed, this is the lesson of France's "cohabitation" government in 1986–1988. Executive power was divided between a liberal president and a conservative prime minister. While the two officials often disagreed, they also avoided conduct that would lead to gridlock, in large part because the public liked the sharing of power.[51]

In short, a two-person presidency of members of different parties would sharply reduce the incentive for members of Congress to vote purely on the basis of party affiliation. Instead, they could attend more to the merits of the executive branch's legislative proposals.

Of course, members of Congress have their own political battles to fight, and the minority party in the House or the Senate might be inclined to block the majority's initiatives in order to improve its chances of regaining the majority in the legislature. Presidential politics are by no means the only source of partisan conflict in Washington. However, to the extent that legislative initiatives emerge from the White House, they no longer would be Democratic or Republican initiatives. Rather, they would be bipartisan initiatives.

Moreover, it is difficult to see how battles over control of Congress would generate the same level of voter polarization along party lines as have battles over the presidency. The public and the political parties care so much about the presidential election because of the president's dominance in the national government, because presidents often have "coattails" and carry with them into Congress members of their party, and because the office will not be contested again for four years. As Justice Robert Jackson wrote in the *Steel Seizure* case, the president is the "focus of public hopes and expectations. In drama, magnitude and finality his decisions so far overshadow any others that almost alone he fills the public eye and ear." Hence, as Matthew Shugart and John Carey have observed, capturing the presidency dwarfs all other electoral goals.[52]

A two-person presidency would recalibrate the balance of power between the executive and legislative branches, but it would not leave congressional elections with the kind of prominence that would drive voter participation in the way a presidential election creates public interest in elections now. The House and Senate still would share the legislative power, and Speakers of the House and majority leaders of the Senate still would share power with their legislative colleagues.

Speaker John Boehner's battle with Representative Eric Cantor for control of the House Republican policy agenda in 2011 provides a useful illustration of the limits of the authority of legislative leaders. While a president can exercise the executive power unilaterally, a House Speaker or a Senate majority leader needs the support of many colleagues before taking action. Or to put it another way, children frequently aspire to be president of the United States when they grow up, but it is the rare child who aspires to be Speaker of the U.S. House of Representatives or majority leader of the U.S. Senate. And voter turnouts are much higher in presidential election years than in other years.

It is not only the case that members of Congress would have a diminished incentive to battle the White House on partisan grounds. They also would have an enhanced incentive to cooperate with the executive branch. Having a good relationship with someone in the Oval Office is very important for providing high-quality services to the residents of a representative's district or a senator's state. Legislators can serve their constituents by passing legislation, but they often can do more by attracting more spending to their districts or states, cutting through the red tape in the federal bureaucracy or otherwise directing the attention of officials in the executive branch to the needs of their constituents. In a one-party executive branch, presidents respond more favorably to members of their party, so members of the other party have little to gain by cultivating relationships with the White House.[53] In a two-party presidency, on the other hand, the Oval Office should be responsive to requests by legislators on both sides of the aisle, and members of Congress would have much to gain by establishing warm relations with executive branch officials.

Note that a coalition presidency addresses the problem of partisan conflict in two important ways. To the extent that the expansion of presidential power has widened the partisan divide, a two-person presidency could address that cause of partisan conflict. And to the extent that other factors have increased partisan behavior, a coalition executive could address the manifestations of partisan division and keep them in check. This latter effect is particularly important for causes of partisan behavior that cannot be reversed (such as the extension of voting rights to blacks), that are difficult to reverse (such as the increase in income inequality), or that might develop in the future.

Moreover, a two-person presidency addresses the problem of partisan conflict by reinforcing the constitutional design rather than by trying to substitute a new blueprint. The coalition executive would provide a check on partisan conflict through the important constitutional model of dividing power and requiring it to be shared. Accordingly, a two-person presidency would work by strengthening the framers' system of checks and balances for containing the problem of faction.

There is an additional way in which a coalition executive would address the problem of partisan conflict. As mentioned earlier, because of the high level of partisan conflict in Washington, presidents face longer and longer delays between the time when they nominate an executive branch official or judge and the time when the Senate confirms the nominee. As a result, executive branch agencies cannot perform their responsibilities as quickly as they could if they were fully staffed, and backlogs lengthen in federal courts. With a two-person presidency, nominees would be far less likely to provoke partisan opposition, and key positions in the executive and judicial branches would be filled more rapidly.

Similarly, transitions between presidential administrations would occur with far less disruption than under the current system. When control of the White House changes from one party to the other, the new president must replace a large group of political appointees from the opposite party with appointees from the president's party. The new officials face a steep learning curve, unfamiliarity with executive branch operations and all of the other challenges of a new job, including, for many, commuting or moving their families to Washington. With a two-person presidency, political appointees from the previous administration always would fit well with the new administration. Of course, new presidents would want to bring in some of their inner circle and key supporters, but they would not need to replace nearly as many executive branch officers as new presidents do now.

There might be another benefit from the reduced need of presidents to appoint new executive branch officials. Many presidents suffer from an excessive dependence on their past advisers after they move into the White House; personal loyalties can lead presidents to overlook deficiencies in judgment and character. Jimmy Carter, for example, saw his close friend and Office of Management and Budget chief Bert Lance resign under a cloud of corruption accusations. To the extent that there are fewer new appointees and more carryover appointees, the potential for such problems will diminish.

While a coalition presidency could do much to diminish partisan conflict in Washington, it might be necessary to supplement such a reform with the additional reform of a filibuster rule in the House of Representatives. I have argued that partisan conflict should be addressed by giving the minority party greater influence in the shaping of governmental policy. When people feel they are able to participate meaningfully in a policy-making process, they are much more likely to cooperate with other participants in the process. A coalition presidency would provide meaningful participation in the deliberations of the executive branch, and the existing filibuster rule already gives the minority party a say in the deliberations of the Senate. In the House, however, the ability of a bare majority to control the policy-making process deprives the minority of the opportunity to play a meaningful role in the process. It is not surprising that the Republican Revolution in Congress in 1994 came out of the House Republican caucus rather than the Senate Republican caucus. Nor is it surprising that the Senate came to an agreement more quickly and more easily than did the House on an extension of the payroll-tax cut in December 2011.

Adding a filibuster rule in the House would force the majority party to include the minority party in its deliberations, and with a coalition presidency as well, there would be incentives for bipartisan cooperation in all three of the political departments of the national government—the House, the Senate, and the Oval Office.[54]

Would a coalition executive be dysfunctional?

I have argued so far that a two-person, coalition presidency would diminish partisan conflict because both major parties would be represented in the executive branch. But maybe a coalition presidency would worsen partisan conflict by bringing ideological differences into the White House. Currently, the United States resolves the fight for control over the executive branch by letting one party assume responsibility for policy making in the Oval Office. With a two-person presidency, the two parties might end up in a continual battle over the executive branch's policy choices.

Indeed, in Federalist 70, Alexander Hamilton worried that a multiheaded presidency would be plagued by dissension and become too dysfunctional. And he cited the historical example of the ancient Roman Republic to justify his concern. Careful consideration indicates that Hamilton's concerns were not well founded.

The experience of other countries

While it is important to learn from history, lest we repeat past mistakes, historical analogies may not be very instructive. The Roman Republic differed from the United States not only in having a plural executive headed by two consuls but in many other ways. The Republic was far less of a democracy than our government, with most people not entitled to serve in public office or to participate in the electoral process. In practice, public office was open only to the rich and only to those who gained their wealth from landholding rather than from trading in the marketplace. The consuls tended to come from a limited number of families and were elected for terms of one year, making it difficult to establish a policy agenda.

In many ways, the consuls had less power than the U.S. president, but in some ways, they had more power. In addition to serving with a co-consul and other, inferior executive officers, consuls were subject to the preferences of the Roman Senate. The Senate played a highly influential role in shaping executive policy. The consuls were required to seek the Senate's advice on all major policy decisions, and they were expected to follow that advice. On the other hand, consuls acted not simply as leaders of an executive branch separate from legislative and judicial branches. Rather, they called the *comitia centuriata* (popular assembly) into session and initiated legislative proposals before it. In addition, the consuls served as judges.[55]

Even if we were to rely on the example of ancient Rome, it can provide support for a two-person presidency. The plural executive in Rome occurred during the Republic phase of ancient Rome's government, which succeeded the monarchy and was followed by the Roman Empire. During the Republic, Rome experienced its greatest growth and expansion, subjecting "nearly the entire civilized world" to its rule. Thus, wrote José Batlle y Ordóñez, in his classic argument for a collective executive, "Athens, Rome, and Venice reached their grandeur under governments of this type."[56]

While the Republic eventually failed, it flourished for some four centuries, and its collapse can be attributed to the difficulties in governing the much larger and heterogeneous population that it conquered rather than its two-person executive branch. Indeed, while consuls enjoyed veto power over their partners and could spend their terms in conflict, they preferred to cooperate. In any event, it is not plausible to cite ancient Rome for the proposition that single-executive government provides a better model than a plural executive. The Roman Empire may have restored order after the Republic, but it had its own tumultuous periods, many emperors were assassinated, and it brought dictatorial government to its citizens.[57]

The history of other countries also appears to be more supportive of a two-person presidency than it is unsupportive. Consider in this regard the tradition of "strongmen," or *caudillos*, at the helm of Latin American countries. For some two centuries, presidential dictators have been common throughout Central and South America, with some of the more notable examples including Juan Perón in Argentina, Augusto Pinochet in Chile, and members of the Somoza family in Nicaragua. Africa too has experienced more than its share of despotic single-executive rulers, from Idi Amin in Uganda to Jean-Bedel Bokassa in the Central African Republic, Robert Mugabe in Zimbabwe, and Muammar el-Qaddafi in Libya. Eastern European countries suffered for decades under authoritarian rule— Joseph Stalin in the Soviet Union, Nicolae Ceauşescu in Romania, Enver Hoxha in Albania, and Josip Tito in Yugoslavia were long-serving dictators. After the break-up of the USSR, observers predicted a wave of liberalization in the former Soviet states, but many of them experienced a slide into authoritarian presidential rule, including Uzbekistan, Turkmenistan, and Belarus.[58]

I cite these examples not to suggest that a one-person executive invariably leads to the serious abuse of power. No U.S. president has acted as a despot. Rather, the point is that one cannot point to unhappy experiences with two-person rule in some countries and ignore similar—or worse—experiences with one-person rule in other countries.

In fact, plural executives often function successfully. A collegial or collective executive is one of the hallmarks of parliamentary systems. In such systems, the executive branch typically comprises multiple cabinet ministers who share responsibility for the executive branch's decisions. Collective responsibility does not always entail collective decision making—the cabinet may assume responsibility as a whole for decisions that are effectively made by the prime minister. Nevertheless, there is still a strong element of collective action. And collective action clearly exists when cabinet ministers reach decisions through their own deliberations. Among stable democracies worldwide, the overwhelming majority have been parliamentary systems historically.[59]

There are several models for executive branch decision making in parliamentary government. As indicated, the executive branch ministers may make decisions together (the "cabinet government" model); they also may approve decisions made by individual ministers for their own departments (the "ministerial" model). Ministers may simply implement decisions made at the party level (the "party government" model), or they may defer to the leadership of the prime minister (the "prime ministerial" model).[60]

Parliamentary systems typically reflect a combination of multiple models rather than a single model, and different models are more important in different countries. In Austria, for example, ministerial government provides the dominant model, with significant elements of party government, cabinet government, and prime-ministerial government. In Great Britain, on the other hand, ministerial autonomy has been limited, and its political system has featured a powerful prime minister, as well as important elements of cabinet and party government. New Zealand provides a good example of strong cabinet government, with weaker elements of prime-ministerial, ministerial, and party government.[61]

Switzerland provides an important example of a parliamentary-presidential hybrid with a strong element of cabinet government and multiparty representation. As in parliamentary systems, the executive branch in Switzerland is chosen by the legislature rather than the voters. However, as in presidential systems, members of the Swiss executive branch serve fixed terms that cannot be shortened by a no-confidence vote of the legislative branch. The Federal Council serves as the executive authority. The Council is a body of seven department heads (analogous to U.S. cabinet secretaries) who together exercise the executive power, and they have done so effectively.[62]

Since 1959, the Swiss councilors have represented the major political parties, with each of the parties being represented in proportion to their support among voters. For most of that time, there were four major parties; but in 2008, one splintered, and since then, the seven councilors have come from five different parties. Those five parties represent a large majority of the country's population, with a total support of 78 percent of voters in the most recent general election (October 2011) and no other party earning as much as 9 percent of the vote.[63]

While each councilor rotates through one-year presidential terms, the president possesses no greater power than the other department heads. Rather, under the Swiss constitutional principle of "nonhierarchy," each of the seven members possesses the same decision-making authority. Decisions are made by consensus, with resort to a majority vote only in exceptional cases. And once a decision is reached, every member of the Federal Council defends it, even if the member had opposed the policy. The president does assume some additional responsibilities, but they are purely representative and ceremonial in nature.[64]

The seven-person executive reflects important aspects of the Swiss political culture. As indicated, political decisions are based on a consensual model. In addition, decision making occurs through a consociational process. That is, major policy decisions are made after broad consultation with interested groups, including the different political parties, business and labor, environmental activists, and other advocacy organizations (a consultative process that is not that different from what occurs during the legislative process or administrative agency rule-making process in the United States). In addition, public officials frequently seek citizen input through referenda on a wide variety of issues, including annual budgets and major capital projects, and the public can initiate the referendum process. Swiss custom and law reflect a distrust of the charismatic or prominent leader, with the Federal Council maintaining a low public profile.[65]

Although U.S. political culture differs from the Swiss model, it is important to remember that a country's institutions can influence its political culture just as its political culture influences its institutions. Thus, while a single president may reflect the more individualistic nature of American society, a two-person presidency could well foster a more communal ethic in the United States.

Indeed, it may be the case that the Swiss Federal Council has succeeded precisely because it and other parts of the government promise broad participation to the public. Switzerland may be much smaller than the United States, but its population is culturally quite diverse, with citizens of French, German, and Italian origin, as well as a small Romansh community, and Switzerland actually has greater social heterogeneity than does the United States. Yet ethnic differences never have caused serious conflict—and political violence is less common in Switzerland than in the United States. In part, political harmony may reflect the fact that economic and religious differences cut across ethnic lines (i.e., within the French, German, and Italian communities, there are rich and poor, and Catholic and Protestant). But it is also important that the government gives voice to citizens across the political spectrum. Seats in the legislature are based on proportional representation, ensuring participation for small as well as large political parties. As mentioned, the Federal Council includes representatives from all the major parties. In addition, under an unwritten rule of Swiss politics, two of the seven seats on the Council are reserved for representatives of the French or Italian communities. With its broader inclusion of different perspectives, the Swiss executive branch likely has done much to defuse societal tensions.

To be sure, Switzerland experienced serious social conflict along religious lines in the past between its Catholic and Protestant citizens. In the 19th Century, Protestants defeated Catholics in a civil war, and religious conflict remained bitter into the 20th Century. But conflict has faded away, partly because of economic and social integration and the declining influence of religion but also because the introduction of proportional representation ensured that power would be shared between the Protestant majority and Catholic minority.[66]

The ability of the Swiss to forge a consensual model of government out of distinct groups in its population bodes well for the potential for cooperation between presidential partners in the United States. The Swiss government has functioned well, with an exceptional record of stability. Indeed, it is difficult to argue that the U.S. government has performed more effectively. Of course, there are criticisms and calls for change in Switzerland. Commentators have observed that because of the Federal Councilors' dual roles as department heads and leaders of government, they find it difficult to manage all their responsibilities. This has led both to insufficient attention to governing and to an administrative branch with too much power. In addition, the one-year term for the presidency makes it difficult for Swiss presidents to develop relationships with heads of state from other countries. That said, the problems with the Swiss government do not stand out among countries—the Swiss express greater trust in their government than do citizens of most other European Union countries, and their dissatisfaction lies more with the legislature. In addition, there have not been the kinds of abuse of power with the Federal Council that have occurred with U.S. presidents.[67]

In sum, while a single president with all the executive power is firmly established in the United States, other countries function very well with an executive branch where power is shared among multiple cabinet ministers from multiple parties acting collectively. From the experience of other countries, we cannot assume, as Hamilton did, that a plural executive would dissolve into dissension and be unable to operate as a team. Rather than providing support for the Hamiltonian view, the international experience indicates that plural executives can operate in an effective manner.

Still, one might ask, even if multiperson executives function well in other countries, how do we know that a coalition presidency would function well in the United States? Hamilton may have been incorrect with regard to international experience, but he might have been correct in his understanding of a plural executive for the new national government. Cabinet ministers may work well together when they all belong to a single party, but two presidents from different parties might bog down in conflict, just as multiparty coalitions in parliamentary systems may fail to act in a productive fashion.

To some extent, it would be good if different worldviews led the two presidents to disagree and therefore initiate fewer rule-making processes, issue fewer executive orders, or commit forces to fewer military operations. One of the key reasons for considering a two-person presidency is to ensure that White House policies emerge from a deliberative process with executives who have different governing philosophies. Such a process may lead to less activity, but it should lead to better activity. As discussed in chapter 5, a bipartisan executive would make for a more effective decision-making process.

But would the two presidents bicker too much and become too paralyzed by their inability to share power? Was Hamilton correct about that possibility? The short response to this concern is to cite the Swiss Federal Council. The executive branch functions well in Switzerland even with multiple decision makers, representing different ideologies, who must reach a consensus before acting. Similarly, as discussed later in this chapter, the French experience with cohabitation governments illustrates how two executives from different political parties can collaborate effectively. There is no reason to think that elected officials from different parties in the United States are more prone to conflict than are elected officials from different parties in other countries.

More importantly, my argument does not rest solely on the evidence from Switzerland, France, and other countries. In the next section, I discuss other reasons to be confident about the functioning of a two-person presidency.

Would two presidents cooperate?

While Alexander Hamilton was concerned about dissension and rivalry between multiple executives, it is more likely that two presidents would develop a meaningful willingness to cooperate with each other. Consider in this regard the productive working relationships that develop between U.S. senators from the Democratic and Republican Parties. Senators Orrin Hatch (R-UT) and Ted Kennedy (D-MA) often collaborated on legislation, and there have been many important statutes sponsored by other Democrats and Republicans. Examples include the Hill-Burton Act for hospital construction, the Bayh-Dole Act for intellectual property rights in scientific discoveries, the Gramm-Rudman-Hollings Act for a balanced budget, the McCain-Feingold Act for campaign finance reform, and the Sarbanes-Oxley Act for securities reform.[68]

Of course, legislators do not always collaborate across party lines, and there are many examples of uncooperative relationships. Nevertheless, if cooperative relationships sometimes emerge from conditions that are not particularly favorable to their development, we can expect cooperative relationships to frequently emerge from conditions that promote their development. A two-person presidency would provide the right conditions for cooperative relationships.

For example, sociopsychological research supports the view that two presidents would work in a cooperative fashion. When people share the same social position, they often identify with each other more than would be expected by their other differences. Indeed, when social psychologists have identified factors that foster the development of good relations between individuals from groups that ordinarily are in conflict, they have found it important for the individuals to have an equal social status. The great Jean Renoir antiwar movie *La Grande Illusion* explored this phenomenon in its depiction of aristocratic officers identifying with aristocratic officers of the enemy more than working-class soldiers from their own country.[69]

There are other important reasons why we can expect cooperative working relationships between two presidents. In particular, the presidents would not have incentives to develop a relationship of conflict.

With multiple-party coalitions, coalition members can hope to establish their dominance at the next election by frustrating the goals of the other parties, just as the minority party in the United States can hope to reclaim the presidency by frustrating the goals of the current president. In many shared leadership situations, one executive might hope to achieve preeminence by outmaneuvering the other. In the two-person presidency that I discuss, however, neither president could hope to become dominant over the other president. A constitutional amendment to adopt an executive branch with two presidents would clearly establish their role as equals and their entitlement to fixed four-year terms of office. In addition, they could be reelected only with a presidential partner.

Not only would the two presidents lack an incentive to be in conflict; they also would have a very important incentive to work cooperatively. Having reached the pinnacle of political life, their focus would turn to making important contributions and establishing a meaningful and enduring legacy.[70] George W. Bush's decision to invade Iraq and overthrow Saddam Hussein is illustrative. While there were a number of reasons for his decision, it appears that he was influenced by the potential for introducing democratic governance to the Arab Middle East and providing a model that could spread to neighboring countries. The possibility of transforming a major region of the world overcame his opposition during the presidential campaign to policies of "nation building."

Similarly, when Barack Obama pressed his health care legislation in 2009 and 2010, he was driven by the desire to accomplish a goal that had been pursued by Democratic (and Republican) presidents from Franklin Delano Roosevelt to Bill Clinton. Even though his advisers warned him that the pursuit of health care reform was unwise when the public wanted its president to devote his energies to the economy, Obama wanted to do something more than secure his reelection. He wanted to secure his legacy, and "for greatness he needed health care."[71] If the two presidents spent their terms locking horns, they would not be able to implement key policies that would enhance their reputations. Accordingly, they likely would come to accommodations that would allow them to implement meaningful policy changes.

In fact, public officials often exhibit flexibility in their positions in order to achieve their political goals—policy positions are driven as much by political considerations as by core personal beliefs. Consider some important, recent examples: As governor of Massachusetts, Mitt Romney promoted the state's 2006 health care reform that was based on an individual mandate to purchase health care coverage. But during his presidential campaign in 2011 and 2012, Romney attacked Obama for promoting the same kind of individual mandate in the 2010 U.S. health care overhaul. U.S. Senator Arlen Specter moved more to the left after switching from the Republican Party to the Democratic Party in 2009. Evan Bayh took more liberal positions when contemplating a bid for the 2008 Democratic presidential nomination than when preparing for reelection in 2010 as a U.S. senator from Indiana. And after Democrats lost their majority in Congress in 1994, Bill Clinton famously "triangulated" in his policy initiatives, moving to the right and staking out positions between those of congressional Democrats and Republicans.[72]

For an earlier example of a candidate changing views, consider U.S. Senator Thomas Watson. As a member of the Populist Party and vice presidential candidate in the 1890s, he championed the rights of African Americans. But by 1904, he added his voice to those who supported the disenfranchisement of blacks, and in 1920, Watson ran as an avowed racist in his successful campaign for the U.S. Senate from Georgia. Just as other elected officials exhibit quite a bit of flexibility in their positions, so would presidents in a coalition executive.[73]

In other words, the ideological views of candidates and elected officials are as much means as they are ends. While candidates and officials may choose positions out of their basic beliefs (ideological views as ends), they more often stake out positions because they view the positions as useful for getting elected or exercising power (ideological views as means). During my six years in the Indiana House of Representatives, I saw elected officials frequently champion ideological positions purely for the electoral benefits that the positions would provide. As the electoral calculus shifts, elected officials modify their positions accordingly. Similarly, co-presidents would modify their positions to enact new policies.

Relationships in Congress across party lines are informative. While there are important examples of collegial and productive relationships between Democratic and Republican senators, there are fewer examples of collaborative relationships between Democratic and Republican representatives. Very likely, this reflects the fact that the majority party in the House need not work with the minority party to pass legislation. In the Senate, with its filibuster and the ability of individual members to hold up action, the minority party generally can block the majority's initiatives, just as presidential partners would be able to block each other's initiatives. And just as the filibuster and individual holds encourage the majority party to work with the minority party in the Senate,[74] so would the veto power of each of the two presidents encourage cooperation in a bipartisan White House. Indeed, presidential pairs would have greater incentives to work cooperatively than do U.S. senators from different parties.

My predictions about the behavior of two presidents may be based on educated guesses, but they also are well supported by principles of game theory (the academic study of strategic behavior). Game theory can identify the kinds of relationships that are likely to encourage cooperative strategies. And a two-person presidency would incorporate the key elements of cooperative relationships.

Thus, for example, when individuals have an ongoing relationship, they are much more likely to choose cooperation with another person than if they have a one-shot relationship. Consider in this regard how much more congenial are the relationships that people have with the person who services their car than with the person who would sell them a new car. Because the two presidents would anticipate a many-year relationship, they would have a strong incentive to cooperate. Indeed, as discussed in chapter 2, it would be helpful to eliminate term limits for the two presidents. Cooperation is more likely in relationships with an indefinite time horizon than when there is a finite time horizon. Other factors that promote cooperation are frequent interactions, regular communication between the individuals in the relationship, and the ability to retaliate with one's own noncooperation when another person is not cooperative. All these factors would be features of a relationship between presidential partners.[75]

Cooperative strategies also are more likely in two-person relationships than in many-person relationships. When many persons are involved, there can be problems identifying noncooperators, so participants may choose to be free riders and exploit the cooperation of other participants. Thus, economic cartels such as OPEC are more stable the fewer the number of members that they have. The more members in a cartel, the more difficult it is to detect cheating (as for example when an OPEC country exceeds its quota for oil production).[76]

Other insights from game theory are useful. When two people are involved in negotiations, they are more likely to reach a balanced agreement when they come to the negotiation from symmetrical positions. If there are asymmetries in their wealth, their needs, their costs from a delay in reaching agreement, or other factors that might affect their perception of a fair deal, then negotiations are more likely to become difficult or break down.[77]

To some extent, asymmetry between two presidents would be inevitable. People are different, and one president might be a more aggressive negotiator than the other. Moreover, there would be asymmetry if one of the presidents' political parties enjoyed greater power in Congress. Nevertheless, the two presidents would be in a symmetrical relationship with respect to the most important element of balance between them—the amount of power that they exercise. As I have indicated, the willingness of president partners to work cooperatively depends in large part on the fact that each of them would possess exactly half the executive power. No maneuvering could change that symmetry and give one or the other president the upper hand in the relationship.

If there were tactics that could change the balance of power between the two presidents, then the relationship could easily devolve into the dissension that Hamilton worried about. Cooperation is far less likely between two people if the benefits from not cooperating can become large relative to the benefits of mutual cooperation. Thus, when Eric Cantor took uncompromising positions in his negotiations on behalf of House Republicans with Barack Obama during the 2011 effort to raise the U.S. debt ceiling, he calculated that noncooperation could enhance his ability to gain greater power. By staking out his

claim as the true representative of Republican values, he might succeed John Boehner as Speaker of the House.[78]

Presidential partners, on the other hand, would not realize any
increase in power by not cooperating with their counterparts. No
matter how intransigent they became, they still would share the executive power on a fifty-fifty basis. Rather than a potential enhance-
ment in authority, the alternative to cooperation would be a failure to
leave a legacy of accomplishment. The unattractiveness of that alternative would drive the two presidents to find common ground.

To put it another way, elected officials engage in conflict not because they value conflict for its own sake but because they can use
it as a way to achieve their chief goals of accumulating power and
enacting favored public policies. If conflict cannot yield an increase
in power or improve the chances of implementing policy, then public
officers will turn to cooperation instead.

The inclination of people to adopt cooperative strategies in balanced relationships extends even to relationships among individuals
who enter the relationship from highly antagonistic positions—as
one might expect with presidents from different parties. An important illustration comes from the example of trench warfare in Europe
during World War I at the Western Front of battle. When small
units faced each other for extended periods of time, the British or
French foot soldiers often would develop cooperative strategies with
their German counterparts. Each side realized that noncooperation
would result in both sides being bloodied, while cooperation would
be mutually beneficial.[79] Or consider how Barack Obama and Hillary
Clinton developed a cooperative relationship as president and secretary of state after they fought bitterly against each other for the 2008
Democratic nomination.

Importantly, with a two-person Oval Office, people who cannot
work well with partners would be discouraged from running for president. If they had a strong need to make decisions on their own, they
would recognize that other positions would be better fits for them.

To be sure, some discordant thinking would be beneficial between
president partners. As I discuss in chapter 5, it is not desirable to have
too much similarity of viewpoint. If officers in the executive branch

are overly cohesive, they become prone to the possibility of "group-think." Two presidents from different parties sharing decision making with each other are in a better position to avoid groupthink than a single president sharing decision making with like-minded advisers. In other words, we want decision makers to bring different perspectives that they need to reconcile, and two presidents in a coalition executive would come to the table with sufficient incentive to reconcile their differences.

The French experience in 1986–1988 with shared executive power also provides reassurance about the risks of dissension between presidential partners. For twenty-six months, the president and prime minister came from opposing political parties rather than the same party. Even though the executive power was not divided equally and even though the president and prime minister were positioning themselves as candidates for the next presidential election, the coalition executive regime worked reasonably well and did not provoke any crises or otherwise break down.[80]

France has a semipresidential system, and its president enjoys more power than is typical for a parliamentary president, especially with regard to foreign policy. As a result, the president rather than the prime minister becomes the dominant national official.[81] During his presidency from 2007 to 2012, for example, Nicolas Sarkozy over-shadowed the prime minister, François Fillon.

However, when the president and prime minister come from different parties, the two can jockey for power. And that is in fact what happened between March 1986 and May 1988 when France was headed by a president from the left (François Mitterrand) and a prime minister from the right (Jacques Chirac). The United States analogue to that arrangement would be to have a Democratic president and a Republican Speaker of the House, with the Speaker also having significant executive power. Although Mitterrand and Chirac battled over domestic policy, Chirac's legislative majority generally prevailed. On foreign affairs, the two parties had similar policies on major issues, and Mitterrand and Chirac avoided public confrontations when disagreements arose.[82]

Interestingly, the fact that Mitterrand and Chirac planned to run for president at the next election fostered cooperation. The public had a generally favorable view toward the sharing of power across party lines, and Mitterrand and Chirac both felt pressure to strengthen their support among voters in advance of the election. Their desire to avoid actions that would antagonize voters made them less willing to push boundaries and threaten the stability of the government.[83]

Elections in France produced two more popular cohabitation arrangements, in 1993–1995 and in 1997–2002, making cohabitation the norm for most the period between 1986 and 2002. While cohabitation invited constant competition between the president and prime minister, Robert Elgie found that there were "well-established procedures" which "minimized the overall extent of the conflict within the executive" and which "ensured the continuity of the system." Indeed, as I have argued would be the case in a coalition presidency, cohabitation government in France featured a significant level of cooperation between the president and prime minister in part because cooperation could "work to the mutual advantage of both."[84]

That said, cohabitation had its problems. While there was cooperation, there also was conflict between the president and prime minister, and France ultimately amended its constitution in 2000 so that elections for the president and the National Assembly take place the same year, reducing the likelihood of cohabitation governments. It is not surprising that conflict occurred—without an equal division of power, the structure of the cohabitation governments permitted the two executives to compete for authority.[85] The coalition executive that I propose would not allow for that kind of maneuvering. Moreover, while French presidents and prime ministers could hope to escape cohabitation government at the next election, presidents in my proposed coalition government could not escape shared governance through new elections.

There is one additional argument to consider. Perhaps presidents in a coalition executive would fail to cooperate with their partners to protect against a viable primary challenge when they run for reelection. Presidents might fear that if they appear too accommodating, they will be attacked for compromising their parties' principles.

This is certainly a plausible result, but I think improbable. The argument fails to account for changes in primary voting or other changes in public behavior that a coalition presidency would likely trigger. Currently, primary voting is dominated by a political party's core supporters, and candidates may need to stake out ideologically strong positions. But in a two-person presidency, the ultimate outcome will be determined largely during the primaries. The Democratic and Republican nominees typically will finish in the top two positions in November. Accordingly, as discussed in chapter 2, people who currently do not affiliate with a political party would recognize that their votes would matter only if they voted in the primary elections. This would drive more independent voters into the primary electorate, and less extreme positions would have greater appeal.

In addition, it is difficult to see why even partisan voters would begrudge the cooperative behavior of their party's nominee. It would be abundantly clear that the two presidents would have no choice but to cooperate to get anything done. And again, it is important that nothing could change that reality. Unlike the current structure, in which voters can hope that their party captures more power in the next election, that possibility would not exist for an executive branch overseen by a two-person presidency. In the end, voters want their elected officials to solve problems, not to let the country's problems go unaddressed.

The resistance to a plural executive in the United States

One might wonder whether the lack of enthusiasm in the United States for a collective executive represents a political example of the "tomato effect." The tomato effect refers to the phenomenon of a practice being rejected because it does not conform to existing theories, even though empirical data demonstrate the validity of the practice. It takes its name from the reluctance of Americans to eat tomatoes during the colonial period and subsequent years. Until the 19th Century, Americans eschewed the tomato, believing it was poisonous because it belonged to a family of plants with some deadly poisonous species. Yet as Americans were shunning the tomato, it had become a staple of diets in Italy, France, and other European countries.[86] Even though Europeans ate tomatoes on a regular basis without any harm, Americans took the view that it did not make sense to eat poisonous food. Eventually, reality overtook theory, and the tomato became a staple in the American diet too.

Perhaps the American antipathy toward a plural executive reflects the same kind of thinking as the previous antipathy toward the tomato. Just as we once were slower than Europeans to recognize the virtue of tomatoes, we are slower than Europeans today to recognize the virtues of a plural executive.

A plural executive must be structured properly

Does it matter that collegial executive branches are found largely in parliamentary governments? Maybe the United States has a unitary executive because it has a presidential rather than parliamentary system of government.

As part of a larger study of presidential government, Matthew Shugart and John Carey considered the adoption of a plural executive in a presidential system as a way to counteract the ills of a highly polarized society. They undertook a comparative analysis of presidential and parliamentary governments, looking at both theory and practice. They found that plural executives can make sense in both presidential and parliamentary systems as a way to address the problem of partisan conflict. Similarly, Arend Lijphart has discussed the importance of power sharing in the executive branch for deeply divided societies.[87]

Sounding some of the themes discussed earlier in this chapter, Shugart and Carey identified two key ways in which a one-person presidency aggravates, rather than ameliorates, partisan conflict. First, they observed that one-person executive systems suffer from a "majoritarianism," in which the lack of meaningful representation for minority voices hampers the ability of the executive branch to bridge partisan divides in the society. With their winner-take-all elections, presidential systems give their executives and the executives' party full control over the policy making of the executive branch while shutting the opposition parties out. Minority parties therefore feel disempowered.[88]

In contrast, in parliamentary systems, where multiple parties often are represented in the executive branch, different ethnic, political, or religious groups can participate in the shaping of national policy. This shared participation makes for more cooperation across class boundaries. Thus, for example, Switzerland's multiparty executive council likely has facilitated cohesion among the German, French, Italian, and Romansh populations, as well as the Catholic and Protestant communities in Swiss society. I shall have more to say about the problem of majoritarianism in one-person presidencies in chapter 6.[89]

Shugart and Carey discussed a second feature of presidential systems that diminishes the influence of minority voices and that was mentioned earlier. Because presidents are elected for fixed terms, their tenure in office is not dependent as much on their relations with the legislature as is the case for the executive branch in parliamentary systems. A parliamentary legislature can bring down the executive branch (the cabinet) with a vote of no confidence. Accordingly, the parliamentary cabinet has a constant incentive to develop and maintain a majority coalition of legislators that will support the government's initiatives. U.S. presidents, on the other hand, can generally serve their full four-year term. As a result, they operate under a weaker incentive to form a durable coalition with members of the legislature from different parties or even their own party.

At the same time, legislators from other parties have little to gain by cooperating with the president. In the United States, obstruction can enhance the out-of-power party's chances of capturing the Oval Office again. In addition, because the public assigns credit or blame for the country's performance largely to the president and the president's party, the opposition realizes little political benefit from cooperation. Thus, few Republicans backed Barack Obama's economic-stimulus proposal in 2009 or his health care legislation in 2010.[90]

If a one-person executive does more to exacerbate rather than mitigate partisan conflict, can a two-person executive dampen partisan conflict in the United States? Yes—both of the conflict-heightening features of a one-person presidency can be addressed by a plural executive. With the sharing of power across partisan divides, the majority party no long would wield exclusive control of executive power, and the minority party would have a more meaningful stake in the shaping of national policy. In addition, there would be much stronger incentives for cooperation between the executive branch and legislators on both sides of the aisle. Thus, as Shugart and Carey concluded, under the right conditions, "collegial presidentialism may offer the best possibility for resolving conflicts peacefully in deeply divided societies."[91]

And it is important to have the right conditions. While Switzerland's executive council has functioned well in its presidential-parliamentary hybrid system, other countries have had less satisfactory experiences with plural executives in their presidential systems. Uruguay tried a plural executive between 1952 and 1966, Cyprus did so between 1960 and 1963, and Bosnia and Herzegovina has done so since 1995.

Uruguay's experiment suffered from a few key problems. The country reserved representation for only the two major parties, even when a strong third party emerged; it fixed the minority party's representation in the executive council at three of the nine seats, regardless of the actual percentage of votes cast for the two major parties; and it adopted a plural executive that was too large (nine members).[92]

While Uruguay found that shared power can suffer when the minority's level of representation is too low, Cyprus found that shared power can suffer when the minority's representation is too high. Cyprus divided its executive powers almost equally between a Greek president and Turkish vice president until civil war broke out after three years. Greek Cypriots felt that the relatively equal power sharing was not fair in a country in which the Greek majority included 78 percent of the population while the Turkish minority comprised only 18 percent.[93]

The difficulties with governance in Bosnia and Herzegovina also suggest that divisions of power will fail when multiple presidents are treated equally but represent constituencies of very different sizes. Since the country's organization under the Dayton Accords of 1995,

Bosnia and Herzegovina has featured a tripartite executive branch, with representation from the Bosniac, Croat, and Serb communities. Each group has a president, and decisions are made by consensus, with the qualification that decisions may be made by two of the presidents if all attempts at reaching a consensus have failed. The presidents take turns serving as chair of the presidency, with rotations every eight months. But the Bosniac-Croat-Serb equality in the executive branch does not reflect their representation in the population. Bosniacs account for 48 percent of the population, Serbs 37 percent, and Croats only 14 percent.[94] The executive branch in Bosnia and Herzegovina is viewed as highly dysfunctional, and indeed it has struggled to make important decisions.

That said, the political system generally is highly dysfunctional in Bosnia and Herzegovina. The country suffers from a weak central government and two semisovereign provinces (the "entities" of the Federation of Bosnia and Herzegovina and the Republika Srpska). In other words, the problems in Bosnia and Herzegovina lie more deeply than in its executive branch. Hence, experts regularly call for broad constitutional reform.[95]

As Shugart and Carey indicate, we can draw two important lessons from the experiences of Uruguay, Cyprus, and Bosnia and Herzegovina. First, a sharing of presidential power among different political parties can work only when the allocation of power fairly reflects the balance in popular support among the parties. The public cares very much about proportionality. Second, the executive branch should include a small number of presidents. Decision making can become unwieldy in large groups. Shugart and Carey recommend keeping the executive branch to no more than two or three persons (though the Swiss experience with a seven-member executive suggests that Shugart and Carey may have been too conservative on this point).[96]

A two-person, coalition presidency in the United States would satisfy both of the conditions suggested by Shugart and Carey. Indeed, a key factor that distinguishes the United States from Cyprus in the early 1960s is the balance in support between the major parties. While the Greek-Turk ratio was more than four to one in Cyprus, the Democratic-Republican ratio in the United States is quite close to one to one. Of course, at particular times, the public may shift more toward the Republican Party and elect a Ronald Reagan or a George W. Bush, while at other times move more toward the Democratic Party and elect a Bill Clinton or a Barack Obama. But neither party has established a persistent presence in the Oval Office since the Roosevelt-Truman span of twenty years of Democratic presidents that ended in 1952. And no candidate has won even 54 percent of the popular vote since Reagan picked up nearly 59 percent of the vote in his 1984 reelection campaign.

In sum, consideration of sociopsychological research, game theory, and international experience indicates that a plural executive can do much to defuse partisan conflict, as long as the plural executive is properly structured. This last point is worth emphasizing. My argument for a two-person presidency relies on the fact that it is designed to neutralize, rather than to aggravate, partisan conflict.

The inadequacy of other proposals

Do we really need to adopt a two-person presidency to defuse partisan conflict? Are there not other reforms that would be effective and less radical? No. A review of other proposals demonstrates that they would not provide the needed relief or would raise their own problems.

Some scholars have argued that we should address partisan conflict by giving the majority party greater control over the institutions of government. In this view, partisan behavior is a problem when the United States has divided government (i.e., when one party controls the presidency and the other party controls at least one of the houses of Congress). Divided government, it is said, causes gridlock and prevents the president and Congress from working cooperatively to solve pressing national problems such as high budget deficits. Unified government, on the other hand, would create greater opportunities for creative, effective government and secure the benefits of strong political parties.[97]

Indeed, there is much to be said for strong political parties. As pro-party scholars observe, the framers may have seen little good to be gained from political parties when they drafted the Constitution, but they nevertheless became the fathers of our two-party system.[98] Today, the Democratic and Republican Parties play dominant roles not only in the selection of candidates for public office but also in the shaping of policy.

Many experts in law and politics think that this has been very good for the United States, that our two-party system has "quasi-constitutional value." In this view, the two-party system fosters political stability and diminishes rather than aggravates the problem of faction. For example, because the Democratic and Republican Parties are necessarily large coalitions of multiple constituencies, they do not pursue the kinds of narrow interests that smaller parties would pursue. In other countries, parties might represent interests based on ethnicity, religion, or geography, and they can exercise disproportionate power in negotiations to form a governing coalition. In Israel, for example, the ultra-Orthodox Shas Party has been able to extract major concessions even when it polls less than 10 percent of the popular vote.[99] In the United States, the party tents are larger and less prone to narrow interest takeover.

There are benefits not only from a two-party system but from political parties generally. It is difficult for voters to be heard when they speak alone. Political parties allow individuals to band together, aggregate their voices, and gain strength in numbers. Political parties also promote competition that is beneficial to the public. As discussed in chapter 3, members of the party out of power can serve as watchdogs over elected officials of the party in power, thereby supplementing the checks and balances of the separation of powers. Larry Kramer has argued that political parties also supplement the "federalism" check on the national government. Because political parties create common interests and dependencies between federal and state elected officials, federal officials often will defer to state interests. Indeed, writes Kramer, the parties supply the check on a too-expansive federal government that state governments were expected to provide but do not provide.[100]

Given the benefits of political parties, many scholars would try to capture their advantages and reduce their disadvantages by borrowing from British-style parliamentary systems the simultaneous control of the executive and legislative branches by one party. In this view, the problem of partisan gridlock lies in the nature of a presidential system of government. When the president is from one party, and the other major party enjoys a majority in the House or the Senate, there is no mechanism to resolve the conflict when the executive and legislative branches are at odds with each other. If the U.S. political system did more to promote one-party control of both the executive and legislative branches, the president and Congress would have a much greater ability to implement a coherent vision, and voters could decide at the next election whether they wanted to continue the implementation or change course.[101]

But one-party government raises its own concerns. In particular, it deviates strikingly from the principle of a separation of powers. The framers consciously divided power to protect against the abuse of power. To be sure, dividing power makes it more difficult to implement change, but that was an important part of the constitutional plan. The framers understood that they were creating a government prone to inertia.

And one need not subscribe to original intent to reject undivided governmental power. Unified executive and legislative branches that promote one political party's agenda may not serve the country's interests well. Efficient lawmaking does not guarantee good lawmaking. When one political party controls all the power, it can easily overreach and enact policies that suffer from excess. Moreover, letting one party run the government leaves the opposition disempowered and inclined toward obstruction. In other words, the answer to a dysfunctional system of checks and balances is not to abandon checks and balances altogether.[102] Rather, we need to look for ways to fix the Constitution's system of divided and shared power. A two-person presidency would do that by discouraging the kind of partisan behavior that has dominated Washington over the years.

Bruce Ackerman has proposed reforms that are designed both to capture the benefits of parliamentary government and to preserve the checks and balances of the United States' separation of powers. Rather than a British-style system, in which one party exercises relatively unchecked power, Ackerman recommends a "constrained parliamentarianism." Constrained parliamentarianism would begin with a British-style parliament but include several mechanisms and institutions to cabin the authority of the parliamentary majority and its prime minister. For example, the public would play an important role through the limited use of referenda, there would be a strong constitutional court with an appointment process favoring moderate and nonpartisan nominees, an integrity branch of the government would protect against public corruption, and a regulatory branch would promote an administrative bureaucracy characterized more by professional expertise than by political allegiances.[103]

There is much good in Ackerman's constrained parliamentarianism. It would alleviate the problem of gridlock from divided government while still employing checks and balances. It would address the problems of fixed terms and term limits for presidents—in a constrained parliamentary system, the legislature could bring down a misguided executive without waiting for the expiration of a four-year term while also allowing the public to reelect an effective executive for more than two terms.

However, constrained parliamentarianism would not respond to one of my basic concerns—the failure of political systems to recognize the interests of people who do not support the majority party or majority coalition. Just as do other parliamentary political systems, constrained parliamentarianism gives disproportionate power to the majority. Even if there are checks on the majority's exercise of power, it would possess 100 percent of the executive power and effective control of the legislative power, even though it might win only a bare majority or substantial plurality of the popular vote. That much power for a majority or plurality makes for a fundamentally unfair system of government.

In contrast, a two-person executive would promote government based on broad consensus rather than government based on the preferences of a mere majority. As Arend Lijphart has argued, while we should view majority rule as a necessary feature of democracy, we should not view it as a sufficient feature. We also can try to maximize the size of the majority to give as many people as possible a voice in their government.[104]

And broad, consensual democracies can maximize the majority while also preserving the interest in good governance. The empirical evidence suggests that consensual democracies are at least as effective as majoritarian governments in managing the economy and more effective at representing the interests of both majority and minority citizens.[105]

In short, a coalition executive responds to the key argument in favor of a parliamentary system without inviting the disadvantages of parliamentary government. A two-person presidency addresses concerns about partisan conflict and the resultant gridlock between the executive and legislative branches. And it does so by broadening rather than narrowing the extent to which executive power is shared across party lines. In addition, a coalition executive provides a much simpler response to the problem of partisan conflict. Changing to a parliamentary system would require many more changes to the U.S. political system. If we can overcome partisan conflict by just restructuring the executive branch, why try to restructure the legislative branch as well?

Other proposals to defuse partisan conflict also are inadequate. Some scholars have proposed nonpartisan commissions to draw lines during political redistricting. In their view, the gerrymandering of legislative districts explains the growing partisan divide in Congress. Over time, more districts have become safe Democratic or safe Republican seats, so elections are decided on primary day rather than Election Day. Since primary voters tend to lie closer to the ideological extremes than Election Day voters, gerrymandering can lead to more polarized members of Congress. The problem with this theory is that the Senate has become just as polarized as the House. Moreover, even with House seats, empirical analysis indicates that gerrymandering has not played an important role in promoting the increase in partisan behavior. After the 2001 redistricting, for example, there was little change in the number of safe congressional districts. And when districts were drawn by nonpartisan commissions or courts, states actually ended up with a greater number of safe seats.[106]

Curbing other excesses in political competition

I have argued that a two-person presidency would respond to the problem of partisan conflict. A two-person presidency also would help curb some of the other excesses of political competition in the United States. As Robert Frank and Philip Cook have written, winner-take-all markets with high payoffs "result in inefficient patterns of . . . investment" by those who compete in the market.[107] Frank and Cook mostly use examples from entertainment, professional sports, and book publishing, but they also indicate how their analysis applies to candidates for public office, especially candidates for the presidency. Political races are winner-take-all affairs in the United States, and the payoff for the presidential election is quite substantial in an era of an imperial president governing the world's leading superpower.

In winner-take-all markets with high payoffs, each contestant or candidate will perceive an added personal benefit from greater and greater investments in time and money. In terms of overall social benefit, however, much of the additional investments would be better spent on other activities or needs.

Why is this so? From the perspective of the individual candidate for president, additional time on the campaign trail and greater spending for television ads will increase the chances of winning by some amount. And the payoff can be huge since the candidate either wins everything or loses everything. Hence, the personal benefits from more campaigning and more spending appear to be high. But the other major-party nominee will match the time and money, and the two candidates will end up in an escalating time and money race. To some extent, voters will benefit from the greater information they receive from the greater efforts by the candidates. However, in the end, the voters will choose one of the two candidates no matter how much time and money the candidates invest. Hence, there are real limits to the social value of increased candidate campaigning and spending. Americans will get one president whether the candidates campaign for one year and altogether spend $200 million or campaign for four years and altogether spend $2 billion.[108] In short, because the payoff from becoming president has become so great and the winner takes all the payoff, individuals overcompete to become president.

With a bipartisan presidency, the payoff from winning would drop significantly since there would be two winners who share the power of the executive branch. Candidates would perceive a reduced benefit from their investments in time and money than they do now, and campaigns should become shorter and less expensive.[109]

Even if candidates would not perceive a reduced benefit from campaign spending, it is likely that potential donors would. Presidential campaigns should become less expensive under a two-person presidency because it will matter less who wins. With a one-person presidency, donors can influence the choice between a Democrat and Republican for the Oval Office. With a two-person presidency, donors could only promote the candidacy of one Democrat over other Democrats for one Oval Office seat or the candidacy of one Republican over other Republicans for the other Oval Office seat. And it generally is much more significant when voters choose between a Democrat and Republican than when they choose among Democrats or among Republicans. Democrats differ more with Republicans than they do with each other, and Republicans differ more with Democrats than they do with each other. Donors would understand that with shared governance, there would be much less change from administration to administration than occurs when an administration of one party is succeeded by an administration of another party. Hence, they would not feel the same level of pressure to try to influence the outcome on Election Day.

Note how lowering the stakes of presidential elections is a far more effective strategy for campaign finance reform than the measures that have been tried to date. When the stakes are high and rising ever higher, candidates—and their supporters—face unremitting pressure to do whatever it takes to win. Thus, when a campaign finance law cuts off one mode of fund-raising or spending, the money moves to another outlet. After Congress limited contributions to candidate committees, for example, contributors funded independent committees, and spending on campaigns continued to rise. Or when public financing of presidential campaigns appeared to provide insufficient funding, Barack Obama in 2008 became the first major-party nominee to opt out of the public financing system. As long as the political system encourages very high spending, there will be very high spending in one form or another. We will see lower spending only when we lower the payoff from spending.

The high stakes of presidential elections generate other problematic behavior by candidates. Just as top athletes cut ethical and legal corners to set records or win championships, candidates for the White House cut ethical and legal corners in their effort to win election. Violations of campaign finance laws occur with some regularity, and candidates take other questionable action. Obama misrepresented his mother's health insurance status to dramatize the need for reform of the health insurance industry, and Bill Clinton refused to commute the death sentence of a mentally retarded man in Arkansas because he did not want to appear soft on crime.[110] Lowering the stakes of winning the presidency will reduce the pressures to sacrifice ethical and legal principles for electoral gain.

If presidential candidates faced less pressure during the campaign, society would benefit in a number of other ways. For example, fewer capable individuals would be discouraged from running by the need to mount a four-year effort and raise hundreds of millions of dollars.

Lowering the stakes of presidential elections also would encourage greater public service by people who aspire to the presidency. The framers expected a politics of virtue to determine our president. Just as voters chose George Washington as their first president because of his great service to the country, the framers expected future presidents to earn their way to the White House through a career of devoted public service. In the U.S. presidential election process, however, the candidates most likely to succeed are not necessarily those who have made major contributions to the public good but those who are the most ambitious and most willing to make whatever sacrifices are required to advance their candidacies.[111] Obama had served in the U.S. Senate only two years before launching his presidential run, and there was nothing particularly noteworthy about his record of accomplishment as a member of Congress, as a state legislator in Illinois, or in positions he held before commencing his career in elected office. Similarly, John Edwards became the Democratic nominee for vice president in 2004 after serving only one term in the Senate.

This is not to say that a pool of the most ambitious people excludes all of the most capable individuals. Obama has accomplished much during his presidency. Nor is it to say that candidates with a strong record of service will make the best presidents. Herbert Hoover brought a remarkable record to the White House. During and after World War I, he organized food aid to millions of starving people in Europe and the Soviet Union. He also served effectively as secretary of commerce in the administrations of Warren Harding and Calvin Coolidge, implementing important initiatives in child health, conservation, highway safety, home ownership, and scientific research. When Republicans prepared to nominate a presidential candidate in 1928, Hoover was the obvious choice. With his record of achievement, he could appeal even to liberal Democrats as a reformer who would "purify capitalism of its . . . commercialism, its waste, and its squalor."[112] Yet Hoover left a legacy as one of the least successful presidents when he handled the Great Depression poorly. Past accomplishments are no guarantee of future success in public service.

Still, there is a legitimate concern when ambition becomes more important than achievement. Presidential politics have evolved to the point that they both deter accomplished persons from running for president and discourage aspiring presidents from trying to make important contributions to society before they launch their campaigns for the White House. The already-accomplished person will recognize that a lengthy record provides fodder for attacks by opponents. For many such people, it will not be worth it to endure the criticism. The not-yet-accomplished candidate, on the other hand, will be reluctant to press for major social reforms before ascending to the Oval Office. Potential candidates always will be calculating the impact of their activities on a future presidential run. After watching Mitt Romney suffer in the presidential nominating process because of his leadership on health care reform while governor of Massachusetts, other elected officials might forgo such accomplishments.

Of course, a record of achievement can help one's chances for election, but the Romney example illustrates the fact that doing the right thing for the community may be the wrong thing for a presidential bid. Inevitably, what is socially valuable will diverge to some extent from what is politically expedient. And when serving the public good diverges from serving one's presidential aspirations, the ever-increasing pressures from presidential politics will push would-be candidates more and more to serve their presidential aspirations. Society will suffer from too much posturing for the presidency and not enough commitment to the common welfare.[113]

In short, just as reform of the executive branch is needed to address the ills of heightened partisan conflict, it also is needed to counteract the excesses of competition for election to the Oval Office. By lowering the stakes in presidential elections, a two-person presidency would provide exactly that kind of reform.

If a two-person presidency would defuse partisan conflict at the national level, might it also defuse partisan conflict at the state level? Perhaps we should adopt two-person governors. Having bipartisan governors would make for better government at the state level, and shared governance in gubernatorial offices would promote greater harmony among legislators and voters.

That said, the argument for two governors is not as strong as for two presidents. First, while the major parties are closely balanced at the national level, they are not always balanced at the state level. Some states vote reliably Democratic; other states vote reliably Republican. More importantly, the imperial presidency problem is not paralleled by an imperial governor problem. State chief executives do not exercise foreign policy powers, their domestic powers are more modest than those of a president, and state legislatures often exercise stronger checks on the domestic power of governors. For example, simple majorities in the state house and senate may be sufficient to override a veto. On balance, it may make sense for some states to take advantage of their role as laboratories of experimentation for novel public policies and to adopt a bipartisan governorship. If it proves effective, then there is an even stronger case for adopting a two-person presidency. And constitutional amendments typically emerge from models developed by states.[114]

To this point, I have argued on behalf of a two-person presidency as a way to mitigate dysfunction in Washington. The imperial presidency could be reined in, and partisan conflict could be moderated.

A plural executive would reduce the negative effects of the United States' current constitutional structure. There also is an important argument for a plural executive in terms of its positive effects. Two presidential partners may well provide more effective leadership than can be provided by a single president. Why this is so is the topic of chapter 5.

5

A bipartisan executive and presidential decision making

I n chapters 3 and 4, I argued that a two-person, coalition presidency would compensate for the Constitution's failure to cabin the power of the executive branch or contain partisan conflict in Washington. There is a third key argument for a presidential partnership—two heads are better than one. Experience with decision making in other settings demonstrates that we get better results when we have shared decision making. Two presidents likely would come to wiser, more prudent judgments than single presidents. Shared decision making also makes for a better process. As discussed in the next chapter, a coalition executive would ensure that a far broader range of the public feels that it has a voice in the shaping of governmental policy.

The advantages of shared decision making would be particularly valuable for the modern presidency. As the executive branch has assumed major policy-making responsibilities, and is not simply charged with implementing legislative policy, it will function more effectively when its decisions reflect a broader range of political perspectives.

Article II and the single president

Despite the merits of a two-person presidency, the framers saw things differently. They felt that a single president makes for a more effective executive branch. Hence, Article II of the Constitution clearly calls for one president at a time: "The executive Power shall be vested in *a* President of the United States of America" (art. II, § 1, cl. 1; emphasis added).

The delegates to the constitutional convention debated and rejected proposals for a plural executive. Elbridge Gerry favored annexing a council to the executive, George Mason and Edmund Randolph recommended three executives rather than one, and the New Jersey plan also called for a multimember executive. But most delegates opposed the idea of a plural executive, and they cited concerns about continual disagreements among multiple executives and ineffective leadership, particularly in military matters. To be sure, the delegates worried that a single executive could assume the excessive power of a monarch, but they also worried that a plural executive would lack sufficient energy and authority. Ultimately, the delegates voted for a single executive, by a vote of seven states to three.[1]

Alexander Hamilton discussed the logic of a single executive in Federalist 70, and he offered several arguments. In the next section, I explain why his thinking was misguided.

Shared decision making

Hamilton's primary argument for a one-person presidency rests in the need for a well-functioning executive branch. A single president can act decisively and with dispatch, wrote Hamilton, whereas multiple persons with executive power would be prone to deliberation and dissension.

Was Hamilton correct that a single executive provides better leadership? When presidents primarily implemented congressionally determined policies, he may well have been right. But in a White House that has assumed considerable policy-making power, decision making would be improved with a plural executive. Indeed, in other important policy-making settings, society has recognized the advantages of shared decision making and substituted that approach for unilateral decision making. Family decisions are shared by both spouses, and medical decisions are shared by patients and physicians.

The constitutional framers also preferred shared decision making for policy makers in the national government. When the Constitution took effect, it provided for twenty-six U.S. senators, and sixty-five U.S. representatives. The Constitution did not specify the number of Supreme Court justices, but the first Congress set the initial number at six in the Judiciary Act of 1789. Recall the earlier quote from Woodrow Wilson: "The whole purpose of democracy is that we may hold counsel with one another, so as not to depend upon the understanding of one man."[2]

The advantages of shared decision making

A preference for shared decision making is not surprising. It is commonly said that two heads are better than one, and it is not difficult to identify activities in which two or more people working together are more effective than either one alone. Consider, for example, the solving of a crossword puzzle with the help of a family member or friend. One person may know more about literature and music, the other about politics and history. Similarly, when contestants on *Who Wants to Be a Millionaire?* use one of their "lifelines" and ask for help from the studio audience, the choice of the audience majority is correct 91 percent of the time.[3]

Groups outperform individuals not only on puzzles or game shows but also when making other kinds of decisions. Much research has been devoted to comparing individual and shared decision making, and overall, experts agree that shared decision making is superior to individual decision making.[4] While there are times when individual decision making achieves better results, consideration of the empirical data indicates that two presidents generally would make better decisions than one president.

For example, groups outperform individuals when making decisions for which there are no obviously correct answers but that instead entail the application of judgment to multiple plausible alternatives.[5] These are the kinds of decisions that presidents face regularly: Which policy should be adopted to deal with a hostile foreign government in a country such as Iran or to pacify a conflict-ridden country such as Afghanistan? What kind of legislative proposal to overhaul the immigration system will best balance the goals of achieving real reform and securing majorities in a politically diverse Congress?

Groups also outperform individuals the greater the complexity of a decision. When faced with complicated questions, individuals tend to oversimplify the matter. Groups, on the other hand, can draw on their broader range of information and talent to give adequate attention to the different, important nuances of the decision. This advantage of groups is important for the executive branch. Presidential decisions frequently involve considerable complexity. Consider in this regard questions involving reform of financial markets and the proper way to regulate the credit default swap market that collapsed in the worldwide financial crisis of 2008.[6]

The benefits of group decision making have been demonstrated in a number of disciplines. For example, groups of physicians outperform individual physicians when making life-and-death decisions for patients. People suffering a heart attack fare better when their physicians practice with other physicians. They are more likely to receive appropriate care and more likely to survive their attack than are patients who receive care from solo practitioners.[7]

Groups do a better job when making other informed judgments, such as creating an investment portfolio. Standard investment theory recommends a diversified portfolio, to decrease the risk of loss, and experimental data indicate that groups generate higher expected values at a lower total risk. It appears that team members improve portfolio quality by vetoing the selection of excessively risky investments—investments whose greater risk cannot be justified by a sufficient gain in expected payoff.[8] The public would benefit from a presidential partner who would veto policies for the country that are excessively risky.

Groups also generally outperform individuals in strategic bargaining games and in game situations that require players to anticipate the dynamics of the game over multiple rounds. It appears that groups learn to act strategically more quickly than do individuals, and they employ a more effective learning process, *even in groups with as few as two members.*[9]

Reasons for the gains from shared decision making

There are several factors that might explain the better decision making of groups. As indicated with the crossword puzzle example, a group of people will know more information than any single individual will. In a world of uncertainty, decision making will benefit from the pooling of knowledge. Thus, for example, collaboration by scientists can lead to more rapid advances in medical knowledge. When researchers studying Alzheimer's disease at different companies and universities began to share their data with each other, they accelerated the generation of information that was being sought to promote the early diagnosis and treatment of the disease.[10]

Groups not only bring larger pools of information to the decision-making process; they also are better able to process large amounts of information.[11] This benefit of shared decision making would be particularly advantageous to presidential pairs shaping public policy. Consider, for example, the number of factors that influence the choice of climate legislation and all of the data that inform those factors: How fast are carbon emissions growing, and how great are their impact? What kinds of conservation measures are available, and how much can they cut carbon emissions? What is the potential for wind, solar, and biofuel power?

A group also brings a wider range of perspectives. A single person is more likely to undervalue or not recognize some important considerations. Thus, the Supreme Court invites amicus briefs from people who might be affected by its decisions, so the justices can take into account all of the relevant factors.[12]

Groups tend to rely on a broader spectrum of ways to solve problems. When a matter is complicated, it often is not obvious how it should best be addressed. Accordingly, it may be necessary to try a number of strategies before a good solution is reached. Indeed, the range of problem-solving strategies may be as important as the problem-solving skills of group members. In a study that looked at this question, researchers found that a group of good problem solvers that employs a diversity of problem-solving approaches can outperform a group of problem solvers whose problem-solving skills are stronger but who employ problem-solving approaches that are alike.[13]

Similarly, in a study that looked at how difficult scientific problems were solved for major firms, the most important factor was the heterogeneity of the scientists trying to solve the problems. For example, solutions were more often found when biologists, chemists, and physicists worked on the challenge than when chemists alone searched for a solution. And when the British government cracked the Nazi's secret codes during World War II, it did so by bringing together not only mathematicians, engineers, and cryptographers but also linguists, classicists, historians, philosophers, and crossword puzzle experts.[14]

With all of these advantages of group decision making, it is not surprising to find that group members achieve new levels of understanding in their decision making and develop into more sophisticated thinkers than do people deciding alone.[15]

Of course, even single presidents do not make decisions alone. They consult with members of their cabinet and other advisers, so they enjoy many of the benefits of shared decision making. Nevertheless, there are critical differences between decision makers and those who advise decision makers. Advisers are less likely than decision-making partners to challenge a decision maker's preferences. Decision making with advisers can be compromised by "groupthink" and other negative consequences of collective thinking that occur when people of like mind decide together. Consider in this regard the difference between a Supreme Court with nine justices and a Supreme Court with one justice and eight (experienced) law clerks.[16]

Like-minded thinking is problematic not only when groups try to reach a final decision; it also can undermine decision making at the brainstorming stage of the process. When members of a group bring divergent perspectives to the table and engage in critical debate of each other's ideas, they are more creative in their generation of potential solutions to problems.[17]

A two-person, coalition presidency would enhance the diversity of viewpoints in the executive branch, and that would make for better decision making. Single decision makers ultimately decide on the basis of their own preferences; multiple decision makers must take into account differences in perspective among each other.

Does it matter that I propose only two presidents rather than a larger group of executives? Two-person groups may not realize all of the benefits of shared decision making, but they secure many of them. For example, two-person groups outperform individuals when involved in strategic thinking. And most experts doubt that either Francis Crick or James Watson alone would have figured out the structure of DNA, but the two of them together did by bringing together their different ways of analyzing problems.[18]

Avoiding bad decisions

Looking at past presidential decisions, there is good reason to think that the United States would have fared better with a presidential partnership. Consider the following examples of bad decisions that could have been avoided.

In March 2003, after months of planning, George W. Bush concluded that the United States needed to invade Iraq in order to prevent Saddam Hussein from threatening the world with weapons of mass destruction. It turned out that Hussein harbored no such weapons, and the United States continues its efforts to stabilize Iraq after conflict that has cost dearly in terms of lives and dollars. It was a terrible mistake by the president and ultimately contributed to the repudiation of the Republican Party by voters in November 2008.[19]

But what if a single president did not have sole authority to make decisions for the executive branch? What if Bush had shared decision-making authority with Democrat Al Gore, the man he had defeated in November 2000? Almost certainly, the United States would not have invaded Iraq, and the world would be a very different place today. To be sure, many Democratic members of Congress voted to authorize the invasion of Iraq, including twenty-nine out of the fifty Democratic senators. However, their support was based on misinformation about Iraq's capability and intentions to use weapons of mass destruction. Under a two-person, coalition presidency, it is unlikely that intelligence reports would have been so misleading. But even if Bush still would have secured the support of Democratic members of Congress, he would not have persuaded Gore to launch a war with Iraq. Gore was an outspoken opponent of the idea of the war, publicly criticizing Bush's hawkish posture toward Iraq in the months before the invasion.[20]

Under a two-person presidency, Richard Nixon would not have been able to drag the United States through the Watergate crisis. He could not have subverted federal agencies if he served with a presidential partner. In addition, he would not have authorized the burglary of the Democratic National Committee's headquarters—in a two-person presidency, Nixon would have had no need to worry about a challenge to his reelection bid from the Democratic candidate.

A two-person presidency would make for better decision making also because it would reduce the incentive for single presidents to overcompensate for perceived vulnerabilities. There is good reason to think that some Democratic presidents have pursued misguided military operations to mitigate public perceptions that Democrats are weaker than Republicans on national security matters. For example, the United States probably would have been better off if Barack Obama had chosen to rely more heavily on targeted attacks against terrorists, like the successful raid on Osama bin Laden's hideout, and to eschew the troop surge in Afghanistan that was difficult to justify in terms of its costs in lives and dollars.[21] But Obama may have felt that less aggressive action would open him up to attacks by Republicans during his reelection campaign in 2012, a concern that would not exist with a two-person presidency.

Or consider John Kennedy's ill-conceived, poorly executed, and disastrous invasion of Cuba at the Bay of Pigs in 1961. Not only did the anticommunist recruits fail to topple Fidel Castro, but the fiasco resulted in sympathy for Cuba and widespread condemnation of the United States. In a two-person presidency with Richard Nixon, the Republican nominee in the 1960 presidential election, Kennedy may well have rejected the operation. The record of the planning indicates that Kennedy would have been less likely to agree with Nixon on an invasion than to authorize the invasion when acting alone. A key reason for Kennedy's interest in an attack on Cuba was to establish his anticommunist credentials. He did not want to validate any suggestions that he was soft on communism.[22] To do so might have cost him enough votes from political independents to sabotage a re-election bid. However, in a two-person presidency, Kennedy would not have needed to secure votes from independents; he would have needed votes only from Democrats and therefore would not have had to move to the right.

All of this is not to say that a two-person presidency would prevent all problematic exercises of executive power. In contrast to his criticism of presidential secrecy as a U.S. senator and presidential candidate, Barack Obama became even more aggressive in some ways than his predecessor, George W. Bush, had been in maintaining executive branch secrecy. Two years into Obama's presidency, his administration had filed criminal charges against more federal employees (five) for disclosing government secrets than had been charged under all previous presidents (three).[23] In other ways, we might expect presidential pairs to try to expand their power. But the division of executive power would supplement the external checks on the executive branch with an internal check, and that should make it less likely that the executive branch would exercise its power inappropriately.

Perhaps a second president would provide an effective check on a wayward colleague. But might a second president also block desirable policies? Of course, there would be some trade-offs from a move to a two-person presidency. But as I discuss in the next section, the usual disadvantages from group decision making would be less of a concern with a two-person presidency. Moreover, when we consider historical examples of visionary presidential decision making, it appears that for the most part, the same policies would have been implemented under a two-person presidency.

The disadvantages of shared decision making

Shared decision making generally works better than individual decision making, but not always. At times, groups make poorer decisions. A person making a bad choice may persuade a person who would otherwise make a good choice to join in the bad choice. In the case of a two-person presidency, however, there is good reason to think that the pitfalls of group decision making would be avoided.

One pitfall for groups is the problem of extreme decision making, a problem that may seem counterintuitive. Indeed, it is often said that groups are less likely than individuals to take extreme positions. And it is easy to think of examples that illustrate the moderating force of groups. Justice Clarence Thomas has espoused an exceptionally narrow view of Congress's power under the Commerce Clause but has not been able to persuade a majority of the justices to share his understanding. Similarly, Justices William Brennan and Thurgood Marshall believed that the death penalty was always unconstitutional but were never able to secure a majority for that perspective.[24] In this view, the need to reach consensus results in a moderating effect from shared decision making. And I have argued that a two-person presidency would discourage strongly partisan decisions in the executive branch.

Sometimes, however, shared decision making may result in more extreme decisions than individual decision making, under what is termed the "choice shift." Studies have found that some groups are willing to accept greater risk than would be predicted by the individual risk preferences of their members, while other groups are more conservative than would be predicted by the risk preferences of their members. If a majority of members of the group are relatively tolerant of risk, there may be an amplification of risk preferences; if a majority of members of the group are relatively risk averse, there may be an attenuation of risk preferences.[25]

It seems unlikely that choice shift would be a significant feature of a two-person presidency. As indicated, choice shift occurs when members of a group share a predisposition in the same direction and then amplify each other's predisposition. But with two presidents from different parties, it is likely that they would bring contrasting rather than similar predispositions on key policy issues, and their participation would have the moderating effect that intuition suggests about shared decision making. Thus, for example, a two-person presidency is likely to result in the appointment of nonideologues to executive branch offices and the federal courts. Persons with strongly held conservative or liberal views would not likely receive the support of presidents from different parties.[26]

As mentioned earlier, the nature of a two-person presidency also suggests that a related pitfall of shared decision making would be avoided—the "groupthink" problem. Irving Janis has argued that an excessive tendency toward uniform thinking by members of a group can lead to defective decision making and ill-fated political decisions. Important examples include the Kennedy administration's decision to authorize the Bay of Pigs invasion of Cuba and the Johnson administration's escalation of the Vietnam War. Studies examining the groupthink effect have found that it is especially a problem of highly cohesive groups, as can happen when presidents surround themselves with loyal and trusted advisers. On the other hand, groups are less likely to fall into the groupthink trap when they are composed of members with highly dominant personalities.[27] One would expect that differences in political philosophy would prevent coalition presidents from becoming too cohesive; one also would expect them to have highly dominant personalities.

A two-person presidency also would not be as susceptible as one might think to another drawback of group decision making. In Federalist 70, Alexander Hamilton observed that a single president can act with dispatch, and one would expect groups to take longer to reach the consensus needed to take action. Generally that is the case. At times, however, groups may be able to act more quickly. With their wider pool of knowledge and broader range of perspectives and problem-solving skills, they may be able to choose a course of action more quickly than would a member of the group acting alone.[28]

Indeed, that result has been suggested by an important simulation of monetary policy making that compared individuals and groups. In that study, participants played Federal Reserve governors and steered a computer economy by changing interest rates. While the differences in decision time were not statistically significant, the groups actually made their decisions more quickly than did the individuals.[29] It appears that for one-time decisions, groups act more slowly than do individuals. However, when multiple decisions are made over an extended time period—as would be the case in a two-person presidency—and groups have the opportunity to develop a working relationship, they may become more efficient than individuals.

There is another reason to think the executive branch would act more quickly under a two-person presidency. While presidents make the ultimate policy decisions, they cannot make those decisions if they are waiting for an analysis of the issues by executive branch officials. And as mentioned in chapter 4, partisan conflict in Washington has led to longer and longer delays in Senate confirmation of presidential appointees. Democratic senators have been slower to support the nominees of Republican presidents, and Republican senators have been slower to support the nominees of Democratic presidents. As a result, key positions in the executive branch remain unstaffed for months or years, even when the need to fill those positions is pressing. When the Obama administration was grappling with the financial crisis after it assumed office in 2009, for example, many senior positions at the Department of Treasury remained vacant. Because senior positions would be filled more readily when nominations emerge from a bipartisan executive, the decision-making process overall could become more efficient.

But even if two presidents would act with less dispatch, that should not be a significant concern. Recall the discussion in chapter 3 that presidential dispatch is less important for an executive branch that has become much more of a maker than an executor of public policy.

What about emergency decision making? Would not the ability to act rapidly be especially important in situations such as an unexpected attack on American soil? There is no reason to think that two presidents would be unable to respond as quickly as a single president. Presidents always confer with trusted advisers before making even emergency decisions. In addition, at times of crisis, public officials close ranks and put aside their differences so they can face severe threats with a unified front. Countries such as Israel, with the collective leadership of parliamentary coalitions, are as quick to respond in emergencies as countries that have a single-person presidency.

In an important way, a two-person presidency would provide more effective leadership than a single president in times of crisis. As the internment of Japanese Americans during World War II and the torture of suspected terrorists after 9/11 indicate, it is all too easy for a president to act in authoritarian and unconstitutional ways during an emergency. The founding fathers thought that Congress and the courts would check presidential abuses of power, but these external checks have rarely worked. Having a two-person, coalition presidency provides the kind of internal check on the executive branch that is necessary precisely in emergencies, when other checks are not effective.

Would a coalition executive sacrifice visionary, inspired leadership?

Two presidents could engage in endless compromise rather than promoting a new way of doing business in Washington. We might never have had a New Deal with a Herbert Hoover–Franklin Delano Roosevelt presidency, a Great Society with a Barry Goldwater–Lyndon Baines Johnson presidency, or a Reagan Revolution with a Jimmy Carter–Ronald Reagan presidency.

However, arguments about visionary leadership often are misguided. As discussed earlier, multiple persons make better decisions than do single persons, especially when they bring different perspectives to the decision-making process. In other words, the better quality of shared decision making outweighs any loss of inspired leadership from the need to compromise.

To be sure, there may be times when single decision makers would outperform multiple decision makers, so there may be situations in which the need to compromise prevents the implementation of an important vision. But I do not argue that shared decision making is *always* superior to individual decision making. Rather, over time, shared decision making generally will result in better decisions. Any loss from not having single decision making will be more than made up by the gains from having shared decision making.

In this regard, while novel approaches can make for important progress, they also can result in disastrous outcomes. Shared decision making would protect the country from a leader with very faulty vision. A George Bush–Al Gore presidency would not have pressed for an invasion of Iraq in 2003, and a Herbert Hoover–Alfred Smith presidency might not have signed the Smoot-Hawley Tariff Act of 1930 and thereby not exacerbated the economic downturn that turned into the Great Depression.

Reducing the risk of a very damaging policy more than compensates for the possibility of missing an exceptionally good policy. As the Great Recession that started in 2007 indicates, the severity of harm from bad policies is much greater than the degree of benefit from wise policies. The unemployment rate may have dropped from 7.5 percent to 4 percent during the Clinton presidency, but the gains were more than undone following the Bush presidency when unemployment rose to 10 percent. Moreover, it is more difficult to undo the harm from a bad policy than to claim the benefit from a forgone good policy. The investor who suffers a 25 percent loss on a stock needs a 33 percent gain from another stock to break even.[30] The investor who passes on a stock that rises 25 percent need only realize a 25 percent gain from another stock to catch back up.

The investment analogy provides other useful insights. For example, the optimal investment strategy entails a diversified portfolio of stocks rather than putting all of one's money in the stock that has the potential for the highest return. Under federal pension law, basic principles of the law of trusts, and the model statute for trustee regulation, trustees have a duty to diversify the investments that they manage. And recall how diversification works. The goal is to identify a range of investments that do not rise and fall in unison. That way, when some investments are not earning a good return, other investments will be rising in value. The volatility of a nondiversified portfolio and its possibility of substantial losses are replaced by the lower risk of a steady, diversified portfolio. Similarly, a coalition executive with its "diversified" presidential pairs and more balanced policies would replace the sharp swings in policy that have occurred when one party pushes its ideology aggressively until the public rebels and votes the other party into power.[31]

Consider in this regard that the excesses of the Johnson administration begat the excesses of the Nixon administration, and the excesses of the Bush administration begat the Obama administration. In short, just as diversification protects against financial harm by spreading a person's money over dissimilar investments, a two-person presidency would protect against political harm by spreading the executive power over dissimilar officeholders.

Another useful analogy comes from investment strategy. The corollary to the visionary political leader is the market-beating mutual fund manager. Some investment managers earn higher returns than the market average for a few years or even a decade or more, and investors often flock to these financial stars. But most managers lag the market, and investors are better off with index mutual funds that reflect the market broadly than with actively managed funds that favor a particular part of the market. Between 1995 and 2008, the S&P 500 stock market index outgained 96 percent of all actively managed stock funds; the broader Wilshire 5000 index had better returns than 86 percent of the actively managed stock funds.[32]

Moreover, even if visionary leaders exist, voters often will choose alternative candidates, just as most investors will overlook the exceptionally successful managers and pick mutual fund managers whose investment philosophies are costly. For every Franklin Delano Roosevelt who ascends to the presidency, a Herbert Hoover, Warren Harding, and Calvin Coolidge also ascend. Abraham Lincoln was preceded by Millard Fillmore, Franklin Pierce, and James Buchanan. And even visionary leaders are a mixed bag. Lyndon Johnson championed the Great Society, but he also escalated the Vietnam War.

The framers too recognized that the benefits of avoiding bad decisions outweigh the losses from missing out on good decisions. When Alexander Hamilton justified the presidential veto in Federalist 73, he argued that the veto's restraint on the legislature would be "much more likely to do good than harm." As Hamilton wrote, the disadvantage from defeating good laws "will be amply compensated by the advantage" of preventing bad laws.[33]

Importantly, the possibility of innovative policy making is already limited by the highly partisan nature of electoral politics in the United States. Because of the filibuster rule in the Senate, for example, presidents can enjoy majority control of Congress by legislators from their own party and still struggle to enact even small changes. Partisan conflict is a greater limitation on presidential initiative than would be a second president. Congressional members from the opposite party are more interested in blocking a president's agenda than in sharing accomplishments. Thus, presidents often do not even try to implement major change, recognizing that partisan opposition will preclude its success. For example, political analysts generally agree that the second term of the Clinton presidency entailed a series of small-bore initiatives rather than major policy changes.[34]

And even when presidents seek substantial change, they may trim their sails in the face of partisan politics. The health care legislation passed in 2010 provides a useful illustration. While the Patient Protection and Affordable Care Act will expand access to health care for millions of Americans, it also is notable for what it will not do. When Barack Obama was advocating for health care legislation before and after his election in November 2008, he spoke of the need for major reform of the health *care* system. However, he actually proposed legislation to reform the health *insurance* system.[35] The primary effects of the health care law will be to make public and private insurance more accessible for the previously uninsured by (1) broadening the eligibility criteria for Medicaid, (2) prohibiting insurers from charging higher premiums or denying coverage to persons with heart disease, cancer, or other "preexisting" medical conditions, and (3) providing subsidies to low- and middle-income families for the purchase of health care insurance. With these changes, more than thirty million Americans could gain access to insurance.

However, the legislation will fall short of major reform both in terms of access and affordability. The law will not achieve universal coverage. According to estimates, thirty-four million Americans will become insured by 2019 because of the new law, but twenty-three million Americans will remain uninsured. The legislation will do much less to address the high costs of health care. Many experts believe that costs will not come down until the United States discards the fee-for-service compensation of physicians and hospitals that pays them more to do more—regardless of whether doing more is good for the patient—or until the country overhauls in other ways the financing of health care. In the health care legislation, much smaller steps were taken to cut spending. Hospitals will be paid less under Medicare for each patient that they serve, and pilot programs will test other cost-cutting approaches; but the legislation actually will increase overall spending for health care in the United States. Instead of ensuring the provision of cost-effective care, the law will ensure the provision of care to more people. To put it another way, rather than fixing a health care system that everyone agrees is flawed, the law puts more of the uninsured into a broken system. Thus, the majority of Americans who currently receive health care insurance as a benefit of employment will see little change in their health care coverage.[36]

In a two-person, coalition executive branch, presidents might actually enjoy greater freedom to enact innovative and important legislation. A partner in the Oval Office would share a president's interest in making change and creating a legacy for the ages, and their proposals would not automatically provoke partisan opposition. The effect of a second president easily could be not to stifle policy initiatives but to channel them in a more balanced direction. Instead of health care legislation that primarily entails reform of the health care insurance industry without addressing the serious problems with the way the United States finances and delivers health care, an Obama–John McCain administration might have been able to push for a real overhaul of the U.S. health care system.

Notably, Republican nominee McCain's campaign proposal was more radical than that of Obama and with some important tweaks could have done more to target fundamental problems with the health care system. McCain wanted to promote real competition among health care plans by replacing employer-provided insurance with a tax credit that would enable individuals to purchase their own coverage and encourage insurance companies to compete for their business.

But the tax credit was pegged at only half the cost of an insurance policy, and insurers would have been free to turn away applicants with a history of heart disease, cancer, or other preexisting medical conditions. If the tax credit were worth the full cost of a low-priced but good-quality health care plan and insurers were required to take all comers, then the McCain plan would have taken the form of the very important proposal from the Committee for Economic Development in Washington, DC.[37] That proposal would achieve health care coverage for all Americans, and its competition-promoting features could generate meaningful cost-saving measures by insurers.

In any event, an Obama-McCain administration probably would have proposed a bill at least as significant as what eventually passed. The individual mandate to purchase insurance at the heart of the legislation began as a Republican idea and was championed by a Republican governor, Mitt Romney, as the key feature of the health care plan enacted in Massachusetts in 2006.[38] If McCain had shared the White House, Republicans would not have felt the need to run away from their own ideas.

Of course, with a bipartisan executive branch, Congress probably would have enacted health care reform decades earlier. Senator Ted Kennedy passed up the opportunity to fashion health care legislation with Richard Nixon because he thought he could get a better deal later with a Democratic administration. His failure to forge an agreement with Nixon became his greatest legislative regret.[39]

In short, overcoming the obstacles of partisan obstruction could more than compensate for the limitations of sharing the executive power with a presidential partner. A two-person presidency is just as likely to generate more visionary proposals as to generate fewer visionary proposals.

Shared leadership in the corporate world

It is useful to consider a similar debate in the corporate sector. Many people believe that a company needs one person at the helm, so as to provide a clear vision and direction, clear accountability, and clear authority for the business.[40] In this view, a single person should hold the two key corporate leadership positions, chief executive officer (CEO) and board chair. Similarly, one might argue, the United States should have a single president.

There are important responses to this argument. First, many experts support a splitting of the CEO and board chair roles between two persons. In this view, an independent board chair provides important oversight of the CEO. In other words, an independent board chair supplies a check and balance for corporate management. Thus, we have an argument similar to a key argument for a two-person presidency. As discussed in chapter 3, a second president would provide a needed check and balance for the executive branch. In addition, when corporations face a complex set of challenges, it is unlikely that one leader will possess the skill set necessary to handle all of the challenges. A pair of corporate officers with complementary talents can provide a broader range of abilities than can a single CEO. Accordingly, leadership teams have been successfully employed at many major companies, including Disney, Goldman Sachs, and HP.[41]

What do the empirical data tell us about the choice between splitting or combining the CEO and board chair roles? Some data indicate that companies that split the roles outperform companies that combine the roles, but other studies come to the opposite conclusion. While the empirical data in favor of splitting roles may be stronger, the studies overall suggest that other aspects of a company's leadership structure have a bigger impact on a company's financial performance.[42]

But even assuming one-person leadership makes sense in the corporate world, that does not weaken the argument for a two-person presidency. If a CEO has to share power with a separate board chair, there would be a real diminution in the CEO's authority. In terms of charting a course for the corporation, CEOs are in a significantly better position to do so when they also sit in the board chair's seat. Without a board chair with whom to share authority, the CEO can implement a corporate vision without being blocked by a corporate officer with an independent power base. In contrast, a president's ability to implement change stands to benefit from a partner in the Oval Office. Although the president would have to share decision making with a colleague, the diminution in authority could be more than offset by the mitigation of partisan conflict. As mentioned earlier, a president may be better off trying to work with one presidential partner of the opposite party, who has an incentive to cooperate, than to work with many senators and representatives of the opposite party who are inclined to be uncooperative.

There is another important lesson from the business world. Bold vision does not appear to be a critical factor in explaining corporate success. In a study of companies that have thrived during times of uncertainty, Jim Collins and Morten Hansen found that the highly successful executives were not distinguished by greater boldness or creativity. Rather, they were characterized by their greater reliance on empirical evidence and their greater discipline.[43]

Visionary leadership and historical examples

Finally, the evidence suggests that the great accomplishments of such visionary presidents as Thomas Jefferson, Franklin Roosevelt, and Lyndon Johnson might well have occurred had they served with presidential partners. While Jefferson's Louisiana Purchase elicited strong opposition from most Federalists, it was supported by John Adams, the Federalist nominee who was defeated by Jefferson in the presidential election preceding the Purchase. The major statutes enacted in the Roosevelt and Johnson administrations could have been passed over the objections of a second president. When FDR and LBJ pressed their legislative initiatives, their political party enjoyed a dominant majority, and there often was strong bipartisan support for the proposals in Congress. Social Security passed in 1935 with overwhelming support on both sides of the aisle, support sufficient to overcome a presidential veto. Medicare and Medicaid also passed the Senate and House with veto-proof majorities in 1965. Even the Civil Rights Act of 1964 and Voting Rights Act of 1965 passed with veto-proof majorities.[44]

Major legislation in other administrations also could have passed under a coalition presidency. During the Nixon administration, for example, Congress passed the National Environmental Protection Act, the Clean Water Act, the Clean Air Act, the Occupational Safety and Health Act, and the Consumer Product Safety Act.[45] Had Hubert Humphrey served along with Richard Nixon, he would have supported all of those laws (some of which were passed with Nixon's approval, others over his veto). It is not clear that many of the key legislative achievements by other presidents would have been blocked in a two-person presidency. Indeed, when Barack Obama and a Democratic Congress enacted their health care law over Republican opposition in 2010, critics of the bill observed that major legislation in the past had secured broad, bipartisan support.

Am I being too rosy about the way in which a two-person presidency would operate? Is it really possible that a coalition presidency would preserve most of the good decisions of a one-person presidency while avoiding most of the bad decisions? Yes. A key reason why the potential benefits of a plural executive outweigh the potential losses is that most examples of visionary presidential thinking reflect presidential policy making rather than presidential execution of congressional policy. As discussed in chapter 3, the framers reserved policy making for deliberative processes among public officials who bring a diversity of perspectives to the table. If the framers and I are correct that policy making is better when it emerges from a deliberative process, then it is not surprising that a two-person presidency would end up making a lot of the good decisions while escaping a lot of the bad decisions of a one-person presidency.

What about Abraham Lincoln and the ending of slavery? Are there some times when only a single, decisive leader will suffice? Perhaps the public tolerates the disadvantages of a one-person presidency as a kind of insurance policy for exceptional moments or periods in history when the country needs a truly visionary president alone at the helm.

It is difficult to assess the slavery question in terms of the choice between a one-person and a two-person presidency. While responsibility for some policies can be assigned to a particular presidential administration, the slavery question and its legacy spanned at least the first thirty-six presidential administrations in the United States, from 1789 through the passage of the Civil Rights Act of 1964 and the Voting Rights Act of 1965. And federal enforcement of the civil rights laws continues to vary from one administration to the next. The federal response to racial discrimination between 1861 and 1864 would have played out differently in a Lincoln–Stephen Douglas or Lincoln–John Breckinridge administration,[46] but it also would have played out differently between 1789 and 1860 and from 1865 onward.

Moreover, although a Civil War may have been inevitable, it also is possible that a two-party presidency throughout the 19th Century might have fostered a more conciliatory resolution of conflict between the North and the South. Indeed, it is not clear that the slavery question could have been resolved in a manner any less damaging to the country than the way it was resolved, with the long delay between the founding of the United States and the elimination of slavery, the 750,000 military deaths and other devastation wrought by the Civil War, and the harms from the prolonged Jim Crow era that followed.[47] Other countries acted more responsibly to end slavery. For example, Great Britain abolished slavery in the home country in 1772 and in most of the British Empire with the passage of the Slavery Abolition Act of 1833.

Finally, it may well be the case that a one-person presidency was needed during the more formative years of the United States when unique problems such as slavery had to be resolved. For a more mature United States, however, there is good reason to conclude that the benefits of a two-person presidency outweigh the disadvantages.

Upon careful examination, it is difficult to base a preference for a single president on the possibility of extraordinary leadership. The visionary leadership argument appears to rest much more on myth or superseded historical considerations than on the realities of political decision making in the contemporary United States.

Concerns about accountability

In Federalist 70, Alexander Hamilton invoked an additional important argument in favor of a single president—the need for accountability. In an executive branch governed by multiple decision makers, voters might have difficulty assessing responsibility. Which of the two presidents should they reward or blame for decisions they like or dislike?[48]

The accountability concerns seem exaggerated. If the executive branch operated like a jury and did not disclose its reasoning, the interest in accountability could indeed be compromised. Or if the executive branch's power were divided among a dozen or more executive councilors, accountability could be difficult to assess. However, with two presidents sharing power equally, they would be equally responsible for any decisions that they made, and voters would rightly hold them equally responsible. A successful administration could be rewarded by reelection of both presidents, and an unsuccessful administration could be punished by replacement of both presidents.

Of course, at times, one of the two presidents might drive particular decisions more than the other president. If that happened, it would be clear to the public, and voters could fairly hold the more responsible president more accountable. And to the extent that one or the other president took greater responsibility for particular decisions, accountability could actually improve with a coalition executive. When a single president assumes responsibility for all policy decisions, voters often cannot hold the president accountable for particular unpopular decisions. Assume, for example, that a voter disagreed with Barack Obama's escalation of the Afghanistan War but approved of his health care legislation. The voter could cast only one vote when Obama ran for reelection in 2012 so could not register both disapproval of his foreign policy and approval of his domestic policy. With a two-person presidency in which the two executives assume primary responsibility for different issues, it would be possible for voters to support one of the executives and not the other.

Moreover, the existing separation of powers in the national government already complicates accountability. When Congress and the president must work together to pass legislation, voters have to figure out whether the president or Congress is more responsible for a new law or a failure to enact a law. Did Congress pass an individual mandate to purchase health care insurance in 2010 because Obama wanted health care reform to take that path, or did Obama agree to an individual mandate because that was the path preferred by the Democratic majority in the House and Senate? Sorting responsibility can become particularly challenging when control of the executive and legislative branches is divided by party. Who should voters have blamed for the failure to adequately address long-term budget deficits when the debt ceiling was raised in August 2011, Obama or Republican members of Congress?[49]

Recall also the discussion in chapter 3 about how shared decision making sometimes can facilitate the ability of the public to assign responsibility for presidential decision making. As Jide Nzelibe and Matthew Stephenson have observed, voters have to worry whether single decision makers act on the basis of solid policy considerations or whether they act out of inappropriate biases.[50] When two presidents from different political parties agree on a common course of action, there is much less reason to worry about the influence of inappropriate biases. Each of the two presidents can weed out the other's misguided predilections.

There is another key reason why a two-person presidency might actually improve the accountability of the executive branch. As Michael Fitts has observed, the one-person presidency may suffer from being held *too* accountable for the performance of the economy, international developments, or other matters that presidents might influence. Because of its unitary nature, especially in contrast to the very plural nature of Congress, the presidency has become a focal point for public attention, credit, and blame. In the view of voters, there is a much greater causal relationship between presidential action (or inaction) and public events than is deserved by the president's actual ability to influence what happens in the country or the world. Thus, a president's reelection chances depend much more on how the U.S. economy is performing than on the president's responsibility for the economy's performance.[51]

A coalition presidency can correct the overaccountability problem in two ways. First, because the executive power would be diminished by dividing it and requiring it to be shared, the public would not view the White House as so influential. The executive branch could lose much of its dominance. In addition, even to the extent that voters saw the executive branch as the dominant branch in the national government, there no longer would be a single person who assumed the public spotlight to the extent that the president currently does. With two presidents sharing decision-making responsibility, voters would recognize that neither of the two presidents could control what happens in the Oval Office.

Finally, accountability concerns should be less of an issue with a two-person presidency. As discussed earlier, shared decision making results in better decision making. Voters therefore would have fewer reasons to hold presidents accountable for unwise policy choices and therefore a diminished need to use their ballots to elect new leaders.

The cultural desire for a single president

After considering the arguments in favor of a divided executive power, we would do well to wonder whether the usual justifications for the one-person presidency fully explain why the United States continues to have its unitary executive structure. Might there be additional reasons for retaining a form of leadership that has not worked well for a long time and that has been rejected by most stable democracies?[52]

Much of the enthusiasm for a single president may reflect a tendency for the public to develop exaggerated expectations as to what its leaders can accomplish. For many people, there seems to be an important psychological drive for an all-powerful savior who can solve serious problems and deliver individuals from their travails—a "myth of leadership becomes more pronounced in times of social or political uncertainty." Thus, just as the framers turned to a president despite their experience with a king, so did the Israelites ask for a king despite their enslavement by the Egyptian pharaohs and despite the warnings they received about the royal abuse of power.[53]

More recently, corporate boards have adopted the position that a poorly performing company can be saved by hiring a star CEO, despite empirical evidence to the contrary. Candidates and presidents appear to recognize the public's desire for a savior and appeal to it in the way they speak about the presidential role and the results they promise to achieve.[54]

When people find a savior, they typically attribute qualities of omnipotence and omniscience to their new leader—until the inevitable disappointment sets in (as happened with a number of voters who supported Barack Obama in 2008). But while their faith is still strong, followers derive much comfort from leaders who convey characteristics of strength, conviction, and certainty and who can thereby address people's fears and doubts. The comfort and enhanced self-esteem of followers is augmented by the fact that they share their faith with other followers.[55]

What the savior phenomenon tells us is that to the extent there is unrealistic thinking in the debate between a single executive and a plural executive, the problem may lie more with the arguments for a single executive. People underestimate the effectiveness of collective leadership and exaggerate the effectiveness of individual leadership. As Bruce Ackerman has observed, "It is downright embarrassing for a constitution to ask free and equal citizens to place so much trust in the personal integrity and ideals of a single human being."[56]

The superhero status of presidents is damaging not only because it is unrealistic. In addition, it undermines citizen participation in the democratic process. To the extent that people expect to be rescued by their leaders, they default on their own responsibility to participate in the political process and to push for changes in public policy. In particular, the savior phenomenon encourages voters to believe that they can solve the dysfunction in Washington simply by changing their elected officials rather than by making the changes in the political system that really could correct the dysfunction.[57]

To sum up this chapter, a two-person presidency can be justified not only for its ability to serve the checking function on the executive branch that the other branches are failing to serve and for its ability to foster a more bipartisan ethic in Washington, DC. It also can be justified as a way to improve the decision making of the executive branch.

These benefits of a two-person presidency do not exhaust the potential advantages of a shared executive power. The next chapter considers other important benefits from a coalition presidency. In particular, it discusses the ability of presidents from two political parties to represent a broader range of the public than is represented by a president from one party.

6

Representation for the public in Washington

Representation for the public in the executive branch

Many scholars have criticized the "winner-take-all" nature of presidential elections in the United States. Whether the most successful candidate secures 43 percent (Bill Clinton in 1992) or 61 percent (Lyndon Johnson in 1964) of the popular vote, whoever receives a majority of votes in the Electoral College gains 100 percent of the executive power. The runners-up are left with nothing.[1]

Winner-take-all elections therefore suffer from a failure to provide real representation to substantial numbers of voters, particularly those from third parties.[2] It is virtually impossible for a Libertarian or Green Party candidate to muster enough votes to come in first. In contrast, countries with proportional representation systems may offer seats in their executive branches to multiple parties.[3]

Winner-take-all elections also can give inadequate representation to the interests of the majority. A president can be elected not only with a bare majority of support but even with less than a majority of the popular vote. Because of third-party candidates, for example, a number of recent presidents were elected with less than 50 percent of the popular vote. "Minority" presidents include Harry Truman, John Kennedy, Richard Nixon, and Bill Clinton. Because of the Electoral College's role in presidential elections, George W. Bush was elected in 2000 not only with a minority of the popular vote but also with fewer votes than Al Gore (47.87 percent versus 48.38 percent). For the more than 50 percent of the electorate that did not vote for Truman, Kennedy, Nixon, Clinton, or Bush, there was an absence of real representation in the White House.[4]

But even if the president commands a majority vote, a considerable part of the electorate will not be represented by its preferred candidate. Indeed, even when a president wins in a landslide with 60 percent of the popular vote, 40 percent of the voters will lack a voice in the executive branch.

As a result, after every presidential election, much of the public feels unrepresented in the Oval Office. They do not believe that their voices are heard or that their interests are considered important. Without an ability to share in the executive power, they have a diminished sense of a stake in the operations of government and become more likely to oppose the president's agenda simply to improve the chances that their preferred candidate will prevail at the next presidential election.[5]

The winner-take-all nature of the presidency exacerbates in another way the minority's sense of being unrepresented in the White House. As mentioned, presidents may enter office after winning a bare majority or just a plurality of the vote. But because they still gain the entire executive power and govern with a cabinet of loyalists, they can easily develop an inflated sense of support for their policies and exercise their authority as if they were elected with a broad mandate to implement their campaign promises.[6]

They also are inclined to view the opposition as representing narrow interests that were rejected by the electorate and deserving of dismissal. When Barack Obama met with Republican legislators shortly after taking office and was presented with their ideas, he reminded them that "elections have consequences" and that he won. However, the substantial opposition to his health care legislation reflected in large part the fact that he really had a mandate from only 53 percent of the voting public, and his failure to acknowledge that reality may have played a big part in the Republican takeover of the House of Representatives in November 2010.[7]

Given the unrepresentative nature of the presidency, it is not surprising that Sanford Levinson and other scholars see a need for reforms that would better promote democratic principles. We not only have a too powerful president who can ignore much of the public's preferences, but the Constitution's very high bar to impeachment requires voters to wait until the end of presidents' four-year terms to replace chief executives who wield their immense power irresponsibly.[8] The public simply has too small a voice in the shaping of presidential policy, a diminished voice that does not comport with the idea of a democracy.

With a two-person, two-party presidency, decision making in the executive branch would reflect the preferences of an overwhelming majority of voters. The executive branch would operate truly as a government of and by the people. It would give the United States a political system in which members of the public could feel that their voices have been heard and in which the executive branch's legislative initiatives reflect the will of nearly the entire electorate. This effect is particularly important in highly polarized political systems, as in the United States today. When voters are deeply divided on partisan lines, the disaffection of the losing candidate's supporters is much greater than in a less partisan society.[9]

Representation for members of third parties

There is another important way in which a coalition executive would enhance the opportunity for voters to elect a president whose priorities align well with their own. A two-person executive branch would improve the chances of success for third-party (or independent) candidates. In a single-president system, supporters of third-party candidates often vote for one of the major-party candidates rather than for the nominee of the third party. A Green Party supporter might vote for the Democratic candidate, and a Libertarian Party supporter might vote for the Republican candidate. The third-party voters worry that casting a ballot for their most preferred candidate will end up helping their least preferred candidate get elected.[10]

In 2000, for example, many Democrats preferred Ralph Nader over Al Gore for the presidency. Gore was the Democratic nominee, but he was perceived as too conservative by the more liberal Democrats. Nader brought to his campaign a record as a leading consumer advocate. In 1965, his book *Unsafe at Any Speed* exposed the automobile industry's failure to adopt good safety standards in their cars, and it led to the passage of legislation that created the National Highway Traffic Safety Administration. As a result of Nader's efforts, cars today come equipped with seat belts, air bags, and a back-up braking system in case the primary brakes fail. Nader pursued abuses in other industries, and he exposed lax regulatory oversight by the Federal Trade Commission and other government agencies. In 1971, he founded Public Citizen, a national advocacy organization that promotes consumer and worker concerns. At first, Nader found it easy to interest members of Congress and White House staff in his issues, but by the 1990s, as the country became more conservative, he found fewer receptive ears even in the Democratic Party.[11]

After two half-hearted campaigns in 1992 and 1996, Nader mounted a serious effort for president in 2000 as the nominee of the Green Party. He based his campaign on an anticorporate platform, charging that the differences between Gore and Republican nominee George W. Bush were insignificant and that neither would champion the kinds of progressive policies that the country needed. Nader struck a chord with liberal Democrats after a Clinton presidency that many felt tilted too far to the right. But fearing that Nader might undermine Gore sufficiently to allow Bush to win, most Democrats urged Nader supporters to vote for Gore. In the end, Nader Democrats generally heeded the entreaties to vote for Gore, and Nader won only about 3 percent of the vote. In a two-person presidency, Nader supporters could have voted for him with the assurance that even if they dragged Gore down, either Nader or Gore would secure the second slot in the White House.[12]

Twenty years before Nader challenged Gore and Bush, supporters of the independent candidacy of U.S. Representative John Anderson faced the same dilemma that Nader supporters faced. Many voters preferred Anderson to incumbent Democrat Jimmy Carter or Republican nominee Ronald Reagan, but they too did not want to waste a vote on someone who could not win and instead might doom the chances of their second-choice candidate.

Anderson ran in the Republican primaries, initially not generating much interest; but his performance in a precaucus debate in Iowa sparked a strong response, and he ran fourth in the New Hampshire primary and second in the Massachusetts and Vermont primaries. He had long served in Congress as a moderate Republican who was willing to break with the party, particularly on civil rights and other social issues, and was respected for his understanding of the issues and eloquence during floor debates. During the campaign, Anderson distinguished himself as a candidate who would recognize difficult challenges facing the country and propose solutions even when they might not be popular. For example, he proposed a fifty-cent increase in the gasoline tax to encourage conservation and to help wean the United States from its dependence on foreign oil. Anderson attracted support not only from many Republicans but also from liberal Democrats who had become disillusioned with President Carter. College students were especially receptive to the Anderson message.[13]

By March 1980, however, Anderson's prospects for the Republican nomination began to fade. He ran well behind Reagan in his home state of Illinois and third in both Connecticut and Wisconsin in what had evolved into a three-person race among Reagan, George H. W. Bush, and Anderson.[14] It had become clear that he was not conservative enough for the primary-voting members of the GOP.

In April, Anderson announced that he would run for president as an independent,[15] and it seemed like an auspicious time for an independent candidacy. Democratic dissatisfaction with Carter led U.S. Senator Ted Kennedy to challenge him in the primaries. On the

Republican side, the emergence of Reagan and the party's rightward shift made many moderate Republicans uncomfortable.

At first, Anderson was poised for a serious run. Early in his independent bid, he polled between 22 and 26 percent of the vote, and when voters in June were asked to assume that Anderson had a real chance of winning the election, he was tied with Carter at 31 percent, with Reagan leading at 35 percent. Major national pollsters believed Anderson could win, and polling both before and after the election indicated that voters preferred Carter over Anderson by only about 7–8 percentage points in a head-to-head comparison.[16]

But Kennedy's reconciliation with Carter at the Democratic National Convention prevented the defection of disaffected Democrats that the Anderson campaign had counted on. Moreover, Anderson's remaining Democratic supporters feared that they would pave the way for a Reagan victory by voting for Anderson, and Anderson's Republican supporters feared they would guarantee a Carter win by voting for Anderson.[17]

In the end, Anderson received only 7 percent of the vote. With a two-person presidency, the Anderson supporters could have voted for him with the assurance that their second choice—either Carter or Reagan—would become one of the two presidents if Anderson came up short.[18]

The best showing among modern third-party candidates was registered by Ross Perot in 1992, who garnered 18.9 percent of the popular vote.[19] Perot had never held elected office but was a successful businessman who could draw on his personal wealth to fund his campaign. Hence, he did not face the fund-raising problems of other third-party candidates. He ran as a straight-talking candidate who would rise above politics to address the country's budget deficits, protect American jobs, and promote greater citizen input into the shaping of governmental policy. Voters had become dissatisfied with Republican incumbent George H. W. Bush, and Democratic challenger Bill Clinton had his own detractors; so voters were unusually receptive to an alternative. But Perot faltered when faced with negative press reports and suspended his campaign in the summer of 1992 before resuming it in the fall.

Nader, Anderson, and Perot all proved to be weak candidates in the end. Even if all of their supporters had voted for them rather than engaging in strategic voting, they would have lost. Still, their efforts suggest that under a two-person presidency, third-party candidates would occasionally be strong enough to win one of the two slots. In particular, the close polling results between Carter and Anderson indicate that a second-place finish would be feasible for third-party candidates who did not have to fight perceptions that their campaigns were lost causes. With the much better chances of success, the pool of individuals interested in a third-party (or independent) candidacy should become much stronger. In short, a two-person presidency could convert third-party candidates from being at best spoilers who can determine which of the major-party candidates wins election to candidates who can win in their own right.[20]

But what if several strong third-party candidates emerged? Might the popular vote be hopelessly splintered and result in presidential pairs who together represent less than a majority of the public? This would be highly unlikely. The major-party duopoly in the United States makes it difficult enough for even one third-party candidate to mount a meaningful challenge.[21] In any case, it would be easy to protect against the problem of coalition presidents who do not represent a sufficiently large majority of the population. The electoral rules could require a minimum percentage vote for election, and instant-runoff voting could be used to identify the two candidates with the broadest support.[22]

The more interesting question is how to deal with the emergence of a third party that develops substantial and sustained support. Should the United States have a three-person presidency?

A strong third party seems unlikely. Elections for other offices would still be winner-take-all affairs, and that would make it difficult for a third party to grow. Moreover, the United States does not have the degree of ethnic or other sociocultural divisions that drive the development of multiple parties in other countries. Voters might coalesce around a particular third-party candidate for one election cycle but not affiliate themselves with the candidate's party over the longer term. In 1998, for example, Jesse Ventura ran as the nominee of the Reform Party and won election as the governor of Minnesota with 37 percent of the vote. In 2006, by which time the Reform Party had evolved into the Independence Party, the party's nominee secured less than 7 percent of the gubernatorial vote in the state.

But what if a third party's presidential candidates consistently won at least 20 percent of the vote after the adoption of a two-person presidency, or it was able to elect 20 percent of the legislators in Congress? At some point, it would make sense to expand the executive branch to ensure representation for all three parties. Much like the Swiss Federal Council has seven seats and allocates them proportionally to the major Swiss political parties, the U.S. executive branch could be expanded to ensure proportional allocation of presidential slots to the major U.S. political parties.

For example, if the Democratic and Republican Parties each had 40 percent support and a third party 20 percent, it would make sense to have two Democratic presidents, two Republican presidents, and one third-party president. If such an expansion occurred, it would be important to maintain the requirement of consensus among all of the presidents. Just as the two presidents in a two-person presidency would have to agree on all decisions, so would the five presidents in a five-person presidency have to agree on all decisions. Otherwise, two parties could form a majority coalition and ignore the interests of the other party. As mentioned earlier, decision by consensus is an important feature of the Swiss Federal Council.

Consideration of third parties indicates that the number of presidents should be the minimum necessary to provide representation in the executive branch to the major political parties. Currently, the United States has a two-party duopoly, so only two presidents would be needed to ensure fair representation. In a country that had three major parties of roughly the same size, three presidents would be needed. And if the parties differed in size, then some parties would deserve more representatives in the executive branch than other parties, and the number of presidents would increase accordingly, as in the example above of a five-person executive branch.

If my goal is to promote more proportional representation in government, why not propose a parliamentary system of government in which political parties are awarded legislative seats in proportion to the votes that they receive? That way, even small minorities could elect preferred officials.

As discussed in chapter 4, a parliamentary system addresses many of the problems with a winner-take-all electoral system, but it does not adequately address the winner-take-all problem of a one-person presidency. When a single party forms the cabinet in a parliamentary system, other parties lack an adequate voice in the executive branch's decision making. And even in coalition governments, there still is only one prime minister. A two-person presidency is able to represent a broader swath of the electorate than is a prime minister in a parliamentary system.

Fairness to the winning candidate

Some people may object to a two-person presidency on the ground that the candidate with the second-highest number of votes would exercise equal power to the candidate who received the most votes. Even though Barack Obama topped John McCain by a margin of 53 percent to 46 percent in the popular vote, they each would have had 50 percent of the power in a two-person presidency.

Perhaps there would have been a 7 percent level of unfairness (Obama's power being 3 percent too low and McCain's power being 4 percent too high). But that pales in comparison to the unfairness of Obama possessing 100 percent of the power after securing only 53 percent of the vote. The actual level of unfairness was 93 percent (Obama's power being 47 percent too high and McCain's power being 46 percent too low). Indeed, winner-take-all presidential systems generate the highest levels of electoral unfairness among governmental systems.[23] Until the vote counts exceed a 75-25 ratio, a two-person presidency is fairer than a one-person presidency.

The unfairness of a one-person presidency is exacerbated by the fact that the United States holds one vote on one day that decides control for thousands of decisions that will be made over a 1,460-day stretch. The majority wins not only on Election Day but on every day thereafter for four years. Majority rule can quickly become rule that ignores the interests of half the public for long stretches of time.

To be sure, on a decision-by-decision basis, the majority ordinarily should prevail. When a choice must be made, the majority's preferences rightly take priority over the minority's preferences.

However, over a series of many decisions, majority rule can be unjust. We generally trust majority rule because the composition of the majority will vary from one decision to another. I may lose when voting with friends on a choice of restaurant, but I may win when voting on a choice of movie. Over the long haul, I will win many times even if not most of the time. Majority rule becomes unfair when some people are persistently in the minority, so they always lose out. As U.S. Supreme Court Justice Byron White wrote, the Constitution is violated when "a particular group has been . . . denied its chance to effectively influence the political process."[24] And with a one-person, one-party presidency, members of the other party are effectively denied their ability to influence executive branch policies for four years.

Congress has long recognized the need to protect minority interests with its filibuster rule in the Senate. It takes the votes of only forty-one senators to block action, and that prevents the majority party from running roughshod over the minority party on Capitol Hill. During the George W. Bush administration, the filibuster was frequently used to protect the interests of Democratic voters; subsequently, the filibuster was frequently used in the Barack Obama administration to protect the interests of Republican voters. A two-person presidency would complement the filibuster rule by protecting minority interests in the Oval Office.

Representation and the framers

In addition, a two-person presidency would bring the executive branch closer to the framers' vision of representation. As the one elected official with a national constituency, the president is supposed to represent all Americans, not just residents of a single state or electoral district, not just members of a particular interest group or political party. As James Madison wrote in Federalist 10, the constitutional structure would foster a national government that would promote the "aggregate interests of the community" rather than the selfish interests of particular factions in society. And as George Washington explained during his presidency, "I have sought the happiness of my fellow citizens" by overlooking "all personal, local, and partial considerations" and by contemplating "the United States as one great whole."[25]

Traditional scholarship has echoed this nonpartisan view of presidential representation, though for different reasons. According to the standard characterization, presidents stake out moderate policy positions out of self-interest. In order to maximize their political support, they must appeal to the median voter. And some presidents have done so. However, modern presidents generally have maintained the partisan views that secured their nomination and have not made significant moves to attract the other party's voters. A strategy of reinforcing core support by tailoring policies to the political base and persuading enough independents to move in the president's direction is usually more successful than moderating policies and risking alienation of the base. This is especially the case when voters are highly polarized in their party affiliations.[26]

While single presidents generally keep their partisan stripes, two presidents from different parties would necessarily take a broader perspective. Their need to reach a consensus would preclude their maintaining strongly partisan positions. With a two-person presidency, the executive branch would look much more like what the framers intended.

A two-person presidency not only would make the executive branch more representative of the public; it also would make the national government more representative of the public in a second way. By rebalancing power between the executive and legislative branches, a two-person presidency would result in a more prominent role in the national government for the branch of government that is most representative of the public, the Congress.

Representation of the public in the national government as a whole

As Henry Clay, Daniel Webster, and others have observed, a single president cannot provide the degree of representation that a diverse legislative body can provide. A Congress of 535 can include men and women; blacks, Latinos, Asians, and whites; Christians, Jews, Muslims, agnostics, and atheists; single and married; gay and straight; Democrats, Republicans, and Independents; and so on. Accordingly, the national government derives most of its representative character from the Congress. It is through Congress that any one citizen is most likely to find an elected official who shares that citizen's values, perspectives, and interests. Thus, the national government becomes more representative as a whole as the legislative power increases and less representative overall as the executive power increases.

Principles of representation, then, circle back to the problem of the imperial presidency. To the extent that the executive branch becomes the dominant power center in the national government, the national government as a whole becomes less representative of the public.

One can appeal not only to basic principles of representation to fault the imperial presidency. One also can appeal to principles of original intent. When the president becomes the dominant power center, the national government departs from the framers' vision of representation. As the name reflects, the House of Representatives was seen as the key representative institution in the national government. The framers provided for direct election of representatives but indirect election of senators and presidents.[27] The framers also gave representatives the smallest constituencies and the shortest terms of office to encourage greater contact and closer relationships between voters and representatives than between voters and senators or presidents. In the framers' view, a strong legislative branch with a representative House would provide the most important source of representation for the public. With the imperial presidency's weakening of the legislative branch, however, the framers' vision of public representation is not being fulfilled.

To be sure, the historical record does not provide an entirely consistent picture of original intent. I have observed that the founding fathers viewed the House as the most representative institution in the national government. And there is strong support for that interpretation. The model for the House of Representatives was the British House of Commons, the most representative component of the British government, while the model for the president was the British king, the least representative component of the British government. And leading Federalists, especially John Adams, wanted to preserve this hierarchy of representation. Federalist 52, for example, referred to the House of Representatives as "that branch of the federal government which ought to be dependent on the people alone."[28]

On the other hand, the Federalists recognized that their hierarchy of representation went against a common and important public sentiment. Many Americans rejected the British model of representation and wanted a new form of government in which all elected officials were equally representative of the public. Accordingly, the Federalists promoted that view of the federal government and referred more to the virtues of checks and balances than to hierarchies of representation when explaining the construction of the executive and legislative branches.[29] Still, enough of the hierarchical model of representation survived the constitutional debates such that the legislative branch, and particularly the House of Representatives, became the most representative component of the national government. With an imperial presidency, however, the role of the House and the representative character of the government have declined.

In sum, in terms of both principles of representation and original intent, the expansion of executive power has diminished the representative nature of the national government.

A number of scholars have observed that the modern president is the most representative public official because the entire electorate votes in presidential elections, and the president's constituency therefore includes the entire country. Only the president takes a national perspective on policy matters. Senators represent the interests of their states, and representatives represent the interests of their districts.[30]

This argument, however, confuses the difference between the president and a single legislator with the difference between the executive and legislative branches. Of course, the president is more representative of the public than any other elected official. A member of

Congress may be elected only by residents of Philadelphia or Utah. However, just as the entire electorate is the president's constituency, so it is the constituency of Congress as a whole.[31] Moreover, because of the diversity of its membership, Congress as a whole is more representative of the public than is the president.

In any event, even if presidents represent the entire electorate in theory, they do not do so in practice. As mentioned earlier, modern presidents generally do not moderate their policy positions to make them more representative of the broad public. Rather, they generally hew to the partisan views that are representative of their political base.

A two-person presidency, then, responds to two representation problems of a winner-take-all, one-person presidency. By dividing the executive power, it diminishes the dominance of the less representative presidency over the more representative Congress, thereby making the national government as a whole more representative of the public. By dividing the executive power along political lines, a coalition presidency makes the executive branch itself more representative of the public.

It may be the case that a two-person presidency needs to be supplemented by other reforms to promote broad representation for the public in Washington. As Daryl Levinson and Richard Pildes have observed, Congress would be more representative of the public if the minority party could exercise greater influence.[32] The Senate has done much to protect minority interests through its filibuster rule. But the absence of a filibuster rule in the House allows the majority to exercise undue control of the legislative process in that chamber. As mentioned in chapter 4, adding a filibuster rule to the House of Representatives would provide a useful complement to a two-person executive branch.

Achieving greater representation by dividing the executive branch along political lines

If we would promote public representation in the executive branch by dividing the executive power between two presidents, why divide along lines of party affiliation? Might we not achieve greater diversity by dividing along other lines—gender, race, religion, or geography, for example?

For several reasons, it makes most sense to divide the executive branch along political lines. We are dealing with political representation, so it is appropriate to allocate power along political lines, just as we would allocate positions along religious lines if we were dealing with religious representation. Moreover, other bases for defining representation are either already employed or are not appropriate. Considerations of geography, for example, are taken into account in the composition of the Senate, with its assignment of two seats to each state and the requirement that presidents receive the most electoral votes rather than the most popular votes. Considerations of gender, race, or religion would raise serious equal protection or First Amendment concerns.

Most importantly, the argument for dividing the executive power is not based exclusively on concerns about representation; it also rests on concerns about partisan conflict and the imperial presidency. Dividing the executive power along political lines is the most effective way to address all of the problems caused by the one-person presidency.

I have discussed how a two-person presidency can ensure that decisions in the executive branch represent the views of all or at least a very broad range of voters. The value of providing a voice to all stakeholders has been recognized by the evolution of decision making in other important settings, including the family and the patient-physician relationship. In both contexts, society has moved from a single decision-maker model to a shared decision-making model. Husbands used to be the family's decision maker; now husbands and wives share the responsibility. Physicians once made medical decisions unilaterally for patients; now patients and physicians share in making medical decisions.

The contemporary model of family decision making

It is not surprising that Alexander Hamilton and the other constitutional framers were attracted to the model of a single executive. That not only was the model of political governance in the framers' day; it also was the model of governance in the family.

While family organization had evolved over time, the model of a dominant husband-father took hold by the framers' generation. Before the 16th Century, blood ties were more important than marital bonds in defining family, and there were loose boundaries between different households. One's family included a wide circle of relatives —not just parents and siblings but also aunts, uncles, and cousins. In the three-century period between 1500 and 1800, the family evolved into a form that was both marriage centered and patriarchal. The framers grew up in nuclear families dominated by fathers, and after marrying, they established new nuclear households dominated by themselves.[33]

The husband's legal predominance was clear and strong. Under early domestic-relations law inherited from England, husbands exercised not only their own legal rights but the rights of their spouses on behalf of the spouses in a guardianship-like relationship. The male was the head of the household and enjoyed rights to manage property, to enter into contracts, and to cast votes. His wife lacked all of those rights. Her property became his property, she no longer could contract in her own name—even with her husband—and she was denied the right of suffrage. Moreover, she could not sue or be sued in her own name, her husband was entitled to wages that she might earn, and her husband enjoyed full legal rights to the control and custody of their children.[34]

In the past two centuries, family dynamics have evolved further. Boundaries between the household and the outside world have become more fluid again, and the marital bond has weakened. As employment opportunities and governmental programs have provided women with extrafamilial sources of income, they have become less dependent on their husbands and more equal in the family hierarchy.[35]

For purposes of this book, the important evolution in the family since 1800 has been the change from a patriarchal order to a much more egalitarian relationship between spouses. Today, when there are major decisions to be made for a family, wives share decision-making authority with their husbands. Thus, for example, in a case involving a medical decision for a minor, the Georgia Supreme Court observed that when "two parents have legal custody of a child, each parent shares equal decision-making responsibility for that child."[36]

Shared decision making is justified in terms of evenhandedness. Women have the same stake as men in the operation of a household and the raising of children. Basic principles of fairness demand equal treatment. When the law gave sole decision-making authority to husbands, it ignored fundamental interests of the wife. Similarly, when the Constitution rests executive authority in the hands of a single president, it ignores fundamental interests of voters who supported the defeated presidential candidates. A two-person presidency can ensure that all voters have a meaningful voice in the deliberations of the executive branch.

To be sure, marriages do not work perfectly, as reflected in the U.S. divorce rate. But the point about the marriage analogy is not to argue that two presidents can or should have a marital-like relationship. Rather, the point about the marriage analogy is that decision making is improved by including more stakeholders in the decision-making process. Marriages may not work as well as we would like, but they would work far less well if we assigned decision-making authority to only one person in the relationship.

Moreover, the fact that many marriages end in divorce does not tell us that two-person presidencies will break down. As discussed in chapter 4, a key feature of a bipartisan executive branch would be the inescapable, fifty-fifty sharing of power. Presidential partners would face a choice of cooperating or getting nothing done. There is no noncooperative strategy that would allow them to accomplish their political goals. Spouses, on the other hand, have an option other than cooperation or failure. They can file for divorce and pursue their professional and personal interests either alone or with a different spouse.

The contemporary model of medical decision making

Just as the evolution of family decision making illustrates the value of shared decision making, so does the evolution of decision making in the patient-physician relationship.

Not that long ago, physicians made medical decisions with little involvement by their patients. Indeed, it was common for physicians to withhold even very important medical information from their patients. According to a 1961 study mentioned in chapter 3, 88 percent of physicians generally did not tell patients when they made a diagnosis of cancer. By 1977, only 2 percent of physicians had such a policy.[37]

Physician unilateralism had a long pedigree. Hippocrates advised the physician to conceal "most things from the patient while . . . attending to him . . . revealing nothing of the patient's future or present condition." The modern era of informed consent, under which physicians must disclose all material information to patients and obtain their consent before treating them, did not begin until 1957.[38]

Medical decision making today is based much more on a shared decision-making model under which physicians provide considerable information to patients and engage them in the decision-making process. Instead of a unilateral decision by the physician, medical treatment has become a mutual decision of doctor and patient.[39]

The move to shared decision making reflects a number of considerations. First, it reflects the fact that patients have the greatest stake in the medical decisions made for them. As a basic matter of respect for them as persons, it is essential to ensure that they have a meaningful voice in the decision-making process so that they can exercise their fundamental rights of autonomy and self-determination. It is not surprising that informed consent blossomed during the 1960s, when individual rights received greater recognition and persons in positions of authority no longer were assumed to deserve control over the lives of others.[40] This concern for respect for patients parallels the argument that a two-person presidency shows respect for voters from both sides of the political spectrum.

Fostering patient autonomy is valuable for its own sake; it also is valuable because it can result in greater patient satisfaction and better outcomes. Patients overwhelmingly report a desire to be involved in the decision-making process. They do not necessarily want to have full responsibility for making the decision—they are typically interested in the physician's opinion about the best approach—but they do want to collaborate with the doctor in choosing among the alternatives. When patients are involved in the decision-making process, they report lower levels of anxiety about their condition, a greater sense of control, less discomfort, and, most importantly, greater improvement in their medical condition. Interestingly, in a study that compared patients who preferred shared decision making with patients who preferred either physician decision making or patient decision making, the shared decision makers had better outcomes than either of the other two groups.[41]

While there are significant differences between shared decision making by patients and physicians and shared decision making by political leaders, this last finding from the medical setting is very instructive for the idea of a coalition presidency. The better outcomes for patients can happen for multiple reasons, but an important reason is the fact that patients are more likely to follow the recommendations of their physicians when they are involved in the decision-making process. Giving patients a voice in the shaping of their care makes them more likely to be comfortable with the care. Analogies exist in workplace psychology. Studies have shown that workers are more accepting of their workplace procedures if they have input into the creation of those procedures.[42]

Similarly, members of the public will be more supportive of executive branch proposals if they feel they have had a voice in the shaping of those proposals. With a two-person presidency instead of a one-person presidency, nearly twice as many Americans will feel that they have had such a voice. In other words, just as shared decision making in medicine fosters cooperation between patients and physicians and shared decision making in the workplace fosters cooperation between employees and employers, so can we expect a bipartisan presidency to foster more cooperation between voters and the executive branch.

Should the executive power be divided among more than two persons?

If dividing the executive power between two presidents would make for better representation, why not divide it even further? That way, there would be opportunities for leaders of political movements other than the Democratic and Republican Parties to serve in the executive branch. Other proposals for a plural executive in the United States have suggested that the executive branch expand to three or even twelve members.[43] Moreover, two heads may be better than one at making decisions, but three, five, or seven heads are probably even better than two.

As discussed earlier, it would make sense to expand beyond two presidents only if a third party emerged with significant and sustained support. My proposal for a two-person presidency reflects two key principles—proportional representation for the major political parties in the executive branch and decisions being made by consensus. Because the United States currently has only two major parties, there is no reason to adopt an executive branch with more than two presidents. On the other hand, if a third party did develop meaningful and enduring support, then it should be represented in the executive branch.

In the meantime, however, there would be important disadvantages to having more than two presidents. While having additional presidents could make the executive branch even more representative of the public, it would compromise another key goal of a two-person presidency. Dividing the executive power among more than two persons might overcompensate for the need to weaken executive power. Rather than simply balancing power between the executive and legislative branches, it could turn the executive branch into the weaker branch.

Perhaps as I have argued, a two-person presidency really would be better than a one-person presidency. But would the country ever make such a change? It would require a constitutional amendment, a task rarely achieved, and Alexander Hamilton's arguments for a single executive resonate with many people. Europeans might like their plural executives, but Americans appear to prefer their single executives. In the next chapter, I explain why the prospects for a two-person presidency are better than one might think at first.

7

The prospects for adopting a two-person presidency

There are good reasons to doubt the possibility of the United States adopting a two-person presidency. In the more than 220 years since the ratification of the Bill of Rights in 1791, the United States has adopted only seventeen amendments to the Constitution. Moreover, the desire for a decisive leader who can act with dispatch not only was important to the framers of the Constitution but also has been important to members of the public since then. Shared leadership in the political and corporate worlds may be the norm in parts of western Europe, but not so in the United States. Americans like their Ronald Reagans and Donald Trumps, and if a leader disappoints, people look for a new one. When the administration of George W. Bush ended with economic collapse and U.S. troops bogged down in Iraq and Afghanistan, the public turned to Barack Obama and his promise of change. Rather than changing their system, U.S. voters are inclined to change their elected officials.

Still, the claim that Americans would not support a constitutional amendment for a bipartisan presidency is a prediction rather than an argument. And as Yogi Berra, Niels Bohr, and other notable persons are reported to have said, it is difficult to make predictions, especially about the future. Indeed, during my service as a state representative in Indiana, I often was surprised when bills that seemed destined for passage were voted down, while other bills that seemed doomed to fail were enacted.

Moreover, it would be foolish to claim any ability to predict twenty-five to fifty years into the future. A two-person presidency may be unlikely in the next decade or two, but one simply cannot know how people who are not yet born will think about the proposal.

In fact, there are good reasons to think that the public will be receptive to the idea of a two-person presidency. While Obama changed the course of the federal government in some ways, he was unable to bring about the postpartisan ethic to which he aspired during his 2008 campaign. The public became more polarized politically under Obama than it had been under any other president during the previous sixty years. Partisan conflict in the House and the Senate continued and perhaps worsened, and voters generally had unfavorable views about Congress.[1]

Voter frustration was vented through the creation and growth of the Tea Party, as well as through large gains for the Republican Party in the midterm congressional elections in November 2010. But turning to new leaders failed once again to fix the dysfunction in Washington. House Republicans proposed unpopular reforms such as their idea to turn Medicare into a program with vouchers for private insurance coverage, and public enthusiasm dimmed quickly.[2]

By February 2012, after a year in which Obama repeatedly clashed with Republicans in Congress over an increase in the debt ceiling, an extension of the payroll tax cut, and other measures, public approval ratings for Congress reached new lows. Only 10 percent of Americans approved of the way the legislative branch was handling its job. During the summer of 2011, the *New York Times* described the public mood about Washington politics "as one of doom, disgust and disbelief" and reported a Canadian tourist as observing, "Instead of building the country, you're destroying it."[3]

In a political environment in which voters are highly frustrated with partisan conflict and in which the existing structure of the U.S. political system offers no meaningful path to a bipartisan or postpartisan ethic, the public may be much more receptive to major reform. Voters finally may come to the realization that the problems with politics in Washington lie not in the people they elect but in the system into which they elect them. A two-person presidency may seem radical, but the constant breakdown and gridlock on Capitol Hill demonstrates precisely why radical reform is needed.

Other factors also suggest that adopting a bipartisan presidency is more feasible than might be expected. First, it is not the case that the public has considered and rejected such a reform. Rather, the idea simply has not been debated. Reforms that are even more radical than a two-person presidency, such as the adoption of a parliamentary system, have been considered, but the more radical reforms entail an abandonment of the basic constitutional structure of divided and shared powers. In a parliamentary system, for example, the executive branch governs as an arm of the legislative branch. A two-person presidency would build on the existing constitutional design both by preserving its essential structure of separated powers and by correcting the problems created by a one-person executive. Accordingly, it is the kind of reform that should be acceptable to the public.

Indeed, proposed reforms for other problems have been more successful in the United States when they build on the existing structure instead of trying to substitute a new blueprint. Thus, for example, when planning his health care reform legislation, Barack Obama acknowledged that he would prefer a Canadian-style, single-payer system if he were starting from scratch. However, he decided that it made more sense to work within the existing system in the United States.[4] Accordingly, as discussed in chapter 5, his legislation increased access to health care insurance by making public programs and private forms of coverage available to more persons.

In other words, the Affordable Care Act removed many of the barriers to coverage that had existed in the U.S. health care system, rather than replacing the U.S. health care system with a model based on another country's system. Similarly, reform of the U.S. political system will be more feasible if it tries to fix the problems with the existing system of separated powers than if it tries to borrow a political system from another country.

In the next sections of this chapter, I discuss in greater detail why the public and members of Congress could be receptive to a two-person presidency. Before explaining why that is so, I consider how the interest groups that lobby elected officials would respond to the idea. Even if the public might prefer a particular policy change, well-organized interest groups can block the change by mobilizing a vocal and determined opposition.[5] On the other hand, if important interest groups support a coalition presidency, they have the power to drive political decision making in that direction.

Highly influential interest groups, such as those that lobby on behalf of corporate interests, could easily like the idea of a coalition presidency. While they might prefer one of the two major parties always to be in control of the national government, they may want even more to avoid the uncertainty that exists when power can shift back and forth between Democrats and Republicans. It is difficult to plan for the long term when a new presidential administration might successfully press Congress to enact significant changes in tax or other economic policy. Presidents also can create uncertainty for the private sector by their ability to change public policy through executive orders or the administrative agency rule-making process. As a result, industry spends substantial time and resources on government relations, time and resources that would be better spent on product development. If Democrats and Republicans continuously share executive power, governmental policy will be more stable and predictable and overall more favorable for business.[6]

Just as there are good reasons for influential interest groups to favor a two-person presidency, so are there good reasons for members of Congress to do so.

A coalition executive and the interests of members of Congress

Cabining the imperial presidency

Weakening the executive power by dividing it would level the balance of power between the executive and legislative branches. Instead of presidential domination of policy making in Washington, Congress would enjoy a more equal role in the determination of the nation's governmental policies. In other words, there would be an increase in the relative power of Congress in its relationship with the executive branch, and that should be quite appealing to members of Congress.

But Congress has enabled the development of the imperial presidency by its voluntary transfer of policy-making authority to the executive branch. If Congress intentionally fostered the expansion of presidential power, why should it support a constitutional amendment that counteracts that expansion?

Adding a second president to the executive branch would not undo the delegation of policy-making power to the executive branch, but it would make it more difficult for the executive branch to unduly exploit its policy-making power. Dividing the executive branch would provide a useful limit on the exercise of presidential power.

Indeed, Congress employs a number of strategies to cabin the policy-making power of the executive branch. For example, it monitors executive action through hearings and investigations by its oversight committees, the House Committee on Oversight and Government Reform and the Senate Committee on Homeland Security and Government Affairs.[7] In the past, the House committee has investigated the abuse of detainees held in the Abu Ghraib prison, the leak of classified information that revealed the identity of Central Intelligence Agency agent Valerie Plame, and failures in the response of the Federal Emergency Management Agency to Hurricane Katrina.

Members of Congress also can request a report by the Government Accountability Office (GAO), a watchdog agency that audits governmental programs at the request of a committee or a single member of Congress.[8] In 2011, for example, the GAO produced a study of the effectiveness of U.S. troops who were training security forces in Afghanistan and Iraq and a report on the implementation of a streamlined review process for small mass-transit projects. It also produced an annual review of the President's Emergency Plan for AIDS Relief (PEPFAR), which funds treatment, care, and prevention services for HIV infection overseas, and an analysis of changes in prescription drug coverage by plans that participate in the Medicare Part D prescription drug program.

Congress can discourage disfavored activity by the executive branch as well by withholding funding for the activity, and it can leverage its power to approve presidential appointees to extract concessions before permitting a vote on a nominee. Thus, for example, in March 2011, when Barack Obama decided to appoint U.S. Department of Commerce Secretary Gary Locke as the new ambassador to China, Senate Republicans warned the president that they would block anyone nominated to replace Locke until Obama sent trade agreements with Colombia and Panama to Congress for approval. The trade deals were finally approved in October 2011, and John Bryson was confirmed as the new secretary of commerce on October 20, 2011.[9]

In short, even as Congress has delegated substantial policy-making power to the executive branch, it has employed a number of practices to constrain the president's use of the delegated power. But these approaches have limited impact. They often occur after the president has implemented a policy decision, and they have been inadequate to reverse the development of the imperial presidency. And some oversight devices have failed. As discussed in chapter 3, the Supreme Court found the legislative veto unconstitutional, and Congress allowed the independent counsel statute to expire after it was implemented poorly. A two-person presidency would provide a more effective constraint on the executive branch and reduce the need for Congress to rely on other, less effective strategies.

And because a two-person presidency would be a coalition presidency, it would reduce the use of oversight tools for partisan purposes. At times, House committees launch investigations to score political points rather than because of genuine policy concerns. When U.S. Representative Dan Burton (R-IN) chaired the House oversight committee, the committee conducted a number of frivolous investigations into the activities of Bill Clinton and his associates, including the suicide of White House counsel Vince Foster. Over a five-year period, the committee issued 1,052 subpoenas to the Clinton administration, and during an investigation into Clinton fund-raising during the 1996 campaign, committee staff released an excerpted audiotape from which exculpatory evidence was omitted.[10]

In sum, a two-person presidency offers legislators a more effective check on executive power than exists currently.

Reducing partisan conflict

The heightened partisan conflict in Washington is troubling not only for the public; it also makes congressional service unpleasant. Members of Congress find the partisan atmosphere disagreeable to the extent that prominent members such as Senators Evan Bayh (D-IN) and Olympia Snowe (R-ME) have chosen to leave office rather than continue working in Washington.[11] Legislators spend less time developing solutions for the country's problems and more time locking horns with their colleagues from across the aisle. Defusing partisan conflict would make for a more rewarding experience for members of the legislative branch.

Enhancing constituent services

A two-party presidency provides another important benefit for members of Congress. Unless a third-party candidate prevails, the members always will have a president from their party to whom they can turn for help with constituent concerns. If there is red tape to cut at the Food and Drug Administration or the Department of Agriculture, senators and representatives will be able to pick up the phone and call senior officials who were appointed by a party colleague. The barriers that exist when the White House is in the hands of a president from the other political party will disappear.

Implications for aspirations to higher office

While a coalition presidency would benefit members of Congress in their congressional roles, how would they feel about a two-person presidency in terms of any aspirations they have to run for election to the White House? Many legislators may be more concerned about the presidential power they might wield in the future than about the presidential power that they must face in the present.

On this question, the calculus is more complicated. Having sole control of the Oval Office might be much more appealing than gaining half of the executive authority. For people who crave power, it may be difficult to support a shrinking of the president's influence. On the other hand, senators and representatives might well prefer a system in which their chances of ascending to the White House would roughly double even though they would have to share power with a presidential partner. And in the current environment of a highly partisan Congress, doubling the chances to move out of Capitol Hill and into the Oval Office could be especially attractive.

Is there any way to predict whether the greater likelihood of becoming a president would outweigh the diminution in executive power? While any further analysis is necessarily speculative, we can turn to the way people deal with risk for a possible answer. Principles of risk tolerance suggest that members of Congress might prefer a coalition presidency in which their chances of election to the White House double.

How do considerations of risk tolerance affect the analysis? Some people are risk seeking, some are risk neutral, and others are risk averse. A useful illustration comes from people's preferences when faced with the choice of (a) receiving $50 for certain or (b) having a 50 percent chance of receiving $100 and a 50 percent chance of receiving nothing. For both choices, the expected payoff is $50 (since 100 percent × $50 = $50 = [50 percent × $100] + [50 percent × $0]). A risk-neutral person would be indifferent between the sure $50 and the 50 percent chance of $100. A risk seeker, on the other hand, would choose the 50 percent chance of $100, while a risk avoider would take the certain $50. For the risk avoider, who worries most about taking nothing, the doubling of the chances of success overcome the 50 percent reduction in the payoff. If we apply this example to the question of a two-person presidency, we see that a risk avoider would prefer a 100 percent chance of gaining half of the presidential power in a coalition presidency, while a risk seeker would prefer a 50 percent chance of winning all of the presidential power in a unitary presidency.[12]

Would members of Congress be risk avoiders or risk seekers with respect to their presidential aspirations? While some people like to gamble and other people try to reduce their risk, we can draw some reliable conclusions about the collective risk preferences of individuals. Specifically, when given the choice between a certain $50 and a 50 percent chance at $100, people tend toward risk avoidance and prefer the certain $50. The doubling in the chances of success more than compensates for the reduction by half in the maximum amount of the payoff. In the presidential candidate context, then, the twofold increase in the chances of election should more than compensate for the 50 percent reduction in power. Members of Congress should prefer a coalition presidency, just as people generally prefer the greater likelihood of the $50 payoff.[13]

Of course, a two-person presidency would not result in a simple doubling of the chances of election and halving of the amount of power. There are nuances to consider, some of which would make a two-person presidency more attractive, while other factors would make it less appealing. For example, I have assumed that a member of Congress would view the adoption of a coalition presidency as doubling the chances of election since there would be two seats in the Oval Office instead of one. But members of a dominant political party might see things differently. If they believed that their party's nominee had a greater than 50 percent chance of winning the general election, they might view a two-person presidency as requiring them to cede half of the presidential authority for less than a doubling of their chances of election. If that were the case, then the expected payoff from election would be lower in a two-person presidency than in a one-person presidency. There also could be less than a doubling in the chances of election since third-party or independent candidates might claim one of the two presidential slots.

On the other hand, there are nuances that would favor a two-person presidency. I have assumed that having to share power with a presidential partner would result in a 50 percent reduction in power. But in fact, the reduction in power might be less than 50 percent. As discussed in chapter 4, partisan conflict can greatly limit the ability of presidents to exercise their authority. Barack Obama was much more successful passing legislation during his first two years with a Democratic Congress than he was in his second two years with a Republican House. Because a two-person presidency can reduce the degree of partisan conflict between the executive and legislative branches, the addition of a second president may result in less than a 50 percent reduction in the effective power of the president. In addition, I observed in chapter 2 that term limits should be abandoned for a two-person presidency. With the opportunity to serve more than eight years and to avoid the status of a lame duck, members of Congress may find a two-person presidency preferable to a one-person presidency.

In sum, while one cannot draw firm conclusions on the question, there are several reasons why members of Congress would prefer a bipartisan executive branch.

Congressional support for a two-person presidency is important, since Congress ordinarily initiates the constitutional amendment process. But it also would be necessary for the public to support a coalition executive, both because of the need for the states to ratify an amendment and because members of Congress will be reluctant to support a constitutional amendment that does not have public support.

A coalition executive and the public desire for a bipartisan ethic

There is reason to think that a majority of the public would be receptive to the idea of a two-person presidency. Voting patterns suggest that significant numbers of Americans prefer that control of their government be divided between Democrats and Republicans.

In recent decades, it has been common for one party to occupy the White House while the other party holds a majority in at least one house in Congress. During Ronald Reagan's eight years in office, Democrats enjoyed a majority in the House of Representatives for all eight years and a majority in the Senate for two years. George H. W. Bush faced a Democratic House and Senate all four years of his term, and Bill Clinton saw Republican majorities in both the House and

Senate for six years of his administration. Divided party control also has become more common in state governments.[14]

A number of political scientists have advanced a theory of "cognitive Madisonianism" to explain the voting practices that yield a government whose power is divided between the two major parties. In this view, many voters consciously choose one party's candidate for president and the other party's candidate for Congress to ensure that political power is shared between the Democratic and Republican Parties. Scholars disagree about the extent to which voters consciously seek divided government and their reasons for preferring divided government, but some empirical data suggest that cognitive Madisonianism is an important phenomenon. In one key study, researchers found that cognitive Madisonians comprise 20 to 26 percent of the electorate and that they prefer divided government both to prevent the concentration of power in one party and to promote a wider mix of policy prescriptions.[15] For those voters who prefer divided government, a coalition presidency should be very attractive. They always would be assured that the parties would share the executive power.

But how do we find majority support for a two-person presidency? Would not strong Democratic and Republican voters prefer their party to have full control of the executive power? Indeed, one could easily conclude that Democrats and Republicans alike would prefer the current structure of the executive branch. For example, they each might believe that their candidate generally stands a better than 50 percent chance of winning the White House. Hence, it would not make sense to give up half of the presidential power for less than a doubling of their chances of victory, and a majority of voters would oppose a two-person presidency.[16]

While there are plausible scenarios that would result in the rejection of a two-person presidency, there also are plausible scenarios that would yield support for a two-person presidency. For example, a two-person presidency could be appealing to one side of the political spectrum. Consider the run-up to the 1996 election. Democrats could be fairly confident that Bill Clinton would win a second term, so they would have wanted to retain a one-person presidency. For

Republicans, on the other hand, the prospect of a Clinton reelection would have made a two-person presidency more appealing. We then can imagine the cognitive Madisonians having joined Republicans in support of a two-person presidency, providing majority support for the proposal.[17]

While it is unclear whether partisans would oppose or support a two-person presidency, trends in political party affiliation bode well for a two-person, coalition presidency. We might expect ardent members of a political party to be less receptive than more independent voters to a power-sharing arrangement among the different political parties. Strong Democrats likely would not see much virtue in Republicans having a share of presidential power, and strong Republicans likely would not see much virtue in Democrats having a share of presidential power. Thus, to the extent that members of the public form strong ties with the Democratic or Republican Party, support for a two-person presidency would be weak. But people are becoming less and less likely to identify with a political party in the United States and more and more likely to characterize themselves as independent voters. Since the 1950s, party affiliation has gradually dropped from 77 percent to about 60 percent.[18]

The French experience with shared executive power provides evidence both for and against the proposition that the U.S. public would like a coalition presidency. As discussed in chapter 4, France featured "cohabitation" governments, with presidents and prime ministers from different parties, for much of the time from 1986 through 2002. While voters initially were apprehensive about a system of shared executive power, cohabitation government became popular and had the support of two-thirds or more of the public. But even though the cohabitation governments were popular, voters passed a referendum in September 2000 that synchronized elections for the president and National Assembly and reduced the likelihood of future cohabitation governments. People apparently decided that they were more interested in maximizing their chances of securing all of the power than in maximizing their chances of securing some of the power.[19]

The mixed messages from France might be explained by differences in preference between party activists and other citizens. Polling of the entire electorate showed that shared governance was popular, but those who actually voted on the referendum cast ballots against shared governance. Party activists may have constituted most of the referendum voters. Turnout was only 30.6 percent, well below the usual turnout for referendums in France between 1960 and 2000. Most referendums saw turnouts of more than 70 percent of voters, with only one other referendum falling below 60 percent.[20] In a low-turnout election, voting will be dominated by party activists, and their views may not reflect those of the general populace. If the public were to consider a constitutional amendment for a coalition presidency in the United States, the outcome could well depend on how broadly the public became involved in the process.

The United States already has deviated from a pure unitary executive to a partial plural executive model

There is another reason to think that the public would be receptive to the idea of shared power in the executive branch. As discussed in chapter 3, the United States already has modified the executive branch from a pure model of single-person control to include elements of a plural executive. Congress has established independent commissions such as the Securities Exchange Commission (SEC) to implement federal laws, and a number of federal statutes vest authority for their execution with cabinet secretaries rather than with the president.[21] The Federal Reserve in particular is viewed as an institution that operates with independence from presidential oversight.

While presidents over the past few decades have increased the White House's control over independent commissions and executive branch agencies, presidents do not have the full control over the actions of the executive branch that proponents of the "unitary" executive desire. As critics of the erosion of the unitary executive argue, there should be no limits on the freedom of presidents to fire Federal Reserve chairs, SEC commissioners, or senior officials at other agencies. Nor should presidents by constrained in their direction of policy decisions by administrative agencies, including when they wish to override the exercise of discretionary power by executive branch officials.[22] But over time, Congress has limited presidential oversight of executive branch action.

In short, while a two-person presidency appears to entail a dramatic break with our current single-person presidency, it actually would represent an extension of the existing evolution of the executive branch from a unitary executive model to somewhat of a plural executive model. If the president already shares executive power with Federal Reserve governors, SEC commissioners, and officials at other agencies, it would not be so strange for the president to share executive power with a presidential partner.

The erosion of the unitary executive might suggest a different policy change than my proposal. Why not expand the use of independent commissions to address the problems with the single-person presidency? Congress could do so through the legislative process, and there would be no need for a constitutional amendment.

It is unlikely that greater use of independent commissions could solve the problems with a one-person presidency. Presidents are able to limit commissions' independence through their power to appoint commissioners. If Congress tried to make the commissions even more independent of presidential control, they would invite a presidential veto. Moreover, the Supreme Court has restricted the ability of Congress to limit presidential control of executive branch agencies. For example, Congress is able to deny the president, or public officials who serve at the pleasure of the president, the authority to appoint the commissioners who head independent agencies. In addition, it is difficult to imagine that Congress would propose independent commissions with significant foreign policy authority.[23]

As indicated at the outset of this chapter, amending the Constitution always presents serious hurdles, and the radical nature of a coalition presidency would face particular barriers to adoption. Still, as discussed, there are many considerations that would favor a two-person presidency in the United States. If partisan conflict persists at very high levels in Washington, the public may be receptive to the kind of change that would be entailed by the implementation of a bipartisan executive branch.

8

Conclusion

The problems of the imperial presidency and partisan conflict have plagued national politics in the United States for decades, and despite persistent concerns about the problems, they only are getting worse.

Presidents from both sides of the political aisle press for an expansive executive authority, even when they come into office after criticizing their predecessors' claims of presidential power, and they have taken steps to assert ever more presidential control over the policy making that occurs in the federal government. The founding fathers may have misgauged the extent to which members of Congress would champion the institutional interests of the legislative branch, but they were correct in thinking that presidents would promote the institutional interests of the executive branch.

As the presidency has become more imperial, so have politics become more partisan. With all that is at stake in presidential elections, the political parties have ample reason to fight hard for the executive power. Public polarization has become greater and greater, and party-line voting in Congress has reached higher and higher levels.

Observers often respond to the imperial presidency and partisan conflict by calling on elected officials to act more responsibly or encouraging voters to replace the officials with new officeholders. But the imperial presidency and partisan conflict are not the result of the people we elect but of the system we elect them into. James Madison was correct when he observed that people are not angels and that the governmental structure must be designed to channel official behavior in the desired direction. Presidents aggrandize power, members of Congress facilitate that aggrandizement, and elected officials have become highly partisan because the political system in the United States encourages all of these developments. If Americans are serious about cabining executive power and dampening partisan conflict, they must revise their constitutional system so that it provides better incentives for presidents and members of Congress.

I have explained why a two-person presidency would respond directly to the problems of the imperial presidency and partisan conflict. It would help restore the intended balance between the executive and legislative branches, it would ensure that policy making in the executive branch comes out of a deliberative process by decision makers with diverse perspectives, and it would give presidents and members of Congress greater incentives for bipartisan governing.

I also have discussed other important benefits of a two-person presidency. With multiple decision makers, the quality of decision making would improve. Two heads really are better than one. In addition, with the decision makers coming from different political parties, the government would become more representative of the citizenry. Almost all of the public, instead of about half of it, would feel like it had a voice in the executive branch. The representative quality of the government would improve also because third-party candidates have a much better chance at running second than at running first in a presidential election.

A coalition presidency could overcome other, related problems with the operation of the national government. For example, many observers have called for the elimination of the filibuster in the Senate, on the ground that major legislation effectively requires sixty votes rather than a simple majority of fifty-one. Defenders of the filibuster view it as an important protection for minority interests. Without the minority party's ability to block legislation, the majority party could impose its policies at will.[1] But even accepting the perspective of filibuster critics, filibuster reform represents an effort to treat symptoms of a problem rather than the cause of the problem. The use of the filibuster has increased because party polarization has increased. Reforming the filibuster would do nothing to defuse partisan conflict and would only force it to become manifest in other ways. It is far better to address the problem of party polarization more directly.

While I believe that much good would come from the adoption of a two-person, two-party presidency, I also believe that much would be gained by its consideration even if it is not ultimately adopted. By recognizing the connection between the one-person, one-party presidency and the dysfunction in Washington, DC, reformers are in a far better position to design alternative remedies for the imperial presidency and partisan conflict. Until we have an adequate understanding of the causes of our problems, we cannot identify effective remedies for the problems.

Notes

Notes to Chapter 1

1. Peter Baker, "Tide Turns, Starkly," *New York Times*, November 3, 2010.

2. Ronald Brownstein, *The Second Civil War: How Extreme Partisanship Has Paralyzed Washington and Polarized America* (New York: Penguin, 2007), 343–47 (quote on 343).

3. "Records of the Federal Convention," in *The Founders' Constitution*, ed. Philip B. Kurland and Ralph Lerner (Chicago: University of Chicago Press, 1987), vol. 3, 491. Randolph became the first attorney general and the second secretary of state of the United States.

4. Richard E. Neustadt, *Presidential Power and the Modern Presidents: The Politics of Leadership from Roosevelt to Reagan* (New York: Free Press, 1990), ix–x.

5. "Records of the Federal Convention," *supra* note 3, 491; Alexander Hamilton, "Federalist No. 70" (the text for each of the Federalist Papers can be found at the website of the Library of Congress, http://thomas.loc.gov/home/histdox/fedpapers .html); Gordon S. Wood, *Representation in the American Revolution*, rev. ed. (Charlottesville: University of Virginia Press, 2008), 23.

6. Arthur M. Schlesinger, Jr., coined the term "imperial presidency" during the Nixon presidency (Kevin Drum, "War without End," *New York Times*, September 5, 2004), and popularized it with his book *The Imperial Presidency* (Boston: Houghton Mifflin, 1973).

7. To be sure, it took some 150 years from the adoption of the Constitution to the development of the imperial presidency. It is hardly surprising that the framers' design might not succeed indefinitely.

8. Sanford Levinson and Ernest A. Young, "Who's Afraid of the Twelfth Amend-

ment?," in *Bush v. Gore* issue, *Florida State University Law Review* 29 (2001): 925–73, 928. See also Federalist No. 57 (identifying as the aim of a constitution the selection of rulers who possess the "most virtue to pursue, the common good of the society"); James A. Gardner, "Can Party Politics Be Virtuous?," *Columbia Law Review* 100 (April 2000): 667–701, 668–69. Indeed, it was not until late in the 19th Century that presidential candidates campaigned actively. "Candidates were expected to remain quietly in the background. The office must seek the man, not the man the office. To do otherwise was degrading not only to the candidate but to the dignity of the position he sought." Robert W. Johanssen, "Stephen A. Douglas' New England Campaign, 1860," *New England Quarterly* 35 (June 1962): 162–86, 162. See also James A. Gardner, "Deliberation or Tabulation? The Self-Undermining Constitutional Architecture of Election Campaigns," *Buffalo Law Review* 54 (April 2007): 1413–82, 1423.

9. Gallup polls comparing Obama's job-approval ratings from Democrats and Republicans found an average 68 percent difference between his 80 percent approval from Democrats and the 12 percent approval from Republicans. George W. Bush became the most polarized president during his fourth year in office. Jeffrey M. Jones, "Obama Ratings Historically Polarized," *Gallup Politics*, January 27, 2012, http://www.gallup.com/poll/152222/Obama-Ratings-Historically-Polarized.aspx (accessed November 8, 2012); see also Pew Research Center for the People & the Press, "Partisan Gap in Obama Job Approval Widest in Modern Era," April 2, 2009, http://pew research.org/pubs/1178/polarized-partisan-gap-in-obama-approval-historic (accessed November 8, 2012).

10. And the losing party's members start testing the waters early for a presidential campaign. By the end of July 2009, Republican hopefuls Haley Barbour, John Ensign, Mike Huckabee, Bobby Jindal, and Mike Pence had made visits to the early primary state of Iowa. Thomas Beaumont, "No. 3 House GOP Leader Just Visiting, Not '12 Candidate," *Des Moines Register*, July 24, 2009.

11. Juan J. Linz, "The Perils of Presidentialism," *Journal of Democracy* 1 (Winter 1990): 51–69, 55–56; John Stuart Mill, "Considerations on Representative Government," in *On Liberty and Other Essays*, ed. John Gray (New York: Oxford University Press, 1998), 302 (quotes).

12. B. Dan Wood, *The Myth of Presidential Representation* (New York: Cambridge University Press, 2009), 199–203.

13. 531 U.S. 98 (2000). For a sampling of critiques of the decision, see Michael Klarman, "*Bush v. Gore* through the Lens of Constitutional History," *California Law Review* 89 (December 2001): 1721–65; Cass Sunstein, "Order without Law," *University of Chicago Law Review* 68 (Summer 2001): 757–73; Laurence H. Tribe, "The Unbearable Wrongness of *Bush v. Gore*," *Constitutional Commentary* 19 (Winter 2002): 571–607.

14. In addition to bipartisan commissions, nonpartisan commissions are used, as with the commission created to identify military bases for closure.

15. Ulrich Klöti, "The Government," in *Handbook of Swiss Politics*, 2nd ed., ed. Ulrich Klöti et al. (Zürich: Neue Zürcher Zeitung, 2007), 155.

16. Amy Gutmann and Dennis Thompson, *The Spirit of Compromise: Why Governing Demands It and Campaigning Undermines It* (Princeton: Princeton University Press, 2012), 147–48.

17. Jonathan Alter, *The Promise: President Obama, Year One* (New York: Simon and Schuster, 2010), 244–46 (quote on 244).

18. Robert Axelrod, *The Evolution of Cooperation* (New York: Basic Books, 1984), 124–32; Itzhak Gilboa, *Rational Choice* (Cambridge: MIT Press, 2010), 100–101; Ming Zeng and Xiao-Ping Chen, "Achieving Cooperation in Multiparty Alliances: A Social Dilemma Approach to Partnership Management," *Academy of Management Review* 28 (October 2003): 587–605.

19. Martin Nowak and Karl Sigmund, "A Strategy of Win-Stay, Lose-Shift That Outperforms Tit-for-Tat in the Prisoner's Dilemma Game," *Nature* 364 (July 1, 1993): 56–58, 56.

20. Tony Ashworth, *Trench Warfare, 1914–1918: The Live and Let Live System* (New York: Holmes and Meier, 1980), 24–47; Axelrod, *Evolution, supra* note 18, 73–81. Ultimately, this "live-and-let-live" strategy unraveled when superior officers ordered their soldiers to launch raids on the other side's trenches. Axelrod, *Evolution, supra* note 18, 82–84.

21. To be sure, countries with parliamentary systems may have a dominant prime minister, so even those countries exhibit a preference for an element of individual leadership.

22. Dana D. Nelson, *Bad for Democracy: How the Presidency Undermines the Power of the People* (Minneapolis: University of Minnesota Press, 2008), 17; 1 Samuel 8 (Hebrew Bible); Rakesh Khurana, *Searching for a Corporate Savior: The Irrational Quest for Charismatic CEOs* (Princeton: Princeton University Press, 2002); Peter Baker, "The Education of a President," *New York Times Magazine*, October 17, 2010, MM40 (discussing President Obama's campaign promise to save the planet).

23. Nelson, *Bad for Democracy, supra* note 22, 4–5, 57, 67.

24. José Batlle y Ordóñez, "A Collegial Executive for Uruguay," in *Parliamentary versus Presidential Government*, ed. Arend Lijphart (Oxford: Oxford University Press, 1992), 175–76 (arguing that a preference for a single executive reflects fidelity to a long-standing, but outmoded, norm); Anthony Gottlieb, "Win or Lose," *New Yorker*, July 6, 2010, 73–74.

25. Woodrow Wilson, "Constitutional Government in the United States," in *The Papers of Woodrow Wilson: Volume 18, 1908–1909*, ed. Arthur S. Link et al. (Princeton: Princeton University Press, 1974), 104–14.

26. Sanford Levinson, *Our Undemocratic Constitution: Where the Constitution Goes Wrong (and How We the People Can Correct It)* (New York: Oxford University Press, 2006), 101–21.

27. Daniel R. Ortiz, "Duopoly versus Autonomy: How the Two-Party System Harms the Major Parties," *Columbia Law Review* 100 (April 2000): 753–74; Paul R. Abramson, John H. Aldrich, Phil Paolino, and David W. Rohde, "Third-Party and Independent Candidates in American Politics: Wallace, Anderson, and Perot," *Political Science Quarterly* 110 (Autumn 1995): 349–67, 357; William Poundstone, *Gaming the Vote: Why Elections Aren't Fair (and What We Can Do about It)* (New York: Hill and Wang, 2008), 59–91.

28. Arend Lijphart, *Patterns of Democracy: Government Forms and Performance in Thirty-Six Countries* (New Haven: Yale University Press, 1999), 118. When Israel agreed to a prisoner swap with Hamas in October 2011, Prime Minister Benjamin

Netanyahu called a meeting of the full cabinet to approve the deal. Ethan Bronner, "Deal with Hamas Will Free Israeli Held since 2006," *New York Times*, October 12, 2011.

29. Peter Shane, *Madison's Nightmare: How Executive Power Threatens American Democracy* (Chicago: University of Chicago Press, 2009), 32–37, 143–45.

30. William E. Scheuerman, *The Realist Case for Global Reform* (Cambridge, UK: Polity, 2011), 149–50.

Notes to Chapter 2

1. I am grateful to Cy Orentlicher for suggesting this point.

2. What if the runner-up for nomination by the Democratic or Republican Party ran as a third-party or independent candidate in the general election? Could voters elect two presidents from one party? Most likely, the runner-up would compete with the nominee for second place. But to prevent the election of two people from one party, it would make sense to provide that if a candidate loses in a bid for a party's nomination, the candidate cannot try to run as the nominee of another party or as an independent candidate. Almost all states have provisions like this. Michael S. Kang, "Sore Loser Laws and Democratic Contestation," *Georgetown Law Journal* 99 (April 2011): 1013–75; 1014.

3. In Nebraska and Maine, electoral votes are allocated by congressional district. The candidate with the most votes in a congressional district earns an electoral vote for that district. The two electoral votes that correspond to the Senate seats are given to the candidate who has the highest statewide vote. Alternatively, each state could allocate its electoral votes based on the shares of the popular vote earned by the candidates statewide. For example, in a state with ten electoral votes, a candidate earning 60 percent of the vote would receive six electoral votes.

4. Douglas ran as the nominee of the Democratic Party, and Breckinridge ran as the nominee of a breakaway Southern Democratic Party. Strom Thurmond in 1948 also won a higher percentage of electoral votes than popular votes by running strongly in the South. For voting data, see John Woolley and Gerhard Peters, "Presidential Elections Data," *The American Presidency Project*, http://www.presidency.ucsb.edu/elections.php (accessed November 8, 2012).

5. The typical elector would cast one vote for a party's presidential candidate and the other vote for the party's vice presidential candidate. To avoid ties, one elector was supposed to discard a ballot and vote only for a party's presidential candidate. However, in 1800, no elector for the Democratic-Republicans discarded a second ballot, and Thomas Jefferson received the same number of votes as his vice presidential partner, Aaron Burr. This sent the election to the House of Representatives, where Jefferson ultimately prevailed over Burr, but only after six days and thirty-six ballots. Sanford Levinson and Ernest A. Young, "Who's Afraid of the Twelfth Amendment?," in *Bush v. Gore* issue, *Florida State University Law Review* 29 (2001): 925–73, 928–32.

6. If one president's party won veto-proof majorities in both the House and Senate, that president might be able to work successfully in partisan fashion.

7. Gary L. McDowell, "Bork Was the Beginning: Constitutional Moralism and the

Politics of Federal Judicial Selection," *University of Richmond Law Review* 39 (March 2005): 809–18.

8. Lee Epstein and Jeffrey A. Segal, *Advice and Consent: The Politics of Judicial Appointments* (New York: Oxford University Press, 2005), 25.

9. Alliance for Justice, *The State of the Judiciary: President Obama and the 111th Congress* (Washington, DC: Alliance for Justice, 2011), 4–5, http://www.afj.org/judicial -selection/state_of_the_judiciary_111th_congress_report.pdf (accessed November 8, 2012). Obama also was unusually slow to nominate judges. Ibid. His low rate of judicial appointments continued during his third and fourth years in office. Charlie Savage, "Obama Lagging on Filling Seats in the Judiciary," *New York Times*, August 18, 2012. Obama took office in 2009 with sixty Democrats in the Senate, but the election of Scott Brown in January 2010 after Senator Ted Kennedy's death reduced the Democratic majority to fifty-nine.

10. Carl Hulse, "G.O.P. Blocks Judicial Nominee in a Sign of Battles to Come," *New York Times*, May 20, 2011. After Liu's withdrawal, he was appointed to the California Supreme Court. Maura Dolan, "Accolades as Justice Confirmed," *Los Angeles Times*, September 1, 2011.

11. Neil A. Lewis, "Stymied by Democrats in Senate, Bush Court Pick Finally Gives Up," *New York Times*, September 5, 2003.

12. Gerald N. Rosenberg, *The Hollow Hope: Can Courts Bring about Social Change*, 2nd ed. (Chicago: University of Chicago Press, 2008), 35–36.

13. Ibid., 51–54, 74–104. To be sure, the decision in *Brown* did lead quickly to integration in the border states between the northern and southern United States. Ibid., 50–51. *Brown* can be found at 347 U.S. 483 (1954).

14. Sanford Levinson, "Compromise and Constitutionalism," in "Compromise and Constitutionalism," special issue, *Pepperdine Law Review* 38 (2011): 821–43, 832–34. *Naim* can be found at 350 U.S. 985 (1956) and *Loving* at 388 U.S. 1 (1967). And even when the Court outlawed segregated schools in *Brown*, it did not require immediate compliance with its decision. Rather, it ordered schools to implement its decision with "all deliberate speed." Brown v. Board of Education, 349 U.S. 294, 301 (1955).

15. Lydia Saad, "Public Opinion about Abortion—An In-depth Review," *Gallup*, January 22, 2002, http://www.gallup.com/poll/9904/public-opinion-about-abortion -indepth-review.aspx (accessed November 8, 2012). The two dissenting justices in *Roe*, William Rehnquist and Byron White, came from the Court's conservative wing. *Roe* can be found at 410 U.S. 113 (1973).

16. Institute for Justice, "Five Years after *Kelo*: The Sweeping Backlash against One of the Supreme Court's Most-Despised Decisions," http://www.ij.org/index .php?option=com_content&task=view&id=3392&Itemid=165 (accessed November 8, 2012). The *Kelo* decision can be found at 545 U.S. 469 (2005).

17. Herman Finer, *The Presidency: Crisis and Regeneration: An Essay in Possibilities* (Chicago: University of Chicago Press, 1960), 34–37.

18. Michael O'Malley, *The Wisdom of Bees: What the Hive Can Teach Business about Leadership, Efficiency, and Growth* (New York: Portfolio, 2010), 95–99. See also Craig L. Pearce and Jay A. Conger, "All Those Years Ago: The Historical Underpinnings of Shared Leadership," in *Shared Leadership: Reframing the Hows and Whys of Leadership*, ed. Craig L. Pearce and Jay A. Conger (Thousand Oaks, CA: Sage, 2003),

1–2 (discussing a trend toward shared leadership in corporations to account for the inability of one person to possess all of the necessary leadership skills and knowledge).

A two-person presidency also would counteract the problem of presidents who give an issue undue attention because of the president's strong personal interest in the matter. When George W. Bush pressed for a war against Iraq, many people wondered whether he was influenced too much by a desire to complete his father's military efforts against Saddam Hussein. After the military drove Iraqi troops out of Kuwait, George H. W. Bush stopped U.S. forces from invading Baghdad and toppling Hussein. Some key supporters of the two presidents Bush believed that the first President Bush should have deposed Hussein. Jorge Alberto Ramirez, "Iraq War: Anticipatory Self-Defense or Unlawful Unilateralism?," *California Western International Law Journal* 4 (Fall 2003): 1–28, 17. In a two-person presidency, the co-president would be able to prevent policies driven more by the other president's personal interests than by the country's overall interests.

19. Scott E. Page, *The Difference: How the Power of Diversity Creates Better Groups, Firms, Schools and Societies* (Princeton: Princeton University Press, 2007), 322–24.

20. James O'Toole, Jay Galbraith, and Edward E. Lawler III, "The Promise and Pitfalls of Shared Leadership: When Two (or More) Heads Are Better than One," in Pearce and Conger, *Shared Leadership*, *supra* note 18, 252–254, 256.

21. Leigh Thompson, Erika Peterson, and Susan E. Brodt, "Team Negotiation: An Examination of Integrative and Distributive Bargaining," *Journal of Personality and Social Psychology* 70 (January 1996): 66–78, 75–76; Anne G. Perkins, "Negotiations: Are Two Heads Better than One?," *Harvard Business Review* 71 (November–December 1993): 13–14.

22. Arend Lijphart, "Presidentialism and Majoritarian Democracy: Theoretical Observations," in *The Failure of Presidential Democracy*, ed. Juan J. Linz and Arturo Valenzuela (Baltimore: Johns Hopkins University Press, 1994), 100; Juan J. Linz, "Presidential or Parliamentary Democracy: Does It Make a Difference?," in ibid., 16–17. While scholars generally mark the beginning of the imperial presidency with FDR, it may be more accurate to identify his cousin, Theodore Roosevelt, as the father of the imperial presidency. Terry M. Moe and William G. Howell, "The Presidential Power of Unilateral Action," *Journal of Law, Economics & Organization* 15 (April 1999): 132–79, 157.

23. Linz, "Presidential or Parliamentary Democracy," *supra* note 22, 17.

24. Alan Abramowitz, *The Disappearing Center: Engaged Citizens, Polarization, and American Democracy* (New Haven: Yale University Press, 2010), 15–20, 85–87. Younger people are less likely to vote than older people.

25. For more than a decade, 35–40 percent of Americans have identified themselves as political independents. Jeffrey M. Jones, "Record-High 40% of Americans Identify as Independents in '11," *Gallup Politics*, January 9, 2012, http://www.gallup.com/poll/151943/Record-High-Americans-Identify-Independents.aspx (accessed November 8, 2012).

26. By way of comparison, general elections in presidential years have generated a turnout of about 60 percent in recent years, while general elections in midterm years for governors, senators, and other officeholders have generated a turnout of about 40 percent. The drop-off in general election voting from a two-person presidency, then,

should be no more than 20 percent. Voting data come from Michael M. McDonald, "Voter Turnout," *United States Elections Project*, http://elections.gmu.edu/voter_turnout.htm (accessed November 8, 2012) (using data between 2004 and 2010).

Notes to Chapter 3

1. The text for each of the Federalist Papers can be found at the website of the Library of Congress, http://thomas.loc.gov/home/histdox/fedpapers.html.

2. See also Herman Finer, *The Presidency: Crisis and Regeneration: An Essay in Possibilities* (Chicago: University of Chicago Press, 1960), 37 (discussing the ample powers of Congress and the intent of the framers that it would be "the primary engine of will and decision").

3. Gordon S. Wood, *The American Revolution: A History* (New York: Modern Library, 2002), 66–69, 139–43; Gordon S. Wood, *The Creation of the American Republic, 1776–1787* (Chapel Hill: University of North Carolina Press, 1969), 132–50, 403–13; Eric A. Posner and Adrian Vermeule, *The Executive Unbound: After the Madisonian Republic* (New York: Oxford University Press, 2010), 183. See also Martin S. Flaherty, "The Most Dangerous Branch," *Yale Law Journal* 105 (May 1996): 1725–1839, 1767; Curtis A. Bradley and Martin S. Flaherty, "Executive Power Essentialism and Foreign Affairs," *Michigan Law Review* 102 (February 2004): 545–688, 583–84.

4. Posner and Vermeule, *Executive Unbound, supra* note 3, 183. Sources also include Wood, *American Revolution, supra* note 3, 71–72; Michael D. Ramsey, *The Constitution's Text in Foreign Affairs* (Cambridge: Harvard University Press, 2007), 33, 36–46.

5. For example, the House is a much larger body, with representatives elected from districts with the same number of constituents, while the Senate gives each state the same number of elected officials. Only the Senate plays a role in confirming presidential appointments, while the House must originate revenue bills. U.S. Const., art. II, § 2, cl. 2, and art. I, § 7, cl. 1.

6. The response to the experience with state legislative tyranny included other measures that responded to deficiencies in the Articles of Confederation—the creation of a strong national government and the establishment of an independent judiciary. Wood, *American Revolution, supra* note 3, 152–58.

7. Wood, *Creation of the American Republic, supra* note 3, 521. Antifederalists also worried that to the extent presidents shared power, they often did so only with the Senate, whose members would identify more with the president than with the people. Ibid. Recall in this regard that senators were chosen by state legislatures rather than through direct election until the adoption of the Seventeenth Amendment in 1913.

8. Flaherty, "Most Dangerous Branch," *supra* note 3, 1727–28; Abner S. Greene, "Checks and Balances in an Era of Presidential Lawmaking," *University of Chicago Law Review* 61 (Winter 1994): 123–96, 125; William P. Marshall, "Eleven Reasons Why Presidential Power Inevitably Expands and Why It Matters," *Boston University Law Review* 88 (April 2008): 505–22, 507; Arthur Schlesinger, Jr., *The Imperial Presidency*, with a new epilogue (Boston: Houghton Mifflin, 1989), 208, 420. See also Garry Wills, *Bomb Power: The Modern Presidency and the National Security State* (New York: Penguin, 2010), 2–3.

9. Daniel Farber, *Lincoln's Constitution* (Chicago: University of Chicago Press, 2003), 118–19.

10. Gary Lawson, "The Rise and Rise of the Administrative State," *Harvard Law Review* 107 (April 1994): 1231–54, 1237–41; Geoffrey R. Stone et al., *Constitutional Law*, 6th ed. (New York: Aspen, 2009), 412–13 ("little guidance" quote); Richard B. Stewart, "The Reformation of American Administrative Law," *Harvard Law Review* 88 (May 1975): 1667–1813, 1675 ("transmission belt" quote); Bruce Ackerman, "The New Separation of Powers," *Harvard Law Review* 113 (January 2000): 633–729, 697 (*"make law"* quote).

11. 42 U.S.C. § 7410(a). The machine-gun provision can be found at 18 U.S.C. 922(o) and the air-quality provision at 42 U.S.C. § 7409(b) (authorizing the EPA Administrator to prescribe air-quality standards that, "allowing for an adequate margin of safety, are requisite to protect the public health"). Implementation of the air-quality statute is discussed in David Schoenbrod, *Power without Responsibility: How Congress Abuses the People through Delegation* (New Haven: Yale University Press, 1993), 58–81.

12. 42 U.S.C. § 7413.

13. Endangerment and Cause or Contribute Findings for Greenhouse Gases under Section 202(a) of the Clean Air Act, 74 Fed. Reg. 66496 (final rule December 15, 2009); John M. Broder, "U.S. Issues Limits on Greenhouse Gas Emissions from Cars," *New York Times*, April 2, 2010.

14. Industrial Union Dept. v. American Petroleum Institute, 448 U.S. 607, 639–640 (1980) (upholding 29 U.S.C. 652(8) and 29 U.S.C. 655(b)(5)).

15. Thomas E. Cronin, *The State of the Presidency*, 2nd ed. (Boston: Little, Brown, 1980), 224 (describing presidential frustration with administrative agency employees who adhere to well-established professional norms rather than presidential priorities); Stewart, "Reformation of American Administrative Law," *supra* note 10, 1713–15 (discussing industry capture).

16. Elena Kagan, "Presidential Administration," *Harvard Law Review* 114 (June 2001): 2245–2385, 2255–2309; Nicholas Bagley and Richard L. Revesz, "Centralized Oversight of the Regulatory State," *Columbia Law Review* 106 (October 2006): 1260–1329, 1263–64; Richard H. Pildes and Cass R. Sunstein, "Reinventing the Regulatory State," *University of Chicago Law Review* 62 (Winter 1995): 1–129, 3–4; Peter Shane, *Madison's Nightmare: How Executive Power Threatens American Democracy* (Chicago: University of Chicago Press, 2009), 152.

Lyndon Baines Johnson initiated the practice of OMB review, and subsequent presidents expanded it. Steven G. Calabresi and Christopher S. Yoo, *The Unitary Executive: Presidential Power from Washington to Bush* (New Haven: Yale University Press, 2008), 12–13; Robert V. Percival, "Presidential Management of the Administrative State: The Not-So-Unitary Executive," *Duke Law Journal* 51 (December 2001): 963–1013, 985–89. See also Shane, *Madison's Nightmare, supra*, 148–58.

17. Kagan, "Presidential Administration," *supra* note 16, 2288; Exec. Order No. 12,866, 3 C.F.R. 638 (1993).

18. Kagan, "Presidential Administration," *supra* note 16, 2285–90; Pildes and Sunstein, "Reinventing the Regulatory State," *supra* note 16, 29; John M. Broder, "Obama Abandons a Stricter Limit on Air Pollution," *New York Times*, September 3, 2011; John

M. Broder, "Re-election Strategy Is Tied to a Shift in Smog," *New York Times*, November 17, 2011; John M. Broder and Dan Frosch, "U.S. Review Expected to Delay Oil Pipeline Past the Election," *New York Times*, November 11, 2011; Center for Progressive Reform, *Behind Closed Doors at the White House: How Politics Trumps Protection of Public Health, Worker Safety, and the Environment* (November 2011), http://www.progressivereform.org/articles/OIRA_Meetings_1111.pdf (accessed November 8, 2012).

19. Kagan, "Presidential Administration," *supra* note 16, 2281–84; Peter L. Strauss, "Presidential Rulemaking," *Chicago-Kent Law Review* 72, no. 4 (1995): 965–86; Bill Vlasic, "Carmakers Back Strict New Rules for Gas Mileage," *New York Times*, July 29, 2011; "2017 and Later Model Year Light-Duty Vehicle Greenhouse Gas Emissions and Corporate Average Fuel Economy Standards," 76 Fed. Reg. 74,854 (December 1, 2011). The final rule for 2017–2025 was issued in August 2012. Bill Vlasic and John Broder, "U.S. Sets High Long-Term Fuel Efficiency Rules for Automakers," *New York Time*, August 29, 2012; 77 Fed. Reg. 62,624 (October 15, 2012).

20. Neal Devins, "Signing Statements and Divided Government," *William & Mary Bill of Rights Journal* 16 (October 2007): 63–79, 67; William G. Howell, *Power without Persuasion: The Politics of Direct Presidential Action* (Princeton: Princeton University Press, 2003), 58–59; Kagan, "Presidential Administration," *supra* note 16, 2303–4; Mark E. Rushefsky, *Public Policy in the United States: At the Dawn of the Twenty-First Century*, 3rd ed. (Armonk, NY: M. E. Sharpe, 2002), 227; Nancy Kassop, "Expansion and Contraction: Clinton's Impact on the Scope of Presidential Power," in *The Presidency and the Law: The Clinton Legacy*, ed. David Gray Adler and Michael A. Genovese (Lawrence: University Press of Kansas, 2002), 7–8; Kenneth Mayer, *With the Stroke of a Pen: Executive Orders and Presidential Power* (Princeton: Princeton University Press, 2001), 3; George A. Krause and David B. Cohen, "Presidential Use of Executive Orders, 1953–1994," *American Politics Quarterly* 25 (October 1997): 458–81, 470. See also Joel L. Fleishman and Arthur H. Aufses, "Law and Orders: The Problem of Presidential Legislation," *Law and Contemporary Problems* 40 (Summer 1976): 1–45, 38–39 (discussing Gerald Ford's executive order restructuring oversight of foreign-intelligence agencies to preempt more restrictive legislation).

21. Sources for this and the preceding paragraphs include Phillip J. Cooper, *By Order of the President: The Use and Abuse of Executive Direct Action* (Lawrence: University Press of Kansas, 2002), 26–27, 31; William Hebe, "Executive Orders and the Development of Presidential Power," *Villanova Law Review* 17 (March 1972): 688–712, 690; Mayer, *With the Stroke of a Pen*, *supra* note 20, 52–54; Peter M. Shane and Harold H. Bruff, *Separation of Powers Law: Cases and Materials* (Durham: Carolina Academic Press, 1996), 131; Fleishman and Aufses, "Law and Orders," *supra* note 20, 7–8, 11–12.

22. For an important discussion of how presidential control of administrative agency decision making is actually exerted, see Lisa Schultz Bressman and Michael P. Vandenbergh, "Inside the Administrative State: A Critical Look at Presidential Control," *Michigan Law Review* 105 (October 2006): 47–99.

23. Mistretta v. United States, 488 U.S. 361, 372 (1989); Peter H. Aranson, Ernest Gellhorn, and Glen O. Robinson, "A Theory of Legislative Delegation," *Cornell Law Review* 68 (November 1982): 1–67, 56–59; Morris P. Fiorina, "Legislative Choice of Regulatory Forms: Legal Process or Administrative Process?," *Public Choice* 39 (January 1982): 33–66, 46–54.

For arguments that the Supreme Court should invalidate many grants of power under the nondelegation doctrine, see Michael B. Rappaport, "The Selective Nondelegation Doctrine and the Line Item Veto: A New Approach to the Nondelegation Doctrine and Its Implications for *Clinton v. City of New York*," *Tulane Law Review* 76 (December 2001): 265–372; Schoenbrod, *Power without Responsibility, supra* note 11. See also Gary Lawson, "Delegation and Original Meaning," *Virginia Law Review* 88 (April 2002): 327–404, 333–35 (arguing that delegations of legislative power violate the framers' division of governmental power but not calling for the courts to revive the nondelegation doctrine). These arguments have so far been unsuccessful. The Supreme Court has not struck down a delegation of legislative power to the executive branch since 1935. Erwin Chemerinsky, *Constitutional Law: Principles and Policies*, 4th ed. (New York: Wolters Kluwer, 2011), 335. See also Eric A. Posner and Adrian Vermeule, "Interring the Nondelegation Doctrine," *University of Chicago Law Review* 69 (Fall 2002): 1721–62 (rejecting the existence of a nondelegation doctrine).

24. Lawson, "Delegation and Original Meaning," *supra* note 23, 335–43.

25. In upholding presidential power to conserve federal lands, the Supreme Court observed that it was blessing a longstanding practice of presidents in which Congress had acquiesced and which could be viewed as part of the "administrative power of the Executive in the management of the public land." United States v. Midwest Oil Co, 236 U.S. 459, 471–74 (1915); Edward S. Corwin, *The President, Office and Powers, 1787–1957; History and Analysis of Practice and Opinion*, 4th rev. ed. (New York: NYU Press, 1957), 120–21.

26. Julia Preston and John H. Cushman, Jr., "Obama to Permit Young Migrants to Remain in U.S.," *New York Times*, June 16, 2012; Stephen Labaton, "Administration Will Strengthen Antitrust Rules," *New York Times*, May 11, 2009.

27. Curtis A. Bradley and Eric A. Posner, "Presidential Signing Statements and Executive Power," *Constitutional Commentary* 23 (Winter 2006): 307–64. Presidents may use signing statements for other purposes, such as for praising the bill's sponsors or supporters or for criticizing "Congress for going too far or not far enough in addressing the problem the bill is supposed to solve." Ibid., 308.

28. Shane, *Madison's Nightmare, supra* note 16, 135–36; Immigration Reform and Control Act, Pub. L. No. 99-603, 100 Stat. 3359 (1986); Marc N. Garber and Kurt A. Wimmer, "Presidential Signing Statements as Interpretations of Legislative Intent: An Executive Aggrandizement of Power," *Harvard Journal on Legislation* 24 (Summer 1987): 363–95, 368–69. See also ABA Task Force on Presidential Signing Statements and the Separation of Powers Doctrine, *Report* (Chicago: American Bar Association, August 2006), http://www.abanow.org/wordpress/wp-content/files_flutter/1273179 616signstatereport.pdf (accessed November 8, 2012); Phillip J. Cooper, "George W. Bush, Edgar Allan Poe, and the Use and Abuse of Presidential Signing Statements," *Presidential Studies Quarterly* 35 (September 2005): 515–32, 522–27, 530 (describing signing statements by George W. Bush as representing "nothing less than a set of audacious claims to constitutional authority").

29. Charlie Savage, "Bush Could Bypass New Torture Ban," *Boston Globe*, January 4, 2006. The statute can be found at 42 U.S.C. § 2000dd.

30. Sources for this and the preceding paragraph include Heidi Kitrosser, "Secrecy and Separated Powers: Executive Privilege Revisited," *Iowa Law Review* 92 (February

2007): 489–543; Gia B. Lee, "The President's Secrets," *George Washington Law Review* 76 (February 2008): 197–261; Mark J. Rozell, "Executive Privilege Revived? Secrecy and Conflict during the Bush Presidency," *Duke Law Journal* 52 (November 2002): 403–21, 405 (observing that "most of President Clinton's uses of executive privilege were indefensible because he asserted this power in circumstances that were far beyond widely accepted norms"); Adam M. Samaha, "Government Secrets, Constitutional Law, and Platforms for Judicial Intervention," *UCLA Law Review* 53 (April 2006): 909–76; Presidential Memorandum on the Freedom of Information Act, 74 Fed. Reg. 4683 (January 26, 2009); Presidential Memorandum on Transparency and Open Government, 74 Fed. Reg. 4685 (January 26, 2009); Peter Nicholas, "Health Executives' Visits Disclosed," *Los Angeles Times*, July 23, 2009; Eric Lichtblau, "Across from White House, Coffee with Lobbyists," *New York Times*, June 25, 2010; Tim Dickinson, "The Spill, the Scandal and the President," *Rolling Stone*, June 8, 2010, http://www.rollingstone.com/politics/news/17390/111965?RS_show_page=0 (accessed November 8, 2012); Jeremy W. Peters, "Efforts to Limit the Flow of Spill News," *New York Times*, June 10, 2010.

When advocacy groups filed Freedom of Information Act requests to find out who attended Cheney's energy meetings, the courts rejected a duty of disclosure for the government. In re Cheney, 406 F.3d 723 (D.C. Cir. 2005). For a developed discussion of the role of executive privilege, see Mark J. Rozell, *Executive Privilege: Presidential Power, Secrecy, and Accountability*, 2nd ed. (Lawrence: University Press of Kansas, 2002).

31. Shane, *Madison's Nightmare, supra* note 16, 18–19.

32. Marlyn Aycock, Mercer Cross, and Elder Witt, *Watergate: Chronology of a Crisis* (Washington, DC: Congressional Quarterly, 1975), 3; Fred H. Altshuler, "Comparing the Nixon and Clinton Impeachments," *Hastings Law Journal* 51 (April 2000): 745–52, 751; Laurence H. Tribe, *American Constitutional Law*, vol. 1, 3rd ed. (New York: Foundation, 2000), 179–81; Frank O. Bowman III and Stephen L. Sepinuck, "'High Crimes & Misdemeanors': Defining the Constitutional Limits on Presidential Impeachment," *Southern California Law Review* 72 (September 1999): 1517–98, 1531; Chemerinsky, *Constitutional Law, supra* note 23, 362–63.

33. Steven G. Calabresi and Kevin H. Rhodes, "The Structural Constitution: Unitary Executive, Plural Judiciary," *Harvard Law Review* 105 (April 1992): 1153–1216, 1215–16; Calabresi and Yoo, *Unitary Executive, supra* note 16, 3–4; Lawson, "Rise and Rise of the Administrative State," *supra* note 10, 1242–46; Lee S. Liberman, "*Morrison v. Olson*: A Formalistic Perspective on Why the Court Was Wrong," *American University Law Review* 38 (Winter 1989): 313–58, 316–17. For contrary views, see Lawrence Lessig and Cass R. Sunstein, "The President and the Administration," *Columbia Law Review* 94 (January 1994): 1–119; Percival, "Presidential Management of the Administrative State," *supra* note 16, 976–80; Peter L. Strauss, "The Place of Agencies in Government: Separation of Powers and the Fourth Branch," *Columbia Law Review* 84 (April 1984): 573–669, 649.

34. For examples of Congress insulating commissions or boards from presidential control by giving their officials fixed terms that overlap presidential administrations, see 15 U.S.C. § 41 (establishing seven-year terms for commissioners of the Federal Trade Commission); 12 U.S.C. § 241 (establishing fourteen-year terms for governors of the Federal Reserve). The Supreme Court has upheld this congressional authority. Humphrey's Executor v. United States, 295 U.S. 602 (1935).

For agency heads who can be fired by the president, Congress has insulated them from presidential control by assigning to them rather than the president the authority to implement various laws, including the statute that governs the food stamps program. 7 U.S.C. § 2013(c). As discussed earlier, recent presidents have curtailed this independence through review of proposed regulations by the Office of Management and Budget.

While presidents can fire or apply other pressure to agency heads who buck presidential preferences, many scholars believe that presidents cannot "dictate the substance of regulatory decisions that agencies are required by law to make." Percival, "Presidential Management of the Administrative State," *supra* note 16, 965–66. To a limited extent, the Supreme Court has upheld the ability of Congress to rest decision-making authority with agency heads. Kendall v. United States, 37 U.S. 524, 610 (1837) (upholding the postmaster general's authority to pay money that Congress had ordered to be paid over the objections of the president and distinguishing between ministerial duties imposed by Congress, which are not subject to the direction of the president, and political duties of an agency official, which are subject to presidential control).

35. David Orentlicher, "Conflicts of Interest and the Constitution," *Washington and Lee Law Review* 59 (Summer 2002): 713–66, 734.

36. Louis Henkin, *Foreign Affairs and the United States Constitution*, 2nd ed. (New York: Oxford University Press, 1996), 31; Harold H. Koh, "Why the President Almost Always Wins in Foreign Affairs," in *The Constitution and the Conduct of American Foreign Policy*, ed. David Gray Adler and Larry N. George, 158–80 (Lawrence: University Press of Kansas, 1996), 159; Charles A. Lofgren, "*United States v. Curtiss-Wright Export Corporation*: A Historical Reassessment," *Yale Law Journal* 83 (November 1973): 1–32, 30 ("commercial relations" quote).

37. Alexander Hamilton, "Federalist No. 69" ("The President is also to be authorized to receive ambassadors and other public ministers. This, though it has been a rich theme of declamation, is more a matter of dignity than of authority. It is a circumstance which will be without consequence in the administration of the government; and it was far more convenient that it should be arranged in this manner, than that there should be a necessity of convening the legislature, or one of its branches, upon every arrival of a foreign minister, though it were merely to take the place of a departed predecessor.")

38. Corwin, *President, Office and Power, supra* note 25, 177–84; Henkin, *Foreign Affairs, supra* note 36, 41; David Gray Adler, "Court, Constitution, and Foreign Affairs," in Adler and George, *Constitution and the Conduct of American Foreign Policy, supra* note 36, 25–26. In *Curtiss-Wright*, the Supreme Court wrote in dictum of the "very delicate, plenary and exclusive power of the President as the sole organ of the federal government in the field of international relations—a power which does not require as a basis for its exercise an act of Congress." United States v. Curtiss-Wright Export Corp., 299 U.S. 304, 320 (1936) (upholding an indictment for a conspiracy to sell arms to Bolivia on the basis of both legislative authorization and inherent executive power). See also ibid., 319; and Shane, *Madison's Nightmare, supra* note 16, 45–46 (both citing Chief Justice John Marshall's invocation of the president as sole organ in a speech to the House of Representatives in 1800 when he served as a member of Congress).

39. David Gray Adler, "The President's Recognition Power," in Adler and George,

Constitution and the Conduct of American Foreign Policy, supra note 36; Adler, "Court, Constitution, and Foreign Affairs," *supra* note 38, 27–38.

40. Terry M. Moe and William G. Howell, "The Presidential Power of Unilateral Action," *Journal of Law, Economics & Organization* 15 (April 1999): 132–79, 147; Brandice Canes-Wrone, William G. Howell, and David E. Lewis, "Toward a Broader Understanding of Presidential Power: A Reevaluation of the Two Presidencies Thesis," *Journal of Politics* 70 (January 2008): 1–16, 4–6.

41. Bradley and Flaherty, "Executive Power Essentialism," *supra* note 3, 554–59, 592–626, 684–86; Cooper, *By Order of the President, supra* note 21, 5–9; Henkin, *Foreign Affairs, supra* note 36, 39–40; David Gray Adler and Larry N. George, introduction to Adler and George, *Constitution and the Conduct of American Foreign Policy, supra* note 36, 3–4. In the *Steel Seizure* case, Justice Jackson wrote a concurring opinion that has been very influential among courts and scholars in understanding the balance of power between Congress and the president. Youngstown Sheet & Tube Co. v. Sawyer, 343 U.S. 579, 640–641 (1952) (Jackson, J., concurring).

The debate over the extent of the president's foreign affairs power centers on the meaning of the "vesting clause" in Article II of the Constitution. According to Article II, "The executive Power shall be vested in a President of the United States of America." U.S. Const., art. II, § 1, cl. 1. According to a minority view, the "executive Power" referred to a commonly understood bundle of powers that belonged to the executive of a country, including foreign affairs powers, and the framers adopted that understanding, albeit with some qualification. Specifically, the framers denied some of the generally understood powers of the executive when they allocated those powers to Congress or the Senate. Thus, for example, Congress has the power to declare war, and the Senate has the power to ratify treaties. But absent a specific grant of power to a person or institution other than the executive branch, the executive branch has all of the government's power to make policy in foreign affairs. Saikrishna B. Prakash and Michael D. Ramsey, "The Executive Power over Foreign Affairs," *Yale Law Journal* 111 (November 2001): 231–356, 252–54; Ramsey, *Constitution's Text, supra* note 4, 54–73.

The vesting clause view has been sharply criticized. In the predominant view, the purpose of the vesting clause serves not as a vehicle for granting broad power to the executive branch but as a declaration that the power to execute the law belongs to a single person. Lessig and Sunstein, "President and the Administration," *supra* note 33, 47–48 n.195. The drafters debated whether to have a single or plural executive, and Article I, Section 1, was designed in large part to indicate that the debate was resolved in favor of a single executive. In other words, the vesting clause should be read as, "The executive Power shall be vested in *a* President of the United States. Edward S. Corwin, "The Steel Seizure Case: A Judicial Brick without Straw," *Columbia Law Review* 53 (January 1953): 53–66, 53. In this view, any executive powers beyond the execution of laws passed by Congress are listed in Article II, Section 2. For example, Article II, Section 2, makes the president commander in chief of the armed forces. As proponents of this view observe, the Constitution created a government of limited, enumerated powers, and it would be odd for the framers to mean something by the "executive Power" more than the power to execute laws passed by Congress.

42. "Records of the Federal Convention," in *The Founders' Constitution*, ed. Philip B. Kurland and Ralph Lerner (Chicago: University of Chicago Press, 1987), vol. 3, 491

(Wilson quote); Bradley and Flaherty, "Executive Power," *supra* note 3, 602. Wilson also cited an executive power to appoint government officials. "Records of the Federal Convention," *supra*.

43. John Hart Ely, *War and Responsibility: Constitutional Lessons of Vietnam and Its Aftermath* (Princeton: Princeton University Press, 1993), 10–11; Louis Fisher, *Presidential War Power* (Lawrence: University Press of Kansas, 1995), 84–87; John C. Yoo, "The Continuation of Politics by Other Means: The Original Understanding of War Powers," *California Law Review* 84 (March 1996): 167–305, 178–79; David Gray Adler, "Clinton, the Constitution, and the War Power," in Adler and Genovese, *Presidency and the Law, supra* note 20, 19, 33–35, 41–43; Jack L. Goldsmith, *The Terror Presidency: Law and Judgment inside the Bush Administration* (New York: Norton, 2007), 37; Charlie Savage, *Takeover: The Return of the Imperial Presidency and the Subversion of American Democracy* (New York: Little, Brown, 2007), 65–67; Frederick A. O. Schwarz and Aziz Z. Huq, *Unchecked and Unbalanced: Presidential Power in a Time of Terror* (New York: New Press, 2007), 161; Louis Fisher, "Parsing the War Power," *National Law Journal*, July 4, 2011, 50.

Scholars disagree whether the Gulf of Tonkin Resolution constituted a declaration of war for the Vietnam War. For an argument that it did, see Ely, *War and Responsibility, supra*, 15–26.

One might argue that the requirement of a congressional declaration of war is satisfied when Congress approves funding for a military mission. Yoo, "Continuation of Politics," *supra*, 174, 279–304. However, the Constitution contemplates prior authorization. Moreover, Congress may feel constrained in its options once the president has committed troops abroad. Even in cases in which Congress would not have authorized the fighting, it may not want to undercut the president once action has been taken. Indeed, in the War Powers Resolution, Congress explicitly stated that appropriations to fund military operations do not constitute an authorization of those operations. 50 U.S.C. § 1547(a)(1); Goldsmith, *Terror Presidency, supra*, 37 n.24.

44. Schlesinger, *Imperial Presidency, supra* note 8, 3–5; Ely, *War and Responsibility, supra* note 43, 3–4; Louis Fisher, "Unchecked Presidential Wars," *University of Pennsylvania Law Review* 148 (May 2000): 1637–72, 1647–48.

45. Fisher, "Unchecked Presidential Wars," *supra* note 44, 1647; Ely, *War and Responsibility, supra* note 43, 3, 5. Congress has the power to declare (rather than to make) war also to avoid the problem of congressional interference with the president's duties as commander in chief. Ely, *War and Responsibility, supra* note 43, 5. For a view that the Constitution leaves room for presidential authorization of force in military operations short of war, see Kenneth B. Moss, *Undeclared War and the Future of U.S. Foreign Policy* (Washington, DC: Woodrow Wilson International Center for Scholars, 2008), 2–3. For a stronger view of presidential authority to initiate war, see Yoo, "Continuation of Politics," *supra* note 43.

46. Goldsmith, *Terror Presidency, supra* note 43, 10, 85–90. See also Dawn E. Johnsen, "What's a President to Do? Interpreting the Constitution in the Wake of Bush Administration Abuses," *Boston University Law Review* 88 (April 2008): 395–419, 398–99, 403–6 (criticizing Bush's use of executive privilege, signing statements, and warrantless wiretaps and his authorization of torture); Robert D. Sloane, "The Scope of Executive Power in the Twenty-First Century: An Introduction," *Boston University*

Law Review 88 (April 2008): 341–51, 347 (discussing Bush's assertion of an expansive executive privilege, disregard of treaty obligations, detention of terror suspects without charges or access to an attorney, and approval of warrantless wiretapping). For an argument defending the policy of warrantless wiretaps, see Gary Lawson, "What Lurks Beneath: NSA Surveillance and Executive Power," *Boston University Law Review* 88 (April 2008): 375–93.

In discussing the infamous "torture memos" that blessed the administration's excessive interrogation techniques, Goldsmith observed that the Office of Legal Counsel's (OLC's) broad rejection of congressional authority to regulate U.S. interrogation practices had "no foundation in prior OLC opinions, or in judicial decisions, or in *any other source of law*." Goldsmith, *Terror Presidency, supra* note 43, 148–49 (emphasis added). See also Schwarz and Huq, *Unchecked and Unbalanced, supra* note 43, 65–81. Goldsmith withdrew the opinions so they could be replaced by appropriate analyses of the lawfulness of aggressive interrogation techniques. Goldsmith, *Terror Presidency, supra* note 43, 144–58.

47. Goldsmith, *Terror Presidency, supra* note 43, 82. While the Supreme Court upheld FDR's executive order authorizing the internment of Japanese Americans in *Korematsu v. United States*, 323 U.S. 214 (1944), experts in constitutional law reject the Court's reasoning. In 1988, Congress issued a formal apology and in 1989 authorized reparations for the internments. For discussion of FDR's thinking, see Greg Robinson, *By Order of the President: FDR and the Internment of Japanese Americans* (Cambridge: Harvard University Press, 2001).

48. Oona A. Hathaway, "Presidential Power over International Law: Restoring the Balance," *Yale Law Journal* 119 (November 2009): 140–268, 173–80. See also Dames & Moore v. Regan, 453 U.S. 654, 679–82 (1981).

49. Bruce A. Ackerman and David Golove, *Is NAFTA Constitutional?* (Cambridge: Harvard University Press, 1995), 13–37, 61–100. Even with approval by majorities in the House and Senate, these agreements do not satisfy the Constitution's requirements for treaties with other countries. Under the Constitution, treaties require a two-thirds majority of senators present at the time of the vote. U.S. Const. art. II, § 2, cl. 2. To be sure, there is support for the view that the framers left room for unilateral action by presidents in reaching some agreements with foreign governments, that they reserved a role for Congress only for major agreements. Moe and Howell, "Presidential Power," *supra* note 40, 137. See also Ramsey, *Constitution's Text, supra* note 4, 179–93. But until the early 1900s, constitutional experts generally agreed that presidential authority to enter into international agreements without Senate approval was greatly limited, and presidents exercised their unilateral authority sparingly. Hathaway, "Presidential Power," *supra* note 48, 171–73.

50. Hathaway, "Presidential Power," *supra* note 48, 144–45, 154–55, 165–66; 22 U.S.C. § 2311(a); 22 U.S.C. § 2753; 22 U.S.C. § 2151t; 22 U.S.C. § 2776(b); Richard F. Grimmett, *Arm Sales: Congressional Review Process* (Washington, DC: Congressional Research Service, February 1, 2012). See also Moe and Howell, "Presidential Power," *supra* note 40, 163–65.

51. Posner and Vermeule, *Executive Unbound, supra* note 3, 26–27.

52. Gordon Silverstein, *Imbalance of Powers: Constitutional Interpretation and the Making of American Foreign Policy* (New York: Oxford University Press, 1997), 195–96.

53. Sloane, "Scope of Executive Power," *supra* note 46, 349–51 (describing the profound influence of foreign policy decisions by the president on foreign policy decisions by other countries). In some ways, the U.S. president is less powerful than a prime minister in a parliamentary government. Prime ministers can rely on their legislative majorities to enact their policy agendas, while U.S. presidents may face a Congress in which the opposition party controls either or both the House and the Senate. As a result, the president's freedom on foreign policy is greater than on domestic policy. Still, the ability of presidents to act unilaterally through administrative agency rule making and executive orders can compensate for legislative obstruction.

54. Flaherty, "Most Dangerous Branch," *supra* note 3, 1727; Benjamin A. Kleinerman, *The Discretionary President: The Promise and Peril of Executive Power* (Lawrence: University Press of Kansas, 2009), 218; Harold H. Koh, *The National Security Constitution: Sharing Power after the Iran-Contra Affair* (New Haven: Yale University Press, 1990): 134–49; William P. Marshall, "Break Up the Presidency? Governors, State Attorneys General, and Lessons from the Divided Executive," *Yale Law Journal* 115, no. 9 (2006): 2446–79, 2470.

55. Ely, *War and Responsibility*, *supra* note 43, ix (observing that Congress was not eager to assume responsibility for military operations during the Cold War with the Soviet Union); Daryl L. Levinson and Richard H. Pildes, "Separation of Parties, Not Powers," *Harvard Law Review* 119 (June 2006): 2311–86, 2351–52 (discussing congressional passivity in the wake of the September 11, 2001, attacks); Sanford Levinson, *Our Undemocratic Constitution: Where the Constitution Goes Wrong (and How We the People Can Correct It)* (New York: Oxford University Press, 2006), 108–9 (discussing the failure of Congress to constrain the president, especially on matters of foreign policy); 2001 Authorization for Use of Military Force, Pub. L. No. 107-40, 115 Stat. 224 (2001); John E. Owens, "Presidential Power and Congressional Acquiescence in the 'War' on Terrorism: A New Constitutional Equilibrium?," *Politics & Policy* 34 (June 2006): 258–303; Neal Kumar Katyal, "Internal Separation of Powers: Checking Today's Most Dangerous Branch from Within," *Yale Law Journal* 115, no. 9 (2006): 2314–49, 2319–20.

At times, Congress has cabined the commander in chief discretion of the president. Jules Lobel, "Conflicts between the Commander in Chief and Congress: Concurrent Power over the Conduct of War," *Ohio State Law Journal* 69, no. 3 (2008): 391–467, 456–60. See also David J. Barron and Martin S. Lederman, "The Commander in Chief at the Lowest Ebb—A Constitutional History," *Harvard Law Review* 121 (February 2008): 941–1112.

56. Stone et al., *Constitutional Law*, *supra* note 10, 395, 438; Tribe, *American Constitutional Law*, *supra* note 32, 662, 668. Yoo, "Continuation of Politics," *supra* note 43, 180–82; John C. Yoo, "Kosovo, War Powers, and the Multilateral Failure," *University of Pennsylvania Law Review* 148 (May 2000): 1673–1731, 1677–79; Bruce Ackerman, "Legal Acrobatics, Illegal War," *New York Times*, June 21, 2011; Michael A. Fitts, "The Legalization of the Presidency: A Twenty-Five Year Watergate Retrospective," *St. Louis University Law Journal* 43 (Summer 1999): 725–40, 726; Morrison v. Olson, 487 U.S. 654 (1988); Moe and Howell, "Presidential Power," *supra* note 40, 168–69.

57. Stone et al., *Constitutional Law*, *supra* note 10, 412–15.

58. Mora v. McNamara, 389 U.S. 934 (1967) (declining to consider a challenge

to the constitutionality of the Vietnam War); Campbell v. Clinton, 203 F.3d 19 (D.C. Cir. 2000) (rebuffing a challenge to President Clinton's bombing of Serbia that was brought by thirty-one members of Congress); United States v. Bolton, 192 F.2d 805, 806 (2nd Cir. 1951) (finding a challenge to the constitutionality of the Korean War as lacking ripeness because the defendant had not refused induction into military duty and it was not clear that he would be sent to Korea even if he did report for duty); Luftig v. McNamara, 373 F.2d 664 (D.C. Cir. 1967) (blocking challenge to the legality of the Vietnam War); Goldwater v. Carter, 444 U.S. 996 (1979); Adler, "Court, Constitution, and Foreign Affairs," *supra* note 38, 35–36.

59. United States v. Curtiss-Wright Corp., 299 U.S. 304 (1936); United States v. Belmont, 301 U.S. 324 (1937); United States v. Pink, 315 U.S. 203 (1942) (as in *Belmont*, involving an agreement between the Soviet Union and the United States to settle claims that resulted from the nationalization of private property by the Soviet Union). Even before the Supreme Court's decisions in *Belmont* and *Pink*, presidents had taken unilateral action to recognize foreign governments, though Congress at times played a collaborative role. Corwin, *President, Office and Powers, supra* note 25, 184–90.

60. Youngstown Sheet & Tube Co. v. Sawyer, 343 U.S. 579 (1952); Hamdan v. Rumsfeld, 548 U.S. 557 (2006) (finding to be illegal the military tribunals created for noncitizens charged with supporting al-Qaeda); Hamdi v. Rumsfeld, 542 U.S. 507 (2004) (holding that U.S. citizens must be given a meaningful opportunity to challenge their detention as enemy combatants); Korematsu v. United States, 323 U.S. 214 (1944) (upholding the World War II internment of U.S. citizens of Japanese descent); Ex parte Quirin, 317 U.S. 1 (1942).

But note that a federal court of appeals limited the reach of the Supreme Court decisions in *Hamdan* and *Hamdi* when it held that enemy combatants are not entitled to habeas corpus relief when they are detained in an active theater of war in a location that is not under the *de jure* or *de facto* control of the U.S. government. Maqaleh v. Gates, 605 F.3d 84 (D.C. Cir. 2010).

The Supreme Court also has sometimes checked presidential power on domestic matters. See United States v. Nixon, 418 U.S. 683, 711–13 (1974) (rejecting President Nixon's assertion of executive privilege to withhold evidence from a criminal trial).

61. Posner and Vermeule, *Executive Unbound, supra* note 3, 35–37; Stephen I. Vladeck, "The Passive-Aggressive Virtues," *Columbia Law Review Sidebar* 111 (October 20, 2001): 122–41, 125.

62. Posner and Vermeule, *Executive Unbound, supra* note 3, 31.

63. William E. Scheuerman, *Liberal Democracy and the Social Acceleration of Time* (Baltimore: Johns Hopkins University Press, 2004), 45–46.

64. 26 U.S.C. § 163(a), (h)(1), (h)(2)(3); Fleishman and Aufses, "Law and Orders," *supra* note 20, 32; Schoenbrod, *Power without Responsibility, supra* note 11, 17.

Congress is able to draft tax laws with much greater specificity than many other laws because it created the Joint Committee on Taxation, a "nonpartisan committee of the United States Congress . . . [that] operates with an experienced professional staff of Ph.D. economists, attorneys, and accountants." Joint Committee on Taxation, "Overview," http://www.jct.gov/about-us/overview.html (accessed November 8, 2012).

To be sure, the executive branch plays a detail-filling role even with tax law. Congress enacted a deduction for home-mortgage interest, but the Department of

Treasury decided that a boat could count as a person's "residence" for purposes of claiming the deduction. 52 Fed. Reg. 48413 (December 22, 1987). Nevertheless, the example of tax law demonstrates that Congress can reserve much more policy-making authority than it has reserved. Other areas in which Congress writes its statutes with precision include the laws that determine the level of Social Security benefits and the amount of the minimum wage. David Epstein and Sharyn O'Halloran, *Delegating Powers: A Transaction Cost Politics Approach to Policy Making under Separate Powers* (New York: Cambridge University Press, 1999), 7.

Or Congress could require administrative agencies to submit major proposed rules to it for approval and then submission to the president for signature. And to deal with time constraints, Congress could provide for an up-or-down vote on the rules without any amendments. Indeed, in the United Kingdom, some regulations, mostly those increasing taxes or other fees, are not valid until approved by Parliament. William Wade and Christopher Forsyth, *Administrative Law*, 10th ed. (Oxford: Oxford University Press, 2009), 765–66.

65. Levinson and Pildes, "Separation of Parties," *supra* note 55, 2357; Daryl J. Levinson, "Empire-Building Government in Constitutional Law," *Harvard Law Review* 118 (January 2005): 915–72, 953–54 (citing Aranson et al., "Theory of Legislative Delegation," *supra* note 23, 55–62, and Epstein and O'Halloran, *Delegating Powers, supra* note 64, 29–33); Schoenbrod, *Power without Responsibility, supra* note 11, 10; Fleishman and Aufses, "Law and Orders," *supra* note 20, 34–35; Leslie Kaufman, "Stung by the President on Air Quality, Environmentalists Weigh Their Options," *New York Times*, September 4, 2011 (reporting on anger by environmentalists when Obama withdrew a proposed rule for reducing smog).

66. Epstein and O'Halloran, *Delegating Powers, supra* note 64, 8–9.

67. Calabresi and Yoo, *Unitary Executive, supra* note 16, 12; Epstein and O'Halloran, *Delegating Powers, supra* note 64, 25. The decision in *Chadha* can be found at 462 U.S. 919 (1983).

As Peter Shane observes, the legislative veto had its disadvantages. In particular, if an agency action could be vetoed by some members of Congress, there was considerable uncertainty about the stability of the action. Shane, *Madison's Nightmare, supra* note 16, 134–35.

68. I am grateful to Mark Graber for the point that policy making should be reserved for multiperson bodies, a point also articulated in Matthew Soberg Shugart and John M. Carey, *Presidents and Assemblies: Constitutional Design and Electoral Dynamics* (Cambridge: Cambridge University Press, 1992), 95. For the quote from Wilson, see Woodrow Wilson, *The New Freedom: A Call for the Emancipation of the Generous Energies of a People* (Englewood Cliffs, NJ: Prentice-Hall, 1961), 72.

69. Scheuerman, *Liberal Democracy, supra* note 63, 39–41.

70. John M. Broder and Michael Luo, "Well-Known Problems of Drilling Agency Still Avoided Fixes," *New York Times*, May 31, 2010.

71. William R. Andersen, *Mastering Administrative Law* (Durham: Carolina Academic Press, 2010), 27–29; John M. Broder, "E.P.A. Sets Poison Standards for Power Plants," *New York Times*, December 22, 2011; Schoenbrod, *Power without Responsibility, supra* note 11, 12.

Delays in issuing rules reflect multiple factors. For example, agencies may be understaffed, or executive branch officials may not want to write the rules. Robert Pear, "U.S. Laws Delayed by Complex Rules and Partisanship," *New York Times*, March 31, 1991.

72. Scheuerman, *Liberal Democracy, supra* note 63, 41.

73. Elisabeth Bumiller, "Candidates' Reactions to Georgia Conflict Offer Hints at Style on Foreign Affairs," *New York Times*, August 10, 2008; Ellen Barry, "War Report Finds Fault with Russia and Georgia," *New York Times*, January 24, 2009; Steven Lee Myers, "Clinton Suggests Tie by Qaeda Arm to Libyan Attack," *New York Times*, September 27, 2012; Maureen Dowd, "Complicity in Duplicity?," *New York Times*, October 3, 2012.

74. To be sure, some policy making in the executive branch occurs through a process with multiple decision makers. In contrast to administrative agencies headed by a single cabinet secretary who serves at the pleasure of the president, independent agencies in the executive branch are led by multiple decision makers who serve terms of a fixed length and who cannot be removed from office by the president. For example, the Federal Reserve has seven governors who serve fourteen-year terms, and the Federal Trade Commission has five commissioners who serve seven-year terms. With these independent agencies, we might expect policy making to reflect a deliberative process among persons of diverse perspectives.

However, independent agency decision making is driven largely by presidential preference. Of course, there are barriers to presidential control of the independent agencies. In addition to the fact that the terms of commissioners may carry over from one presidential administration to another, partisan polarization has made it more difficult for presidents to obtain Senate approval of their commission appointees. In addition, some agencies must have commissioners from both parties, and opposition-party senators can force presidents to appoint party loyalists to the opposition-party commission slots. Still, the data indicate that presidents are able to staff independent agencies with a majority of commissioners who will promote the president's agenda. In a key study, researchers considered presidential appointments to eleven different independent agencies (not including the Federal Reserve) from the presidency of Warren Harding in 1921–1923 through the presidency of George W. Bush in 2001–2008. With the exception of one agency for one president, each president realized a majority of party members for all eleven of the agencies. On average, it took nine to ten months to achieve a majority for an agency, with the time to majority lengthening as Congress became more partisan. But even for Bill Clinton and George W. Bush, majorities were gained on the eleven agencies within an average of twenty months. Moreover, partisan polarization has meant that presidential appointees from the president's party have become reliable supporters of presidential policies. Neal Devins and David E. Lewis, "Not-So-Independent Agencies," *Boston University Law Review* 88 (April 2008): 459–98, 469–73 and n.56, 492–97; Posner and Vermeule, *Executive Unbound, supra* note 3, 6.

75. Posner and Vermeule, *Executive Unbound, supra* note 3, 43–44.

76. The deliberative process between two co-presidents would be superior to the deliberative process that often exists in the U.S. House of Representatives also because it would better respect different political perspectives. Because there is no filibuster rule in the House, the majority can shape policy without the participation of the minority. Barbara Sinclair, *Party Wars: Polarization and the Politics of National Policy*

Making (Norman: University of Oklahoma Press, 2006), 351–53. In a two-person, two-party presidency, both parties would participate equally in the shaping of executive policy.

77. Youngstown Sheet & Tube Co. v. Sawyer, 343 U.S. 579, 637 (1952) (Jackson, J., concurring).

78. Donald Oken, "What to Tell Cancer Patients: A Study of Medical Attitudes," *Journal of the American Medical Association* 175 (April 1, 1961): 1120–28, 1121; David Leonhardt, "Forget Who Pays Medical Bills, It's Who Sets the Cost," *New York Times*, July 26, 2009; David Orentlicher, "Paying Physicians More to Do Less: Financial Incentives to Limit Care," *University of Richmond Law Review* 30 (January 1996): 155–97, 158; Jaime S. King and Benjamin W. Moulton, "Rethinking Informed Consent: The Case for Shared Medical Decision-Making," *American Journal of Law and Medicine* 32, no. 4 (2006): 429–501, 472–73.

79. Finer, *Presidency*, *supra* note 2, 32.

80. Schlesinger, *Imperial Presidency*, *supra* note 8, 382–86, 389–92, 409–11, 491–92.

81. Goldsmith, *Terror Presidency*, *supra* note 43, 216; Schwarz and Huq, *Unchecked and Unbalanced*, *supra* note 43, 203–07; Shane, *Madison's Nightmare*, *supra* note 16, 186–95. Shane also has proposed structural reforms, such as removing barriers to voting, eliminating partisan redistricting, reducing corporate influence in politics, and reducing media costs for candidates. Ibid., 195–202. His proposals are all valuable, but their impact on the imperial presidency may not be very substantial.

82. Levinson, "Empire-Building Government," *supra* note 65, 953–55. See also Moe and Howell, "Presidential Power," *supra* note 40, 144.

83. Posner and Vermeule, *Executive Unbound*, *supra* note 3, 23–25; Levinson and Pildes, "Separation of Parties," *supra* note 55, 2341, 2357–58 (citing Epstein and O'Halloran, *Delegating Powers*, *supra* note 64, 154–60); William G. Howell and Jon C. Pevehouse, *While Dangers Gather: Congressional Checks on Presidential War Powers* (Princeton: Princeton University Press, 2007), 75–113. For discussion of additional, collective-action problems that discourage checking and balancing by Congress and the Supreme Court, see Posner and Vermeule, *Executive Unbound*, *supra* note 3, 20–23. See also Mayer, *With the Stroke of a Pen*, *supra* note 20, 30–31.

84. Terry M. Moe, "Presidents, Institutions, and Theory," in *Researching the Presidency: Vital Questions, New Approaches*, ed. George C. Edwards III, John H. Kessel, and Bert A. Rockman (Pittsburgh: University of Pittsburgh Press, 1993), 376.

85. Moe and Howell, "Presidential Power," *supra* note 40, 148–53; Kagan, "Presidential Administration," *supra* note 16, 2255–2309; People for the American Way, *The Record and Legal Philosophy of Samuel Alito: "No One to the Right of Sam Alito on This Court"* (Washington, DC: People for the American Way, January 2006), 20–25, http://media.pfaw.org/stc/alito-final.pdf (accessed November 8, 2012); Alliance for Justice, *Report on the Nomination of John G. Roberts to the United States Supreme Court* (Washington, DC: Alliance for Justice, 2005), 71–85, http://www.afj.org/afj_roberts_prehearing_report.pdf (accessed November 8, 2012).

86. Bruce Ackerman, "The Emergency Constitution," *Yale Law Journal* 113 (March 2004): 1029–91, 1047–49.

87. Katyal, "Internal Separation of Powers," *supra* note 55, 2323–42. For example, Katyal would strengthen the civil service by modeling it after the foreign service so

that the attractive job opportunities are not reserved heavily for short-term political appointees, and civil service workers enjoy real protection from reprisals if they express dissenting view. On the unwillingness of the Supreme Court to enforce consultation mandates, see Lujan v. Defenders of Wildlife, 504 U.S. 555 (1992).

88. Marshall, "Break Up the Presidency?," *supra* note 54; Christopher R. Berry and Jacob E. Gersen, "The Unbundled Executive." *University of Chicago Law Review* 75 (Fall 2008): 1385–1434. Marshall limits his proposal to an independent attorney general, while Berry and Gersen contemplate other independent executive branch officials.

89. Marshall, "Break Up the Presidency?," *supra* note 54, 2476; Berry and Gersen, "Unbundled Executive," *supra* note 88, 1393–94.

90. Posner and Vermeule, *Executive Unbound, supra* note 3, 25–31, 3–15, 113, 129–33 (quotes on 113 and 133).

91. Ibid., 16, 116–22 (citing Federalist 51). See also Levinson and Pildes, "Separation of Parties," *supra* note 55, 2319.

92. Posner and Vermeule, *Executive Unbound, supra* note 3, 176–87.

93. Ibid., 49.

94. Jide O. Nzelibe and Matthew C. Stephenson, "Complementary Constraints: Separation of Powers, Rational Voting and Constitutional Design," *Harvard Law Review* 123 (January 2010): 617–53, 625–26. Parents who dislike all the testing of their children at schools might place responsibility at the feet of school board or state officials rather than holding Congress accountable for enacting the No Child Left Behind statute that links federal funding for education to the use of student testing.

95. Ibid., 628–36.

96. Nancy L. Rosenblum, *On the Side of the Angels: An Appreciation of Parties and Partisanship* (Princeton: Princeton University Press, 2008), 120–21.

97. Levinson and Pildes, "Separation of Parties," *supra* note 55, 2314–16, 2368–75, 2384–85 (also proposing elimination of the single vote for a straight-ticket ballot to discourage straight-ticket voting).

98. Amy Gutmann and Dennis Thompson, *The Spirit of Compromise: Why Governing Demands It and Campaigning Undermines It* (Princeton: Princeton University Press, 2012), 126–27.

99. Rosenblum, *On the Side of the Angels, supra* note 96, 8–9.

Notes to Chapter 4

1. Zachary A. Goldfarb, "U.S. Rating Downgraded for the First Time," *Washington Post*, August 6, 2011.

2. Richard Hofstadter, *The Idea of a Party System: The Rise of Legitimate Opposition in the United States, 1780–1840* (Berkeley: University of California Press, 1969), 9–29; Arthur M. Schlesinger, Jr., introduction to *History of U.S. Political Parties*, ed. Arthur M. Schlesinger, Jr., 5 vols. (New York: Chelsea House, 1973), 1:xxxiv. While Edmund Burke in England took the view that parties were overall a good institution, he lacked adherents in the United States until some time had passed after the adoption of the Constitution. Hofstadter, *Idea of a Party System, supra*, 29–35. The Madisonian view was elaborated in Federalist 10.

3. As Madison wrote in Federalist 51, "If men were angels, no government would be necessary." The text for each of the Federalist Papers can be found at the website of the Library of Congress, http://thomas.loc.gov/home/histdox/fedpapers.html. Although the Library of Congress attributes Federalist 51 to Madison or Alexander Hamilton, scholars commonly attribute it to Madison. See, e.g., Geoffrey R. Stone et al., *Constitutional Law*, 6th ed. (New York: Aspen, 2009), 22.

4. Jason M. Roberts and Steven S. Smith, "Procedural Contexts, Party Strategy, and Conditional Party Voting in the U.S. House of Representatives, 1971–2000," *American Journal of Political Science* 47 (April 2003): 305–17, 305; Neal Devins and David E. Lewis, "Not-So-Independent Agencies," *Boston University Law Review* 88 (April 2008): 459–98, 477, 493; Nolan M. McCarty, Keith T. Poole, and Howard Rosenthal, *Polarized America: The Dance of Ideology and Unequal Riches* (Cambridge: MIT Press, 2006), 3.

Researchers have calculated measures of partisanship dating back to the formation of the modern Democratic and Republican Parties in 1876, and the measures can be based on roll-call voting, as well as ratings of interest groups. McCarty et al., *Polarized America, supra*, 5, 8. Regardless of the measure used, there is a striking increase in partisanship. Mark D. Brewer, Mack D. Mariani, and Jeffrey M. Stonecash, "Northern Democrats and Party Polarization in the U.S. House," *Legislative Studies Quarterly* 27 (August 2002): 423–44, 423.

5. Nancy L. Rosenblum, *On the Side of the Angels: An Appreciation of Parties and Partisanship* (Princeton: Princeton University Press, 2008), 356–58.

6. Jonathan Oberlander, *The Political Life of Medicare* (Chicago: University of Chicago Press, 2003), 22, 29; Robert A. Caro, *The Years of Lyndon Johnson: The Passage of Power* (New York: Knopf, 2012), 452–54.

7. McCarty et al., *Polarized America, supra* note 4, 16, 23–32; Stanley B. Greenberg, *Middle Class Dreams: The Politics and Power of the New American Majority* (New York: Times Books, 1995), 23–38, 140–41.

8. Daryl L. Levinson and Richard H. Pildes, "Separation of Parties, Not Powers," *Harvard Law Review* 119 (June 2006): 2311–86, 2333; McCarty et al., *Polarized America, supra* note 4, 23–24, 49–50; Roberts and Smith, "Procedural Contexts," *supra* note 4, 306; Alan Abramowitz, *The Disappearing Center: Engaged Citizens, Polarization, and American Democracy* (New Haven: Yale University Press, 2010), 97–98; "SENATE_111 Rank Ordering," Voteview.com, http://voteview.com/sen111.htm (accessed November 8, 2012).

The *National Journal* has analyzed voting records for senators and representatives since 1981 and ranked the members of Congress in terms of how conservative or liberal they are. Typically, Republicans in the Senate fell in the conservative wing of the chamber and Democrats in the liberal wing, but there was a group of a dozen or more centrists that included Republicans and Democrats. For the first time in 1999, all of the Democrats had ratings that were more liberal than any of the Republicans. Richard Cohen, "A Congress Divided," *National Journal* 32 (February 5, 2000): 382–404, 382. See also McCarty et al., *Polarized America, supra* note 4, 30–31 (finding only one Democratic senator to the right of the most liberal Republican during the 1990s).

9. Gerald F. Seib, "Enduring Partisan Divide Stokes Skepticism of Washington," *Wall Street Journal*, November 1, 2009; Levinson and Pildes, "Separation of Parties,"

supra note 8, 2324; James Q. Wilson and John J. DiIulio, *American Government: Institutions and Policies*, 11th ed. (Boston: Houghton Mifflin, 2008), 337. Another measure of party-line voting in Congress shows a similar increase. The number of votes in which a majority of Democrats opposed a majority of Republicans rose from 40 percent in the early 1970s to 70 percent in 1995. Levinson and Pildes, "Separation of Parties," *supra* note 8, 2333 n.83.

10. William P. Marshall, "Eleven Reasons Why Presidential Power Inevitably Expands and Why It Matters," *Boston University Law Review* 88 (April 2008): 505–22, 518–19; Jim Rutenberg and Marjorie Connelly, "Polls Show Obama Gaining among Bush Voters," *New York Times*, October 24, 2008 (reporting approval rating of 22 percent for President Bush just two weeks before Election Day). See also Levinson and Pildes, "Separation of Parties," *supra* note 8, 2323–25 (observing that the "electoral and policy interests of politicians have become intimately connected to political parties"). Democrats regained majorities in the House and Senate in 2006, while Republicans reclaimed control of the House and became a more substantial minority in the Senate in 2010.

11. In the 2007–2008 Congress, there were fifty-one successful filibusters. Jean Edward Smith, "Filibusters: The Senate's Self-Inflicted Wound," *100 Days* (blog), *New York Times*, March 1, 2009, http://100days.blogs.nytimes.com/2009/03/01/filibusters-the-senates-self-inflicted-wound (accessed November 8, 2012). Forty-one senators can block legislation today merely by threatening a filibuster. David E. RePass, "Make My Filibuster," *New York Times*, March 2, 2009. For an important discussion of the filibuster and its greatly increased use in recent decades, see Catherine Fisk and Erwin Chemerinsky, "The Filibuster," *Stanford Law Review* 49 (January 1997): 181–254.

Other sources for this paragraph include Devins and Lewis, "Not-So-Independent Agencies," *supra* note 4, 488–91; Richard H. Pildes, "Why the Center Does Not Hold: The Causes of Hyperpolarized Democracy in America," *California Law Review* 99 (April 2011): 273–333, 281–84, 320–21; Sheryl Gay Stolberg, "A Defining Moment Nears for President," *New York Times*, July 22, 2009; Wilson and DiIulio, *American Government*, *supra* note 9, 336 (reporting that 98 percent of Republicans voted for at least one of the four articles of impeachment against Clinton, while 98 percent of the Democrats voted against all of the articles).

12. Adam Nagourney, "Partisan or Not, a Tough Course on Health Care," *New York Times*, July 26, 2009; David M. Herszenhorn, "Party Lines Barely Shift as Package Is Approved," *New York Times*, February 14, 2009; Robert Pear, "Senate Passes Health Care Overhaul on Party-Line Vote," *New York Times*, December 25, 2009; Robert Pear and David M. Herszenhorn, "Congress Sends White House Landmark Health Overhaul," *New York Times*, March 22, 2010.

One of the three senators who voted for the 2009 economic recovery bill—Arlen Specter—switched parties two months later. Carl Hulse and Adam Nagourney, "Specter Switches Parties: More Heft for Democrats," *New York Times*, April 29, 2009.

13. Jeffrey M. Jones, "Obama Ratings Historically Polarized," *Gallup Politics*, January 27, 2012, http://www.gallup.com/poll/152222/Obama-Ratings-Historically-Polarized.aspx (accessed November 8, 2012) (noting that the public became more polarized in year four of the George W. Bush administration); Sheryl Gay Stolberg, "Where Have You Gone, Joe the Citizen?," *New York Times*, August 9, 2009; Alan

Abramowitz, "Partisan Polarization and the Rise of the Tea Party Movement" (paper presented at the annual meeting of the American Political Science Association, Seattle, Washington, September 1–4, 2011), http://papers.ssrn.com/sol3/papers.cfm?abstract _id=1903153 (accessed November 8, 2012).

14. Sources for this and the preceding two paragraphs include Eric Foner, *Give Me Liberty! An American History*, 3rd ed. (New York: Norton, 2011), 295–301, 305–7; Samuel E. Morison, Henry S. Commager, and William E. Leuchtenburg, *The Growth of the American Republic*, 7th ed. (New York: Oxford University Press, 1980), vol. 1, 318 (quoting Thomas Jefferson).

15. Pildes, "Why the Center Does Not Hold," *supra* note 11, 287–95; Roberts and Smith, "Procedural Contexts," *supra* note 4, 306; Levinson and Pildes, "Separation of Parties," *supra* note 8, 2334–35; McCarty et al., *Polarized America*, *supra* note 4, 51–54; Byron E. Shafer and Richard Johnston, *End of Southern Exceptionalism: Class, Race, and Partisan Change in the Postwar South* (Cambridge: Harvard University Press, 2006), 4, 22–50.

16. Brewer et al., "Northern Democrats," *supra* note 4, 436–38. Thus, voters have not become more polarized in their positions on issues, but they have sorted themselves in a more polarized fashion when choosing their party affiliation. Morris P. Fiorina, Samuel J. Abrams, and Jeremy C. Pope, *Culture War? The Myth of a Polarized America*, 3rd ed. (Boston: Longman, 2011), 8–9.

17. Brewer et al., "Northern Democrats," *supra* note 4, 436; McCarty et al., *Polarized America*, *supra* note 4, 71–138. Income inequality has risen from a number of socioeconomic changes. The wealthy have become even wealthier from increased returns from their investment in education, sharp increases in corporate compensation, and more two-income households with fewer children. At the same time, the poor have become poorer because of declines in labor-union representation, competition from low-wage countries, and higher rates of divorce. McCarty et al., *Polarized America*, *supra* note 4, 166.

18. McCarty et al., *Polarized America*, *supra* note 4, 2–3, 12, 106–7. While the Democratic Party has become somewhat more liberal, the increase in polarization primarily reflects a shift to the right in the Republican Party. Ibid., 11.

19. Ibid., 2, 13.

20. Ibid., 3, 13–14.

21. Ibid., 166–69, 184–86; Jacob S. Hacker and Paul Pierson, *Winner-Take-All Politics: How Washington Made the Rich Richer—and Turned Its Back on the Middle Class* (New York: Simon and Schuster, 2010), 51–54. The health care legislation that passed in 2010 may result in important redistribution of income. David Leonhardt, "In Health Bill, Obama Attacks Wealth Inequality," *New York Times*, March 24, 2010.

22. McCarty et al., *Polarized America*, *supra* note 4, 22; Foner, *Give Me Liberty!*, *supra* note 14, 632–43, 656–58 (quote at 642); Dana D. Nelson, *Bad for Democracy: How the Presidency Undermines the Power of the People* (Minneapolis: University of Minnesota Press, 2008), 88.

23. Roberts and Smith, "Procedural Contexts," *supra* note 4, 307, 315; Thomas E. Mann and Norman J. Ornstein, *It's Even Worse than It Looks: How the American Constitutional System Collided with the New Politics of Extremism* (New York: Basic Books, 2012), 33–37. Other commonly suggested explanations do not seem to have played a

significant role. For example, partisan gerrymandering might explain polarization in the House of Representatives, but it would not explain the similar polarization in the Senate. McCarty et al., *Polarized America, supra* note 4, 64–65. It also does not appear that polarization can be explained by a greater participation of more ideological voters in party primaries. Ibid., 67–70. See also Pildes, "Why the Center Does Not Hold," *supra* note 11, 312–15.

24. Larry J. Sabato, "How the Campaign Season Got So Long," *Wall Street Journal*, October 11, 2011.

25. During my six years of service in the Indiana General Assembly, I saw the same phenomenon occur at the state level between governors and legislators. When a Republican governor, Mitch Daniels, identified the adoption of daylight saving time or the sale of a toll road as legislative priorities, many Democratic members of the Indiana House of Representatives opposed the governor, despite support in their districts for the proposals. And many Republican members of the Indiana House supported the governor, despite opposition in their districts to his proposals.

26. Leon D. Epstein, *Political Parties in the American Mold* (Madison: University of Wisconsin Press, 1986), 40, 82–83; David J. Samuels and Matthew S. Shugart, *Presidents, Parties, and Prime Ministers: How the Separation of Powers Affects Party Organization and Behavior* (New York: Cambridge University Press, 2010), 8; Morison et al., *Growth of the American Republic, supra* note 14, vol. 1, 416–18; Richard P. McCormick, *The Second American Party System: Party Formation in the Jacksonian Era* (Chapel Hill: University of North Carolina Press, 1966), 13, 342.

27. Epstein, *Political Parties, supra* note 26, 84–86.

28. Arend Lijphart, "Presidentialism and Majoritarian Democracy: Theoretical Observations," in *The Failure of Presidential Democracy*, ed. Juan J. Linz and Arturo Valenzuela (Baltimore: Johns Hopkins University Press, 1994), 97.

29. Juan J. Linz, "Presidential or Parliamentary Democracy: Does It Make a Difference?," in Linz and Valenzuela, *Failure of Presidential Democracy, supra* note 28, 19.

30. Epstein, *Political Parties, supra* note 26, 82.

31. Lijphart, "Presidentialism and Majoritarian Democracy," *supra* note 28, 98. Parliamentary systems are typically characterized by unified government—the majority party or coalition controls both the legislative and executive branches. Wilson and DiIulio, *American Government, supra* note 9, 315–17.

32. Hofstadter, *Idea of a Party System, supra* note 2, 40; Samuel Issacharoff and Richard H. Pildes, "Politics as Markets: Partisan Lockups of the Democratic Process," *Stanford Law Review* 50 (February 1998): 643–717, 713; Gerald Leonard, *The Invention of Party Politics: Federalism, Popular Sovereignty, and Constitutional Development in Jacksonian Illinois* (Chapel Hill: University of North Carolina Press, 2002), 18, 26–28; Ronald L. Nelson, "The U.S. Supreme Court and the Institutional Role of Political Parties in the Political Process: What Tradition?," *Widener Law Journal* 15 (2005): 85–108, 88–90; James L. Sundquist, "Needed: A Political Theory for the New Era of Coalition Government in the United States," *Political Science Quarterly* 103 (Winter 1989): 613–35, 614–15. To be sure, many of the founding fathers also became the founding fathers of political parties. Hofstadter, *Idea of a Party System, supra* note 2, 2; Lloyd N. Cutler, "Now Is the Time for All Good Men," *William and Mary Law Review* 30 (Winter 1989): 387–402, 389.

It is true that party influence and party activity have been higher in the past. Cutler, "Now Is the Time," *supra*, 392–93; Issacharoff and Pildes, "Politics as Markets," *supra*, 644. Nevertheless, the role of parties is still far greater today than the framers envisioned. Levinson and Pildes, "Separation of Parties," *supra* note 8, 2324–25.

33. Samuel Issacharoff, "Introduction: The Structures of Democratic Politics," *Columbia Law Review* 100 (April 2000): 593–97, 594 n.5; Donald P. Kommers, *The Constitutional Jurisprudence of the Federal Republic of Germany*, 2nd ed. (Durham: Duke University Press, 1997), 201–10.

34. Paul Frymer and Albert Yoon, "Political Parties, Representation, and Federal Safeguards," *Northwestern University Law Review* 96 (Spring 2002): 977–1026, 982; Robert Bejesky, "Undermining Egalitarian Principles of Federalism? A Cross-National Comparison of India, Mexico, and the United States," *Temple International and Comparative Law Journal* 14 (Fall 2000): 363–400, 369; Paul Frymer, *Uneasy Alliances: Race and Party Competition in America* (Princeton: Princeton University Press, 1999) ("parties" quote), 12; Nathaniel Persily, "Toward a Functional Defense of Political Party Autonomy," *New York University Law Review* 76 (June 2001): 750–824, 793; Rosenblum, *On the Side of the Angels*, *supra* note 5, 116–17, 126–36.

35. Hofstadter, *Idea of a Party System*, *supra* note 2, 2, 9 ("sores" quote and Jonathan Swift quote); James A. Gardner, "Can Party Politics Be Virtuous?," *Columbia Law Review* 100 (April 2000): 667–701, 667–68; Steven G. Calabresi, "Political Parties as Mediating Institutions," *University of Chicago Law Review* 61 (Fall 1994): 1479–1533, 1482–83; Levinson and Pildes, "Separation of Parties," *supra* note 8, 2320; George Washington, "Farewell Address," in *A Compilation of the Messages and Papers of the Presidents*, ed. James D. Richardson (New York: Bureau of National Literature, 1897), vol. 1, 211.

The framers' concerns echoed those of political theorists of the 18th Century who believed that political parties would promote special interests and social conflict rather than encouraging the civically virtuous pursuit of the common good. Hofstadter, *Idea of a Party System*, *supra* note 2, 12–13, 51–53; Schlesinger, introduction, *supra* note 2, xxxiv.

36. When the framers used the word "parties," they used the term to mean interest groups more broadly. Larry D. Kramer, "Putting the Politics Back into the Political Safeguards of Federalism," *Columbia Law Review* 100 (January 2000): 215–93, 269–70. Nevertheless, their concerns still apply with respect to political parties.

37. Cecelia M. Kenyon, "Men of Little Faith: The Anti-Federalists on the Nature of Representative Government," *William and Mary Quarterly* 12 (January 1955): 3–43, 40.

38. Hofstadter, *Idea of a Party System*, *supra* note 2, 11–12.

39. Ibid., 46–47.

40. Stone et al., *Constitutional Law*, *supra* note 3, 21; Levinson and Pildes, "Separation of Parties," *supra* note 8, 2319.

41. Samuels and Shugart, *Presidents*, *supra* note 26, 23.

42. David R. Mayhew, *Divided We Govern: Party Control, Lawmaking and Investigations, 1946–2002*, 2nd ed. (New Haven: Yale University Press, 2005), 4, 61, 210. The Supreme Court struck down the line-item veto in *Clinton v. City of New York*, 524 U.S. 417 (1998).

43. Keith Krehbiel, "Institutional and Partisan Sources of Gridlock: A Theory of Divided and Unified Government," *Journal of Theoretical Politics* 8 (January 1996): 7–40, 11; Keith Krehbiel, *Pivotal Politics: A Theory of U.S. Lawmaking* (Chicago: University of Chicago Press, 1998).

44. Sean Q. Kelly, "Divided We Govern: A Reassessment," *Polity* 25 (Spring 1993): 475–84; John J. Coleman, "United Government, Divided Government, and Party Responsiveness," *American Political Science Review* 93 (December 1999): 821–35, 827 (confirming Kelly's findings); John J. Coleman and David C. W. Parker, "The Consequences of Divided Government," in *The Oxford Handbook of the American Presidency*, ed. George C. Edwards III and William G. Howell (New York: Oxford University Press, 2009), 389–91; Sarah A. Binder, "The Dynamics of Legislative Gridlock, 1947–96," *American Political Science Review* 93 (September 1999): 519–33, 528. Binder also validated the framers' view that dividing power between a House and a Senate would weaken the legislative branch. Interbranch polarization increases legislative gridlock. Ibid., 528. See also George C. Edwards III, Andrew Barrett, and Jeffrey Peake, "The Legislative Impact of Divided Government," *American Journal of Political Science* 41 (April 1997): 545–63, 561–62 (finding that a smaller percentage of important initiatives passes during periods of divided government).

45. Coleman, "United Government," *supra* note 44, 822.

46. Ibid., 823–24, 829–32. Sometimes, intraparty factionalism can increase the likelihood that Congress and the president will enact important legislation during divided government. If a Republican president can work with congressional Republicans and conservative congressional Democrats, legislative success is more likely. Ibid., 831–32.

47. Levinson and Pildes, "Separation of Parties," *supra* note 8, 2340 ("vetoes" quote); William G. Howell and Jon C. Pevehouse, *While Dangers Gather: Congressional Checks on Presidential War Powers* (Princeton: Princeton University Press, 2007), 75–113.

48. Levinson and Pildes, "Separation of Parties," *supra* note 8, 2323–24.

49. In fact, it is not unusual to see presidents act unilaterally in presidential systems characterized by partisan gridlock. Matthew Soberg Shugart and John M. Carey, *Presidents and Assemblies: Constitutional Design and Electoral Dynamics* (Cambridge: Cambridge University Press, 1992), 35–36.

50. Economists generally agreed, however, that the law did prevent the unemployment rate from being even higher than it was.

51. Roy Pierce, "The Executive Divided against Itself: Cohabitation in France, 1986–1988," *Governance* 4 (July 1991): 270–94, 277.

52. Youngstown Sheet & Tube Co. v. Sawyer, 343 U.S. 579, 653 (1952) (Jackson, J., concurring); Shugart and Carey, *Presidents and Assemblies*, *supra* note 49, 31–32. See also David J. Samuels, "Presidentialized Parties: The Separation of Powers and Party Organization and Behavior," *Comparative Political Studies* 35 (May 2002): 461–83, 468–69. Thus, for example, when Israel changed its parliamentary system to provide for direct election of the prime minister, the major parties placed greater emphasis on winning the election for prime minister than on winning legislative seats in the parliament. Samuels, "Presidentialized Parties," *supra*, 475–78.

53. Shugart and Carey, *Presidents and Assemblies*, *supra* note 49, 31. See also Chris-

topher R. Berry, Barry C. Burden, and William G. Howell, "The President and the Distribution of Federal Spending," *American Political Science Review* 104 (November 2010): 783–99 (finding that presidents direct more federal spending to congressional districts held by members of their party); Sanford C. Gordon, "Politicizing Agency Spending Authority: Lessons from a Bush-Era Scandal," *American Political Science Review* 105 (November 2011): 717–34 (discussing the efforts by the administration of George W. Bush to direct federal spending to priority congressional districts for the Republican Party).

54. For a thoughtful discussion of other reforms in Congress to defuse partisan conflict, see Mickey Edwards, *The Parties versus the People: How to Turn Republicans and Democrats into Americans* (New Haven: Yale University Press, 2012), 91–145.

55. Sources for this and the preceding paragraphs include Mary T. Boatwright, Daniel J. Gargola, and Richard J. A. Talbert, *The Romans: From Village to Empire* (New York: Oxford University Press, 2004), 98; Fritz M. Heichelheim, Cedric A. Yeo, and Allen Mason Ward, *A History of the Roman People*, 2nd ed. (Englewood Cliffs, NJ: Prentice-Hall, 1984), 51–53; Eric Posner, "The Constitution of the Roman Republic: A Political Economy Perspective" (University of Chicago, Public Law & Legal Theory Working Paper, October 31, 2010), 7–8, 15, http://papers.ssrn.com/sol3/papers.cfm?abstract_id=1701981 (accessed November 8, 2012); Curtis A. Bradley and Martin S. Flaherty, "Executive Power Essentialism and Foreign Affairs," *Michigan Law Review* 102 (February 2004): 545–688, 564 (discussing the Roman Senate's possession of much of what we would consider the executive power).

For some time, consuls served a single term; but the law was changed to permit reelection, and some consuls served for extended periods. Boatwright et al., *Romans, supra*, 66.

56. Boatwright et al., *Romans, supra* note 55, 120; José Batlle y Ordóñez, "A Collegial Executive for Uruguay," in *Parliamentary versus Presidential Government*, ed. Arend Lijphart (New York: Oxford University Press, 1992), 176.

57. Heichelheim et al., *History of the Roman People, supra* note 55, 229–30, 324–26, 349–51, 400, 408–9, 411–13; Posner, "Constitution of the Roman Republic," *supra* note 55, 3, 8, 29–33.

58. Bruce Ackerman, "The New Separation of Powers," *Harvard Law Review* 113 (January 2000): 633–729, 645–46; Giovanni Sartori, "Neither Presidentialism nor Parliamentarism," in Linz and Valenzuela, *Failure of Presidential Democracy, supra* note 28, 107; Thomas Carothers, "The End of the Transition Paradigm," *Journal of Democracy* 13 (January 2002) 5–21, 9.

59. Douglas V. Verney, *The Analysis of Political Systems* (London: Routledge and Kegan Paul, 1959), 27; Matthew S. R. Palmer, "Collective Cabinet Decision Making in New Zealand," in *Cabinet Ministers and Parliamentary Government*, ed. Michael Laver and Kenneth A. Shepsle (Cambridge: Cambridge University Press, 1994), 233–41; Arend Lijphart, *Thinking about Democracy: Power Sharing and Majority Rule in Theory and Practice* (London: Routledge, 2008), 143; Michael Laver and Kenneth A. Shepsle, "Cabinet Ministers and Government Formation in Parliamentary Democracies," in Laver and Shepsle, *Cabinet Ministers, supra*, 7–8; Michael Laver and Kenneth A. Shepsle, "Cabinet Government in Theoretical Perspective," in Laver and Shepsle, *Cabinet Ministers, supra*, 298–99; Scott Mainwaring, "Presidentialism, Multipartism,

and Democracy: The Difficult Combination." *Comparative Political Studies* 26 (July 1993): 198–228, 204 (observing that of the thirty-one countries that had uninterrupted democratic government between 1967 and 1992, only four had U.S.-like presidential systems).

While stable democracies generally have parliamentary governments, presidential systems have become more common overall among democratic governments as new democracies in Latin American and eastern Europe have favored presidential systems. Samuels and Shugart, *Presidents, supra* note 26, 4–5. Even though presidential democracies are becoming more common and make up a larger percentage of stable democracies, they may not be effective democracies. Only a few Latin American democracies, for example, have provided their citizens good democratic governance (as measured by the fairness of the political process and the protection of basic civil rights). Scott Mainwaring and Timothy R. Scully, "Democratic Governance in Latin America: Eleven Lessons from Recent Experience," in *Democratic Governance in Latin America*, ed. Scott Mainwaring and Timothy R. Scully (Stanford: Stanford University Press, 2010), 365–69.

60. Laver and Shepsle, "Cabinet Ministers," *supra*, note 59, 6–8

61. Wolfgang C. Müller, "Models of Government and the Austrian Cabinet," in Laver and Shepsle, *Cabinet Ministers, supra* note 59, 31; Anthony King, "Ministerial Autonomy in Britain," in Laver and Shepsle, *Cabinet Ministers, supra* note 59, 203–25; Palmer, "Collective Cabinet Decision Making," *supra* note 59, 229–43. In some countries, one model may prevail in a single-party cabinet, while another model may dominate in a multiparty cabinet. Müller, "Models of Government," *supra*, 15–19; Ferdinand Müller-Rommel, "The Role of German Ministers in Cabinet Decision Making," in Laver and Shepsle, *Cabinet Ministers, supra* note 59, 152–53.

62. Lijphart, introduction to Lijphart, *Parliamentary versus Presidential Government, supra* note 56, 5–7; René Rhinow and Annemarie Huber-Hotz, "The Future of the Political System," in *The New Switzerland: Problems and Policies*, ed. Rolf Kieser and Kurt R. Spillmann (Palo Alto, CA: Society for the Promotion of Science and Scholarship, 1996), 18–19. The councilors serve four-year terms.

63. Swiss Federal Chancellery, *The Swiss Confederation: A Brief Guide 2012*, 34th ed. (Bern: Swiss Federal Chancellery, 2012), 42–43, http://www.bk.admin.ch/dokumentation/02070/index.html?lang=en (accessed November 8, 2012); Wolf Linder, *Swiss Democracy: Possible Solutions to Conflict in Multicultural Societies*, 3rd ed. (Houndmills, UK: Palgrave Macmillan, 2010), 12–13; Swiss Parliament, "Elections and Votes," http://www.parlament.ch/e/wahlen-abstimmungen/parlamentswahlen/wahlen-2011/Pages/eckdaten.aspx (accessed November 8, 2012).

64. Linder, *Swiss Democracy, supra* note 63, 10; Ulrich Klöti, "The Government," in *Handbook of Swiss Politics*, 2nd ed., ed. Ulrich Klöti et al. (Zürich: Neue Zürcher Zeitung, 2007), 155; Hanspeter Kriesi and Alexandre H. Trechsel, *The Politics of Switzerland: Continuity and Change in a Consensus Democracy* (Cambridge: Cambridge University Press, 2008), 75–76. New Zealand's cabinet also operates by consensus for many issues. Palmer, "Collective Cabinet Decision Making," *supra* note 59, 236–41.

65. Terry Nichols Clark, "The Swiss Communal Ethic," in *Commonwealth: The Other Road to Democracy—The Swiss Model of Democratic Self-Governance*, ed. Daniel J. Elazar (Lanham, MD: Lexington Books, 2001), 140–45.

66. Sources for this and the preceding paragraph include Arend Lijphart, *Patterns of Democracy: Government Forms and Performance in Thirty-Six Countries* (New Haven: Yale University Press, 1999), 55–59; Arend Lijphart, Ronald Rogowski, and R. Kent Weaver, "Separation of Powers and Cleavage Management," in *Do Institutions Matter? Government Capabilities in the United States and Abroad*, ed. R. Kent Weaver and Bert A. Rockman (Washington, DC: Brookings Institution, 1993), 310–14; Linder, *Swiss Democracy, supra* note 63, 21–28; Kenneth D. McRae, *Conflict and Compromise in Multilingual Societies: Switzerland* (Waterloo, ON: Wilfrid Laurier University Press, 1983), 74–82 (discussing how social cleavages are cross-cutting). Conflict between Catholics and Protestants also characterized the old Swiss Confederation from the end of the 13th Century through the end of the 18th Century. McRae, *Conflict and Compromise, supra,* 39.

67. Linder, *Swiss Democracy, supra* note 63, 4; Rhinow and Huber-Hotz, "Future of the Political System," *supra* note 62, 19–20; Kriesi and Trechsel, *Politics of Switzerland, supra* note 64, 81–83; Andreas Weber (Honorary Consul for Switzerland in Indianapolis), in discussion with author, August 27, 2009 (discussing the absence of abuse by the executive in Switzerland). According to Transparency International's "Corruption Perceptions Index," Switzerland ranks in a tie for eighth best among countries worldwide. (The United States came in at number twenty-four). Transparency International, "Corruption Perceptions Index 2011," http://cpi.transparency.org/cpi2011/results/#CountryResults (accessed November 8, 2012).

68. David M. Herszenhorn, "Senate Feels an Absence on Health Bill," *New York Times*, June 9, 2009; Susan Milligan, "Across the Aisle, a Ballad to Kennedy," *Boston Globe*, July 16, 2008. The Hill-Burton Act was sponsored by Senators Lister Hill (D-AL) and Harold Burton (R-OH) and passed in 1946 as the first major federal health care legislation. Kenneth Wing, "The Community Service Obligation of Hill-Burton Health Facilities," *Boston College Law Review* 23 (May 1982): 577–90, 583–84; Ellyn L. Brown, "The Hill-Burton Act, 1946–1980: Asynchrony in the Delivery of Health Care to the Poor," *Maryland Law Review* 39, no. 2 (1979): 316–75, 316, 318–19.

69. Marilynn B. Brewer and Rupert J. Brown, "Intergroup Relations," in *The Handbook of Social Psychology*, 4th ed., ed. Daniel T. Gilbert, Susan T. Fiske, and Gardner Lindzey (New York: McGraw-Hill, 1998), vol. 2, 577–78; John F. Dovidio and Samuel L. Gaertner, "Intergroup Bias," in *Handbook of Social Psychology*, 5th ed., ed. Susan T. Fiske, Daniel T. Gilbert, and Gardner Lindzey (Hoboken, NJ: Wiley, 2010), vol. 2, 1094–95; Colin Davis, *Scenes of Love and Murder: Renoir, Film and Philosophy* (London: Wallflower, 2009), 80.

70. Elena Kagan, "Presidential Administration," *Harvard Law Review* 114 (June 2001): 2245–2385, 2335; Terry M. Moe and William G. Howell, "The Presidential Power of Unilateral Action," *Journal of Law, Economics & Organization* 15 (April 1999): 132–79, 136.

71. Jonathan Alter, *The Promise: President Obama, Year One* (New York: Simon and Schuster, 2010), 244–46 (quote on 244).

72. Michael Luo, "Romney Faces Another 'Flip-Flop' Question: Has He Changed on Stem Cells?," *New York Times*, June 15, 2007; Katharine Q. Seelye, "Senator Specter Becomes Focus of Anti-Incumbent Fervor," *New York Times*, January 27, 2010; "SENATE_111," *supra* note 8 (finding that Arlen Specter was the twenty-sixth-most-

liberal senator as a Democrat and the sixty-first-most-liberal senator as a Republican in the iiith Congress); Ezra Klein, "The Strange Case of Evan Bayh," *American Prospect*, April 3, 2009, http://prospect.org/article/strange-case-evan-bayh (accessed November 8, 2012); Jonathan Weisman, "In Campaign, One Man's Pragmatism Is Another's Flip-Flopping," *Washington Post*, June 28, 2008.

Ultimately, Bayh decided not to run for reelection. Adam Nagourney, "Democrats Reel as Senator Says No to 3rd Term," *New York Times*, February 16, 2010.

This is not to say that presidential nominees always moderate their positions and promote centrist policies to appeal to general election voters. Many chief executives will succeed politically by maintaining their partisan views and therefore do not try to steer a middle course. B. Dan Wood, *The Myth of Presidential Representation* (Cambridge: Cambridge University Press, 2009), 199–203. But that does not change the point. When presidents need to maintain their ideological biases to succeed politically, they will do so. On the other hand, when success depends on a moderation of positions, presidents will moderate their positions.

73. C. Vann Woodward, *Tom Watson: Agrarian Rebel* (New York: Oxford University Press, 1963), 220–22, 370–72, 473–74.

74. Donald R. Matthews, *U.S. Senators and Their World* (Chapel Hill: University of North Carolina Press, 1960), 99–101. For similar reasons, collaborative relationships often develop between Democrats and Republicans from the different chambers. Republicans might be able to push their agenda through the House without Democratic support, but they will typically run up against a Democratic majority or filibuster in the Senate.

75. Howard Raiffa, John Richardson, and David Metcalfe, *Negotiation Analysis: The Science and Art of Collaborative Decision Making* (Cambridge: Belknap Press of Harvard University Press, 2002), 301; Itzhak Gilboa, *Rational Choice* (Cambridge: MIT Press, 2010), 100–101; Charalambos C. Aliprantis and Subir K. Chakrabarti, *Games and Decision Making*, 2nd ed. (New York: Oxford University Press, 2011), 329.

76. Robert M. Axelrod, *The Evolution of Cooperation* (New York: Basic Books, 1984), 124–32; Gilboa, *Rational Choice, supra* note 75, 100–101; Ming Zeng and Xiao-Ping Chen, "Achieving Cooperation in Multiparty Alliances: A Social Dilemma Approach to Partnership Management," *Academy of Management Review* 28 (October 2003): 587–605; Herbert Hovenkamp and Phillip E. Areeda, *Antitrust Law: An Analysis of Antitrust Principles and Their Application*, 2nd ed. (New York: Aspen, 2005), vol. 12, ¶ 2002fi, 25.

77. Raiffa et al., *Negotiation Analysis, supra* note 75, 115–18.

78. Martin Nowak and Karl Sigmund, "A Strategy of Win-Stay, Lose-Shift That Outperforms Tit-for-Tat in the Prisoner's Dilemma Game," *Nature* 364 (July 1, 1993): 56–58, 56 (describing the relationship in payoffs from the different strategies); Juan Williams, "Cantor Undercuts Boehner," *The Hill*, June 27, 2011.

79. Tony Ashworth, *Trench Warfare, 1914–1918: The Live and Let Live System* (New York: Holmes and Meier, 1980), 24–47; Axelrod, *Evolution of Cooperation, supra* note 76, 73–81. Ultimately, this "live-and-let-live" strategy unraveled when superior officers ordered their soldiers to launch raids on the other side's trenches. Axelrod, *Evolution of Cooperation, supra* note 76, 82–84.

80. Pierce, "Executive Divided," *supra* note 51.

81. Shugart and Carey, *Presidents and Assemblies*, *supra* note 49, 60; Robert Elgie, "'Cohabitation': Divided Government French-Style," in *Divided Government in Comparative Perspective*, ed. Robert Elgie (Oxford: Oxford University Press, 2001), 109–10.

82. Pierce, "Executive Divided," *supra* note 51, 278–84. In general, the prime minister assumes greater power during cohabitation governments in France. Elgie, "Cohabitation," *supra* note 81, 119–20.

83. Pierce, "Executive Divided," *supra* note 51, 277.

84. Elgie, "Cohabitation," *supra* note 81, 106, 112, 116–17, 124; Andrew Knapp and Vincent Wright, *The Government and Politics of France*, 5th ed. (New York: Routledge, 2006), 122–23.

85. Robert Elgie, *Political Institutions in Contemporary France* (Oxford: Oxford University Press, 2003), 125–26; Elgie, "Cohabitation," *supra* note 81, 114, 120–21. Before the constitutional amendment, cohabitation governments typically were created in legislative election years that followed presidential election years. Presidents served seven-year terms, and National Assembly deputies serve five-year terms, so the president's party could lose its majority in a nonpresidential election year, just as many U.S. presidents lose their congressional majorities in the off-year elections. The constitutional amendment reduced the presidential term to five years. Elgie, *Political Institutions*, *supra*, 103. One cohabitation government resulted when Jacques Chirac prematurely dissolved the National Assembly and called for new legislative elections. Ibid., 117.

86. James S. Goodwin and Jean M. Goodwin, "The Tomato Effect: Rejection of Highly Efficacious Therapies," *Journal of the American Medical Association* 251 (May 11, 1984): 2387–90. The deadly nightshade belongs to the same plant family as the tomato, and the leaves and stems of tomato plants contain the same poisons—atropine in particular—that are in the nightshade.

87. Shugart and Carey, *Presidents and Assemblies*, *supra* note 49; Lijphart, *Thinking about Democracy*, *supra* note 59, 80.

88. Shugart and Carey, *Presidents and Assemblies*, *supra* note 49, 30–31. Presidents often try to give voice to minority interests when choosing the members of their cabinets, but the appointments generally reflect a "descriptive" rather than real representation. That is, the cabinet members typically acquiesce in the president's agenda rather than forcefully promoting the interests of the group that they are supposed to represent. Ibid., 31.

89. Parliamentary systems also can suffer from excessive majoritarianism. In the Westminster model of parliamentary government used in Great Britain and other countries, legislative seats are not allocated based on proportional representation but after individual winner-take-all elections for the different seats. Hence, one party typically gains full control of the executive branch. Ibid., 93–94.

90. Ibid., 33–34. The president's diminished incentive to form durable coalitions with members of the legislature is exacerbated by the fact that presidential elections often favor "outsiders" who do not come to the executive branch with longstanding relationships with legislators. Ibid., 33. See also Samuels and Shugart, *Presidents*, *supra* note 26, 9; Kaare Strøm, "Delegation and Accountability in Parliamentary Democracies," *European Journal of Political Research* 37 (May 2000): 261–89, 265–66.

91. Shugart and Carey, *Presidents and Assemblies*, *supra* note 49, 105.

92. Ibid., 101, 104. When Uruguay restored its unitary executive, it still shut the third party out of the executive branch since the two major parties would control the presidential election. Ibid., 101. The Uruguayan experiment lasted until economic problems unrelated to the structure of the executive branch led the country to restore its unitary executive. In other words, the plural executive was essentially the scape-goat for the economic decline. Ibid., 99; Luis Eduardo González and Charles Guy Gillespie, "Presidentialism and Democratic Stability in Uruguay," in Linz and Valen-zuela, *Failure of Presidential Democracy, supra* note 28, 228. Indeed, even after adopting a strong, single-person executive in 1966, Uruguay experienced a military coup in 1973. González and Gillespie, "Presidentialism," *supra*, 231, 237.

Inspired by the Swiss model, Uruguay also experimented with a plural executive between 1918 and 1933, when a unitary president existed side-by-side with a nine-member executive council. In that experiment, the executive powers were sharply divided between the president and the council rather than shared by them. The president was given responsibility for public order, defense, and foreign affairs, while the executive council oversaw domestic policy. Shugart and Carey, *Presidents and Assem-blies, supra* note 49, 97; González and Gillespie, "Presidentialism," *supra*, 227. The first Uruguayan plural executive was abolished by the country's president at a time when the impact of the Great Depression was fueling a fascist trend in government world-wide. González and Gillespie, "Presidentialism," *supra*, 228.

93. Shugart and Carey, *Presidents and Assemblies, supra* note 49, 99–100.

94. Dayton Accords, Annex 4, Article V; Central Intelligence Agency, *The World Factbook*, https://www.cia.gov/library/publications/the-world-factbook/geos/bk.html (accessed November 8, 2012). The country is divided into two entities, the Federa-tion of Bosnia and Herzegovina and the Republika Srpska. The Bosniac and Croat presidents are elected by voters in the Federation of Bosnia and Herzegovina, and the Serb president by voters in Republika Srpska. If a dissenting president declares the majority's decision to be "destructive of a vital interest" of the entity from which the president was elected (the Federation or the Republika), the decision is referred to the entity's legislative body, which has the authority to block the presidential decision from taking effect. Dayton Accords, Annex 4, Article V.2.

95. Edward P. Joseph and R. Bruce Hitchner, *Making Bosnia Work: Why EU Accession Is Not Enough* (Washington, DC: United States Institute of Peace, June 2008), http://www.usip.org/files/resources/1_7.PDF (accessed November 8, 2012). The governmental system in Bosnia and Herzegovina is very cumbersome, with too many seats of power. R. Bruce Hitchner, "From Dayton to Brussels: The Story behind the Constitutional and Governmental Reform Process in Bosnia and Herzegovina," *Fletcher Forum of World Affairs* 30 (Winter 2006): 125–36, 126–27. As one observer has commented on the totality of national and local government, the country has "five presidents, four vice presidents, 13 prime ministers, 14 parliaments, 147 ministers and 700 members of Parliament, all of whom serve a population of just under four million people." Joseph and Hitchner, *Making Bosnia Work, supra*, 2 (quoting Miroslav Lajčák, then the High Ambassador for Bosnia and Herzegovina, an official responsible for overseeing the civilian implementation of the Dayton Accords).

96. Shugart and Carey, *Presidents and Assemblies, supra* note 49, 100, 103–4.

97. Cutler, "Now Is the Time," *supra* note 32, 390–91, 397–400.

98. Hofstadter, *Idea of a Party System, supra* note 2, 2; Cutler, "Now Is the Time," *supra* note 32, 389.

99. Daniel R. Ortiz, "Duopoly versus Autonomy: How the Two-Party System Harms the Major Parties," *Columbia Law Review* 100 (April 2000): 753–74, 753–54 (describing the commonly held view among other scholars about the value of the two-party system); John H. Aldrich, *Why Parties? The Origin and Transformation of Political Parties in America* (Chicago: University of Chicago Press, 1995), 8–9; David K. Ryden, *Representation in Crisis: The Constitution, Interest Groups, and Political Parties* (Albany: SUNY Press, 1996), 119–21. But see Richard L. Hasen, "Entrenching the Duopoly: Why the Supreme Court Should Not Allow the States to Protect the Democrats and Republican from Political Competition," *Supreme Court Review*, 1997, 331–71, 349, 358–60 (calling into question the antifactional role of the Democratic and Republican Parties).

100. Kramer, "Putting the Politics Back," *supra* note 36, 268–87; Samuel Issacharoff, Pamela S. Karlan, and Richard H. Pildes, *The Law of Democracy: Legal Structure of the Political Process*, 3rd ed. (New York: Foundation, 2007), 205; E. E. Schattschneider, *The Struggle for Party Government* (College Park: University of Maryland Program in American Civilization, 1948), 35, reprinted in *The Party Battle* (New York: Arno, 1974); Rosenblum, *On the Side of the Angels, supra* note 5, 120–21,

101. Cutler, "Now Is the Time," *supra* note 32, 398–402; James L. Sundquist, *Constitutional Reform and Effective Government*, rev. ed. (Washington, DC: Brookings Institution, 1992); Lijphart, introduction, *supra* note 62, 15; Sundquist, "Needed," *supra* note 32, 626–31.

102. Sources for this and the preceding paragraph include Stone et al., *Constitutional Law, supra* note 40, 24–25; Thomas O. Sargentich, "The Limits of the Parliamentary Critique of the Separation of Powers," *William and Mary Law Review* 34 (Spring 1993): 679–739, 716–17; Lijphart, *Patterns of Democracy, supra* note 66, 259; Erwin Chemerinsky, "The Question's Not Clear, but Party Government Is Not the Answer," *William and Mary Law Review* 30 (Winter 1989): 411–23, 419–23.

103. Ackerman, "New Separation of Powers," *supra* note 58, 664–70, 694–97.

104. Lijphart, *Patterns of Democracy, supra* note 66, 2.

105. Ibid., 258–300.

106. Abramowitz, *Disappearing Center, supra* note 8, 100–101; McCarty et al., *Polarized America, supra* note 4, 59–67. Some scholars propose wider use of "open primaries," in which a party's primary elections would be open to voters who are not affiliated with the party. Levinson and Pildes, "Separation of Parties," *supra* note 8, 2381–82. There are constitutional barriers to open primary laws. Ibid., 2382–83. More importantly, the empirical evidence does not predict much of an effect on political polarization from open primaries. McCarty et al., *Polarized America, supra* note 4, 194.

107. Robert H. Frank and Philip J. Cook, *The Winner-Take-All Society: How More and More Americans Compete for Ever Fewer and Bigger Prizes, Encouraging Economic Waste, Income Inequality, and an Impoverished Cultural Life* (New York: Free Press, 1995), 19.

108. Ibid., 125–31.

109. It is possible that the campaign cycle will not shorten. Campaigns might last longer than four years currently if they were not artificially limited by the president's

four-year term of office. If that is the case, then a two-person presidency might still yield four-year campaigns. On the other hand, campaign spending does not face the same kind of artificial cap as exists with the length of the campaign cycle. Hence, campaign spending should decline with a two-person presidency.

110. Kevin Sack, "Book Challenges Obama on Mother's Deathbed Fight," *New York Times*, July 14, 2011; Janny Scott, *A Singular Woman: The Untold Story of Barack Obama's Mother* (New York: Riverhead Books, 2011), 338; Marshall Frady, "Death in Arkansas," *New Yorker*, February 22, 1993, 107–8. It is now unconstitutional to execute people who are mentally retarded. Atkins v. Virginia, 536 U.S. 304 (2002).

111. Bruce Ackerman, *We the People: Foundations* (Cambridge: Belknap Press of Harvard University Press, 1991), 68; Malcolm Gladwell, *Outliers: The Story of Success* (New York: Little, Brown, 2008), 239, 246–49.

112. "Gallery Four: The Wonder Boy," and "Gallery 5: The Logical Candidate," Herbert Hoover Presidential Library and Museum, http://hoover.nara.gov/exhibits/Hooverstory/gallery04/index.html and http://hoover.nara.gov/exhibits/Hooverstory/gallery05/index.html (accessed November 8, 2012).

113. Frank and Cook, *Winner-Take-All Society, supra* note 107, 182–83. A similar phenomenon exists with aspiring Supreme Court justices. After watching Robert Bork's nomination fail because of his controversial positions and watching David Souter's nomination succeed after he avoided leaving a paper trail of his views, many prospective justices choose not to engage with important social problems—better to remain silent and viable as a Supreme Court nominee than vocal and unable to be confirmed. As Professor Pamela Karlan observed in responding to her own question as to whether she would want to serve as a justice, "You bet I would. But not enough to have trimmed my sails for half a lifetime." Peter Baker, "Favorites of Left Don't Make Obama's Court List," *New York Times*, May 26, 2009.

114. New State Ice v. Liebmann, 285 U.S. 262, 311 (1932) (Brandeis, J., dissenting); Akhil R. Amar, *America's Unwritten Constitution: The Precedents and Principles We Live By* (New York: Basic Books, 2012), 467.

Notes to Chapter 5

1. "Records of the Federal Convention," in *The Founders' Constitution*, ed. Philip B. Kurland and Ralph Lerner (Chicago: University of Chicago Press, 1987), vol. 3, 491–94; James Madison, *The Debates in the Federal Convention of 1787 Which Framed the Constitution of the United States of America*, ed. Gaillard Hunt and James Brown Scott (Amherst, NY: Prometheus Books, 1987), 37–40, 48–51, 101–4; Theodore B. Olson, "The Impetuous Vortex: Congressional Erosion of Presidential Authority," in *The Fettered Presidency: Legal Constraints on the Executive Branch*, ed. L. Gordon Crovitz and Jeremy A. Rabkin (Washington, DC: American Enterprise Institute, 1989), 226–30.

In Mason's three-person presidency, each executive would represent a different region of the country. Gary L. Gregg II, *The Presidential Republic: Executive Representation and Deliberative Democracy* (Lanham, MD: Rowman & Littlefield, 1997), 91. The New Jersey plan did not specify a number of executives. Madison, *Debates, supra,* 103. See also Charles C. Tansill, ed., *Documents Illustrative of the Formation of the Union of the American States* (Washington, DC: Government Printing Office, 1927), 131–33, 567, 595, 686–87 (record of the Constitutional Convention on June 1, August 18, August 22, and September 7, 1787).

Proposals for a divided executive would recur. John Calhoun believed a two-person presidency, with one president from the North and the other from the South, would defuse the tensions that ultimately led to the Civil War. Gregg, *Presidential Republic, supra,* 91–92.

2. Woodrow Wilson, *The New Freedom; A Call for the Emancipation of the Generous Energies of a People* (Englewood Cliffs, NJ: Prentice-Hall, 1961), 72. The first Congress included twenty-two senators and fifty-nine representatives since Rhode Island and North Carolina had not yet joined the new union. Herman Finer, *The Presidency: Crisis and Regeneration: An Essay in Possibilities* (Chicago: University of Chicago Press, 1960), 149. To be sure, the House and Senate have multiple decision makers to foster the constitutional interest in representation. As discussed in chapter 6, a two-person presidency serves that purpose as well.

3. Samuel Issacharoff, "Democracy and Collective Decision Making," *International Journal of Constitutional Law* (April 2008): 231–66, 255 (citing James Surowiecki, *The Wisdom of Crowds: Why the Many Are Smarter than the Few and How Collective Wisdom Shapes Business, Economies, Societies, and Nations* [New York: Doubleday, 2004], 11). While groups may make for better decision making, there are tasks for which a single talented person would perform better individually than as part of a group. J. Richard Hackman and Nancy Katz, "Group Behavior and Performance," in *Handbook of Social Psychology*, 5th ed., ed. Susan T. Fiske, Daniel T. Gilbert, and Gardner Lindzey (Hoboken, NJ: Wiley, 2010), vol. 2, 1212–14.

4. Alan S. Blinder, *The Quiet Revolution: Central Banking Goes Modern* (New Haven: Yale University Press, 2004), 48–49; Susan G. Straus, Andrew M. Parker, James M. Bruce, and Jacob W. Dembosky, *The Group Matters: A Review of the Effects of Group Dynamics on Processes and Outcomes in Analytic Teams* (Santa Monica, CA: RAND, 2009), vii, 2, http://www.rand.org/pubs/working_papers/WR580 (accessed November 8, 2012).

Studies come to different conclusions on the question whether group members work together in a synergistic way, so that the total effort is greater than the sum of the parts, or whether there are diminishing returns as individuals combine into groups. In other words, 1+1 might be greater than 2, or it might be less than 2 (but still greater than 1). Compare David J. Cooper and John H. Kagel, "Are Two Heads Better than One? Team versus Individual Play in Signaling Games," *American Economic Review* 95 (June 2005): 477–509, 478, 502–4 (reporting synergies in groups), with James H. Davis, "Some Compelling Intuitions about Group Consensus Decisions, Theoretical and Empirical Research, and Interpersonal Aggregation Phenomena: Selected Examples, 1950–1990," *Organizational Behavior and Human Decision Processes* 52 (June 1992): 3–38, 5–10, and John M. Levine and Richard L. Moreland, "Small Groups," in *The Handbook of Social Psychology*, ed. Daniel T. Gilbert, Susan T. Fiske, and Gardner Lindzey, 4th ed. (New York: McGraw-Hill, 1998), vol. 2, 438 (finding diminishing returns in group interactions).

5. Donald G. Ellis and B. Aubrey Fisher, *Small Group Decision Making: Communication and the Group Process*, 4th ed. (New York: McGraw-Hill, 1994), 17–18.

6. Ibid., 17.

7. Jonathan D. Ketcham, Laurence C. Baker, and Donna MacIsaac, "Physician Practice Size and Variations in Treatment and Outcomes: Evidence from Medicare Patients with AMI," *Health Affairs* 26 (January 2007): 195–205.

8. Bettina Rockenbach, Abdolkarim Sadrieh, and Barbara Mathauschek, "Teams Take the Better Risks," *Journal of Economic Behavior and Organization* 63 (July 2007): 412–22, 419–20. See also Cooper and Kagel, "Are Two Heads Better than One?," *supra* note 4, 482 (observing that group members are able to catch each other's errors).

9. Gary Bornstein and Ilan Yaniv, "Individual and Group Behavior in the Ultimatum Game: Are Groups More 'Rational' Players?," *Experimental Economics* 1 (June 1998): 101–8; Martin G. Kocher and Matthias Sutter, "The Decision Maker Matters: Individual versus Group Behavior in Experimental Beauty-Contest Games," *Economic Journal* 115 (January 2005): 200–223, 219–20; Cooper and Kagel, "Are Two Heads Better than One?," *supra* note 4, 478.

10. Blinder, *Quiet Revolution, supra* note 4, 43; Gina Kolata, "Rare Sharing of Data Led to Results on Alzheimer's," *New York Times*, August 13, 2010; Scott E. Page, *Diversity and Complexity* (Princeton: Princeton University Press, 2011), 224–27 (discussing the benefits of collective knowledge).

11. Peter Chalos and Sue Pickard, "Information Choice and Cue Use: An Experiment in Group Information Processing." *Journal of Applied Psychology* 70 (November 1985): 634–41.

12. Dee Ann Kline, "Intuitive Team Decision Making," in *How Professionals Make Decisions,* ed. Henry Montgomery, Raanan Lipshitz, and Berndt Brehmer (Mahwah, NJ: Erlbaum, 2005), 171.

13. Lu Hong and Scott E. Page, "Groups of Diverse Problem Solvers Can Outperform Groups of High-Ability Problem Solvers," *Proceedings of the National Academy of Sciences* 101 (November 16, 2004): 16385–89; see also Blinder, *Quiet Revolution, supra* note 4, 43.

14. Scott E. Page, *The Difference: How the Power of Diversity Creates Better Groups, Firms, Schools, and Societies* (Princeton: Princeton University Press, 2007), 2, 3. In the scientific-problem study, the different problem solvers worked individually for the most part rather than in teams. Karim R. Lakhani, Lars Bo Jeppesen, Peter A. Lohse, and Jill A. Panetta, "The Value of Openness in Scientific Problem Solving" (working paper, October 2006), http://www.hbs.edu/research/pdf/07-050.pdf (accessed November 8, 2012).

15. Kline, "Intuitive Team Decision Making," *supra* note 12, 171; Cooper and Kagel, "Are Two Heads Better than One?," *supra* note 4, 503.

16. Blinder, *Quiet Revolution, supra* note 4, 43–44.

17. Charlan J. Nemeth, Bernard Personnaz, Marie Personnaz, and Jack A. Goncalo, "The Liberating Role of Conflict in Group Creativity: A Study in Two Countries," *European Journal of Social Psychology* 34 (July–August 2004): 365–74. And it is important that the group members share different perspectives that are authentically held. "Devil's advocates" are not as effective at improving the decision-making process as are dissenters who sincerely believe in their divergent viewpoints. Ibid., 367; Charlan J. Nemeth and Margaret Ormiston, "Creative Idea Generation: Harmony versus Stimulation," *European Journal of Social Psychology* 37 (May–June 2007): 524–35, 526.

18. Cooper and Kagel, "Are Two Heads Better than One?," *supra* note 4; Page, *Difference, supra* note 14, 28–29.

19. The repudiation almost came four years earlier. Bush won a narrow victory over John Kerry, prevailing by 50.7 to 48.3 percent in the popular vote and 286–251 in the electoral vote. But the very accurate social science models that predict outcomes of presidential elections based on economic conditions and the advantages of incumbency estimated a popular vote total for Bush around 55 percent. Nolan M. McCarty, Keith T. Poole, and Howard Rosenthal, *Polarized America: The Dance of Ideology and Unequal Riches* (Cambridge: MIT Press, 2006), 197. Hence, it appears that Bush's Iraq policy may have cost him up to 4 percent of the vote.

20. Adam Nagourney, "For Remarks on Iraq, Gore Gets Praise and Scorn," *New York Times*, September 25, 2002.

21. Elisabeth Bumiller, "West Point Is Divided on a War Doctrine's Fate, *New York Times*, May 28, 2012.

22. Irving L. Janis, *Groupthink: Psychological Studies of Policy Decisions and Fiascoes*, 2nd ed. (Boston: Houghton Mifflin, 1982), 15, 30–31.

23. Scott Shane, "Complaint Seeks Punishment for Classification of Documents," *New York Times*, August 2, 2011. In subsequent years, charges were filed against other employees.

The tendency toward excessive secrecy responds to a concern of the framers. In Federalist 70, Alexander Hamilton worried that a plural executive would compromise the nation's interest in secrecy. I am skeptical that a presidential partnership would entail any compromise of security interests. The two presidents would recognize the need to protect the disclosure of highly confidential information. Rather than compromise secrecy, a two-person presidency might help address the problem with excessive executive branch secrecy. As discussed in chapter 3, presidential assertions of privilege and confidentiality have been unnecessary at times and detrimental to the public's interest in open government. A second president is in a better position than the public to understand when an assertion of executive privilege is not justified and may then refuse to support the assertion.

24. Blinder, *Quiet Revolution, supra* note 4, 48; Michael Mello, *Against the Death Penalty: The Relentless Dissents of Justices Brennan and Marshall* (Boston: Northeastern University Press, 1996).

25. Davis, "Some Compelling Intuitions," *supra* note 4, 10–15. For further discussion of choice shift, see ibid. and Peter J. Burke, "Interaction in Small Groups," in *Handbook of Social Psychology*, ed. John Delamater (New York: Springer, 2006), 380–81.

26. Cf. Christopher J. Waller, "A Bargaining Model of Partisan Appointments to the Central Bank," *Journal of Monetary Economics* 29 (June 1992): 411–28 (finding that appointments to the Federal Reserve are likely to be more moderate when the out-of-power party exerts more influence in the confirmation process).

27. Herbert H. Blumberg, "Group Decision Making and Choice Shift," in *Small Group Research: A Handbook*, ed. A. Paul Hare, Herbert H. Blumberg, Martin F. Davies, and M. Valerie Kent (Norwood, NJ: Ablex, 1994), 204–5; Janis, *Groupthink, supra* note 22, 2–47, 97–130; Michael R. Callaway, Richard G. Marriott, and James K. Esser, "Effects of Dominance on Group Decision Making: Toward a Stress Reduction

Explanation of Groupthink," *Journal of Personality and Social Psychology* 49 (October 1985): 949–52, 952.

Groupthink can reflect elements of compliance (group members suppress their doubts about the group's decision) and internalization (group members accept the group's decision). Clark McCauley, "The Nature of Social Influence in Groupthink: Compliance and Internalization," *Journal of Personality and Social Psychology* 57 (August 1989): 250–60. See also Peter Shane, *Madison's Nightmare: How Executive Power Threatens American Democracy* (Chicago: University of Chicago Press, 2009), 59–81 (discussing the groupthink phenomenon in the context of the Vietnam and Iraq Wars).

28. Ellis and Fisher, *Small Group Decision Making, supra* note 5, 47–48.

29. Alan S. Blinder and John Morgan, "Are Two Heads Better Than One? Monetary Policy by Committee," *Journal of Money, Credit and Banking* 37 (October 2005): 789–811, 797–98, 802.

30. If you start with $100 and lose 25 percent, you now have $75. To get back to $100, you need to pick up $25, which would represent a 33 percent increase from $75.

31. John H. Langbein, "The Uniform Prudent Investor Act and the Future of Trust Investing," *Iowa Law Review* 81 (March 1996): 641–69, 646–49; 29 U.S.C. § 1104(a)(1) (C) (regulating pension trustees); *Restatement (Third) of Trusts: Prudent Investor Rule* § 227(b) (1992); Uniform Prudent Investor Act § 3; Michael O'Malley, *The Wisdom of Bees: What the Hive Can Teach Business about Leadership, Efficiency, and Growth* (New York: Portfolio, 2010), 90–93 (discussing how beehives and businesses thrive from the steadiness provided by a diversity of workers).

32. John C. Bogle and David F. Swensen, *Common Sense on Mutual Funds: New Imperatives for the Intelligent Investor*, 10th ed. (Hoboken, NJ: Wiley, 2010), 147. As manager of the Legg Mason Value Trust mutual fund, William Miller posted returns higher than the S&P 500 index for fifteen years in a row from 1991 to 2005. However, a dismal 2008 performance wiped out all of the past years' gains and left the fund as one of the worst performing funds in its class. Tom Lauricella, "The Stock Picker's Defeat," *Wall Street Journal*, December 10, 2008.

33. The text for each of the Federalist Papers can be found at the website of the Library of Congress, http://thomas.loc.gov/home/histdox/fedpapers.html.

34. Jeffrey A. Frankel and Peter R. Orszag, introduction to *American Economic Policy in the 1990s*, ed. Jeffrey A. Frankel and Peter R. Orszag (Cambridge: MIT Press, 2002), 5. See also Juan J. Linz, "Presidential or Parliamentary Democracy: Does It Make a Difference?," in *The Failure of Presidential Democracy*, ed. Juan J. Linz and Arturo Valenzuela (Baltimore: Johns Hopkins University Press, 1994), 39 (observing that congressional obstruction can make it very difficult for presidents to exercise their considerable powers); Terry M. Moe and William G. Howell, "The Presidential Power of Unilateral Action," *Journal of Law, Economics & Organization* 15 (April 1999): 132–79, 155. This limitation is much more an issue for domestic policy. As discussed in chapter 3, presidents enjoy broad discretion when engaged in foreign policy matters.

35. Jeff Zeleny, "Obama Says Benefits from Health Care Overhaul Would Be Immediate," *New York Times*, January 9, 2010 (quoting Obama as saying, "Once I sign health insurance reform into law . . .").

36. Robert Pear, "Health Care Cost Increase Is Projected for New Law," *New York Times*, April 24, 2010; David Orentlicher, "Rationing Health Care: It's a Matter of the Health Care System's Structure," *Annals of Health Law* 19 (Summer 2010): 449–64; Reed Abelson, "Health Care Changes Wouldn't Have Big Effect for Many," *New York Times*, December 25, 2009. The twenty-three million who will remain uninsured include five million illegal immigrants. Pear, "Health Care Cost Increase," *supra*. The thirty-four million estimate for the newly insured may not be realized if some states forgo the option to expand their Medicaid population.

Of course, one would expect greater spending with higher levels of coverage. Nevertheless, the need to curtail health care spending remains.

37. Committee for Economic Development, *Quality, Affordable Health Care for All: Moving beyond the Employer-Based Health-Insurance System* (Washington, DC: Committee for Economic Development, 2007), http://www.ced.org/images/library/reports/health_care/report_healthcare07.pdf (accessed November 8, 2012). The committee's membership comprises leaders from business and education.

38. Richardo Alonso-Zaldivar, "Health Insurance Mandate Began as a Republican Idea," *Boston Globe*, March 28, 2010. When Bill Clinton proposed a mandate on employers to provide health care coverage in 1994, Republicans responded with a proposed mandate on individuals to purchase health care coverage.

39. Angelo Lopez, "Ted Kennedy, Richard Nixon and Universal Health Care," *Everyday Citizen*, September 29, 2009, http://www.everydaycitizen.com/2009/09/ted_kennedy_richard_nixon_and.html (accessed November 8, 2012).

40. Jay Dahya and Nickolaos G. Travlos, "Does the One Man Show Pay? Theory and Evidence on the Dual CEO Revisited," *European Financial Management* 6 (March 2000): 85–98, 87–88; Dan R. Dalton, Michael A. Hitt, S. Trevis Certo, and Catherine M. Dalton, "The Fundamental Agency Problem and Its Mitigation: Independence, Equity, and the Market for Corporate Control," *Academy of Management Annals* 1, no. 1 (2007): 1–64, 13–15; and O'Malley, *Wisdom of Bees*, *supra* note 31, 125–26.

41. Robert A. G. Monks and Nell Minow, *Corporate Governance*, 4th ed. (West Sussex, UK: Wiley, 2008), 242–44; Dahya and Travlos, "Does the One Man Show Pay?," *supra* note 40, 90–91 (observing that while most companies in the United States combine the roles of CEO and board chair, most corporations in the United Kingdom split the roles); James O'Toole, Jay Galbraith, and Edward E. Lawler III, "The Promise and Pitfalls of Shared Leadership: When Two (or More) Heads Are Better than One," in *Shared Leadership: Reframing the Hows and Whys of Leadership*, ed. Craig L. Pearce and Jay A. Conger (Thousand Oaks, CA: Sage, 2003), 252–57; Thuy-Nga T. Vo, "To Be or Not to Be Both CEO and Board Chair," *Brooklyn Law Review* 76 (Fall 2010): 65–129.

42. Vo, "To Be or Not to Be," *supra* note 41, 118–20; Dahya and Travlos, "Does the One Man Show Pay?," *supra* note 40, 94–96; Chia-Wei Chen, J. Barry Lin, and Bingsheng Yi, "CEO Duality and Firm Performance—An Endogenous Issue," *Corporate Ownership & Control* 6 (Fall 2008): 58–65. Empirical data may underestimate the value of split leadership. It is often difficult for non-CEO board chairs, who serve on a part-time basis and come from outside the company, to provide an effective counterweight to CEOs who serve the companies on a full-time basis.

43. James C. Collins and Morten T. Hansen, *Great by Choice: Uncertainty, Chaos, and Luck? Why Some Thrive Despite Them All* (New York: HarperCollins, 2011), 8–10.

44. On the Louisiana Purchase, see David G. McCullough, *John Adams* (New York: Simon and Schuster, 2001), 586. It is not clear that Richard Nixon would have tried to block the Civil Rights Act of 1964 as Johnson's co-president. While Nixon was no great progressive on race relations, there are a few reasons to think he would not have opposed enactment of the act. First, he sometimes did advance civil rights policies, as with his support for the desegregation of schools in the South and his promotion of affirmative action programs. Second, like Johnson, Nixon would have recognized the political risks for the Democratic Party from passage of the act. Third, as Johnson pushed his legislative priorities, he moved power from Congress to the White House, and Nixon would have welcomed the shift. Thus, whether acting on the public interest or out of self-interest, Nixon might have supported the act. Hugh Davis Graham, "Richard Nixon and Civil Rights: Explaining an Enigma," *Presidential Studies Quarterly* 26 (Winter 1996): 93–106, 94–96; Nick Kotz, *Judgment Days: Lyndon Baines Johnson, Martin Luther King, Jr., and the Laws That Changed America* (Boston: Houghton Mifflin, 2005), 61; Robert A. Caro, *The Years of Lyndon Johnson: The Passage of Power* (New York: Knopf, 2012), 502.

45. Jacob S. Hacker and Paul Pierson, *Winner-Take-All Politics: How Washington Made the Rich Richer—and Turned Its Back on the Middle Class* (New York: Simon and Schuster, 2010), 96–97.

46. Douglas came in second in the popular vote, while Breckinridge ran second in the Electoral College.

47. Paul Finkelman, "The Cost of Compromise and the Covenant with Death," in "Compromise and Constitutionalism," special issue, *Pepperdine Law Review* 38 (2011): 845–88, 849; J. David Hacker, "A Census-Based Count of the Civil War Dead," *Civil War History* 57 (December 2011): 307–48, 348.

A two-person presidency raises a number of counterfactual possibilities. With a Lincoln-Douglas or Lincoln-Breckinridge administration, Lincoln might not have become embroiled in a Civil War. It was his election that precipitated South Carolina's secession. Had Lincoln assumed office with a presidential partner more sympathetic to southern interests, the South might not have chosen secession in 1861.

Or with a two-person presidency, the South would not have enjoyed the degree of control over the White House that it exercised from 1789 to 1850. Over that period, nine out of the twelve presidents had been southern-born slaveholders, and because southern presidents more often served a second term, slaveholders sat in the Oval Office for fifty out of the country's first sixty-two years. The South also enjoyed dominance in the House of Representatives, frequent majorities in the Senate, and majority control of the Supreme Court. Finkelman, "Cost of Compromise," *supra*, 863–64, 869–70. By the time of the Compromise of 1850, southern leaders such as South Carolina Senator John C. Calhoun were unwilling to compromise on the slavery question and preferred dissolution of the Union to a resolution of the conflict between the abolitionists and the proponents of slavery. Ibid., 869–70. If there had been greater balance in government, the antislavery movement might have been more forceful and able to prevent the kind of intransigence exhibited by people such as Calhoun. On the other hand, to the extent that southern support for secession reflected the North's economic dominance and fears that western expansion would deprive the South of its political influence, an assurance of shared power in the Oval Office might have made southerners less convinced that their fortunes would be more favorable outside the Union. For many southerners, secession was seen as the only way to preserve their political identity. Mark E. Brandon, *Free in the World: American Slavery and Constitutional Failure* (Princeton: Princeton University Press, 1998), 134, 172.

48. See also Arthur Schlesinger, Jr., *The Imperial Presidency*, with a new epilogue (Boston: Houghton Mifflin, 1989), 386.

49. Linz, "Presidential or Parliamentary Democracy," *supra* note 34, 13.

50. Jide Nzelibe and Matthew Stephenson, "Complementary Constraints: Separation of Powers, Rational Voting and Constitutional Design." *Harvard Law Review* 123 (January 2010): 617–53, 627–31.

51. Michael A. Fitts, "The Paradox of Power in the Modern State: Why a Unitary, Centralized Presidency May Not Exhibit Effective or Legitimate Leadership." *University of Pennsylvania Law Review* 144 (January 1996): 827–902, 884–89. There is a general tendency for people to exaggerate the influence of leaders on events. James R. Meindl, Sanford B. Ehrlich, and Janet M. Dukerich, "The Romance of Leadership," *Administrative Science Quarterly* 30 (March 1985): 78–102.

52. Recall from chapter 4 that most stable democracies have had parliamentary governments with plural executives.

53. Dana D. Nelson, *Bad for Democracy: How the Presidency Undermines the Power of the People* (Minneapolis: University of Minnesota Press, 2008), 17, 22 ("myth" quote); 1 Samuel 8 (Hebrew Bible).

54. Nelson, *Bad for Democracy*, *supra* note 53, 57; Gregg, *Presidential Republic*, *supra* note 1, 1; David Mendell, *Obama: From Promise to Power* (New York: Amistad, 2007), 9; Rakesh Khurana, *Searching for a Corporate Savior: The Irrational Quest for Charismatic CEOs* (Princeton: Princeton University Press, 2002); Peter Baker, "The Education of a President," *New York Times Magazine*, October 17, 2010, MM40 (discussing President Obama's campaign promise to save the planet).

55. Nelson, *Bad for Democracy*, *supra* note 53, 22, 25; Ann Ruth Willner, *The Spellbinders: Charismatic Political Leadership* (New Haven: Yale University Press, 1984), 8 ("superhuman" quote); D Jerrold M. Post, "Narcissism and the Charismatic Leader-Follower Relationship," *Political Psychology* 7 (December 1986): 675–88, 684–85.

Less than two and a half years after Obama took office, he was being pummeled in the press by his supporters. Drew Westen, "What Happened to Obama?," *New York Times*, August 7, 2011; Cenk Uygur, "Obama's Tipping Point," *Huffington Post*, August 9, 2011, http://www.huffingtonpost.com/cenk-uygur/obamas-tipping-point_1_b_921805.html (accessed November 8, 2012). Consider as well how the reputation of former Federal Reserve chair Alan Greenspan plummeted in the wake of the Great Recession. Peter S. Goodman, "Taking Hard New Look at a Greenspan Legacy," *New York Times*, October 9, 2008.

56. Bruce Ackerman, "The New Separation of Powers," *Harvard Law Review* 113 (January 2000): 633–729, 663.

57. Nelson, *Bad for Democracy*, *supra* note 53, 4–5, 57, 67, 97–102.

Notes to Chapter 6

1. Arend Lijphart, "Presidentialism and Majoritarian Democracy: Theoretical Observations," in *The Failure of Presidential Democracy*, ed. Juan J. Linz and Arturo Valenzuela (Baltimore: Johns Hopkins University Press, 1994), 97; Matthew Soberg Shugart and John M. Carey, *Presidents and Assemblies: Constitutional Design and Electoral Dynamics* (Cambridge: Cambridge University Press, 1992), 30–31.

Winners of Senate and House races also earn all of the power. However, this unfairness is mitigated by the fact that the losing party in some races will be the winning party in other races. Thus, the entire Congress ends up with a more proportional system of representation.

2. Hence, Maurice Duverger established the principle that winner-take-all elections generate two-party systems. Maurice Duverger, *Political Parties: Their Organization and Activity in the Modern State*, 3rd ed. (London: Methuen, 1964), 217, 239–45; see also Lani Guinier, "No Two Seats: The Elusive Quest for Political Equality," *Virginia Law Review* 77 (November 1991): 1413–1514, 1429 (discussing underrepresentation of minority groups in winner-take-all elections).

3. Recall from chapter 4 that the seven-member Swiss executive council represents five political parties and nearly 80 percent of the popular vote in its country. And in Germany after the September 2009 elections, the center-right cabinet included eight ministers from the Christian Democratic Union, five ministers from the Free Democratic Party, and three ministers from the Christian Social Union (with none from the Social Democratic Party, the main opposition party). The three governing parties secured 48.4 percent of the popular vote, with the Social Democratic Party garnering 23 percent of the vote and two other parties on the left winning 11.9 and 10.7 percent of the vote. Nicholas Kulish, "Chancellor of Germany Claims Win in Elections," *New York Times*, September 28, 2009. But see James A. Gardner, "Madison's Hope: Virtue, Self-Interest, and the Design of Electoral Systems," *Iowa Law Review* 86 (October 2000): 87–172 (arguing that proportional representation systems encourage the public's pursuit of self-interest, whereas winner-take-all elections are more likely to promote pursuit of the common good).

4. The popular vote percentages were 49.55 for Truman in 1948, 49.72 for Kennedy in 1960, 43.42 for Nixon in 1968, 43.01 for Clinton in 1992, and 49.23 for Clinton in 1996.

5. Douglas J. Amy, *Real Choices/New Voices: How Proportional Representation Elections Could Revitalize American Democracy*, 2nd ed. (New York: Columbia University Press, 2002), 26; Juan J. Linz, "The Perils of Presidentialism," *Journal of Democracy* 1 (Winter 1990): 51–69, 56–57.

6. Shugart and Carey, *Presidents and Assemblies, supra* note 1, 32.

7. Juan J. Linz, "Presidential or Parliamentary Democracy: Does It Make a Difference?," in Linz and Valenzuela, *Failure of Presidential Democracy, supra* note 1, 25; Joseph Rago, "Obama and the Narcissism of Big Differences," *Wall Street Journal*, August 6–7, 2011.

8. Sanford Levinson, *Our Undemocratic Constitution: Where the Constitution Goes Wrong (and How We the People Can Correct It)* (New York: Oxford University Press, 2006), 101–21.

9. Shugart and Carey, *Presidents and Assemblies, supra* note 1, 96.

10. Amy, *Real Choices, supra* note 5, 96–98; Paul R. Abramson, John H. Aldrich, Phil Paolino, and David W. Rohde, "Third Party and Independent Candidates in American Politics: Wallace, Anderson, and Perot," *Political Science Quarterly* 110 (Autumn 1995): 349–67, 354–64; Duverger, *Political Parties, supra* note 2, 226.

11. Justin Martin, *Nader: Crusader, Spoiler, Icon* (New York: Basic Books, 2002), 45–46, 61, 66–82, 99–104, 140–41, 226–28.

12. Ibid., 226–39. Many people believed that Nader did in fact swing the election to Bush. Nader received more than 95,000 votes in Florida, the deciding state in the election, and Bush won Florida by a margin of only 538 votes. Ibid., 267–72; Amy, *Real Choices, supra* note 5, 97.

13. Mark Bisnow, *Diary of a Dark Horse: The 1980 Anderson Presidential Campaign* (Carbondale: Southern Illinois University Press, 1983), 8–9, 15–16, 107–24, 138, 150; Jim Mason, *No Holding Back: The 1980 John B. Anderson Presidential Campaign* (Lanham, MD: University Press of America, 2011), 86–89, 120–29, 141–43, 159–70.

14. Bisnow, *Diary of a Dark Horse, supra* note 13, 166, 175–77; Mason, *No Holding Back, supra* note 13, 183–224.

15. Bisnow, *Diary of a Dark Horse, supra* note 13, 177–206; Mason, *No Holding Back, supra* note 13, 253–67.

16. Bisnow, *Diary of a Dark Horse, supra* note 13, 213, 240, 242; Abramson et al., "Third Party," *supra* note 10, 357; Mason, *No Holding Back, supra* note 13, 305–9.

17. Bisnow, *Diary of a Dark Horse, supra* note 13, 279–80, 304–5.

18. Amy, *Real Choices, supra* note 5, 98. To be sure, there were other factors contributing to Anderson's low vote total. His support began to decline as he adopted a more conventional campaign strategy, becoming more guarded in his relations with the media and more cautious in his positions. And some key miscalculations damaged his presidential bid. On the eve of the Democratic convention, for example, he appeared to flip-flop on how he would respond to the challenge that Kennedy had mounted against Carter. Bisnow, *Diary of a Dark Horse, supra* note 13, 207–13, 274–79; Mason, *No Holding Back, supra* note 13, 281–91, 321–25.

19. Abramson et al., "Third Party," *supra* note 10, 353; Ronald Rapoport and Walter J. Stone, *Three's a Crowd: The Dynamic of Third Parties, Ross Perot, and Republican Resurgence* (Ann Arbor: University of Michigan Press, 2005), 4. Alabama Governor George Wallace received fewer popular votes in 1968 than Perot did in 1992; but Wallace's support was more concentrated in the South, and he picked up forty-six electoral votes to zero for Perot. The best third-party showing in the 20th Century was made by Theodore Roosevelt, who received 27.4 percent of the popular vote (and 16.6 percent of the electoral vote) in 1912, when he ran second to Woodrow Wilson. Rapoport and Stone, *Three's a Crowd, supra,* 4. For voting data, see John Woolley and Gerhard Peters, "Presidential Elections Data," *The American Presidency Project,* http://www.presidency.ucsb.edu/elections.php (accessed November 8, 2012).

20. Abramson et al., "Third Party," *supra* note 10, 355–59; William Poundstone, *Gaming the Vote: Why Elections Aren't Fair (and What We Can Do About It)* (New York: Hill and Wang, 2008), 59–91. To be sure, even if third-party candidates have not been able to win election, they have influenced the major parties. Candidates like Anderson and Perot signal significant public dissatisfaction with the major parties,

and the major parties may respond to the signal by adjusting their positions to capture the third party's supporters. Rapoport and Stone, *Three's a Crowd, supra* note 19, 5; James L. Sundquist, *Dynamics of the Party System: Alignment and Realignment of Political Parties in the United States* (Washington, DC: Brookings Institution, 1983), 28–30; Steven J. Rosenstone, Roy L. Behr, and Edward H. Lazarus, *Third Parties in America: Citizen Response to Major Party Failure*, 2nd ed. (Princeton: Princeton University Press, 1996), 8. But see Marjorie Randon Hershey, *Party Politics in America*, 13th ed. (New York: Pearson Longman, 2009), 40 (observing that the influence of third parties on major-party platforms is uncertain).

A co-presidency also can increase the freedom of primary voters to opt for their preferred candidate. When a president seeks reelection currently, members of the president's party might discourage a primary challenge out of fear that a divisive primary campaign would harm the eventual nominee in the general election. With a co-presidency, a divisive primary will rarely cause any more harm than dropping the president from first to second on Election Day.

21. Of course, the Democratic and Republican Parties are not as strong as they once were, and individuals are more likely to identify themselves as independent. Edward S. Greenberg and Benjamin I. Page, *The Struggle for Democracy*, 7th ed. (New York: Pearson Longman, 2005), 138–39; James Q. Wilson and John J. DiIulio, *American Government: Institutions and Policies*, 11th ed. (Boston: Houghton Mifflin, 2008), 192. However, the decline of the parties has been less than suggested by many political scientists. Much of the fall in party identification has occurred among nonvoters rather than voters. Larry M. Bartels, "Partisanship and Voting Behavior, 1952–1996," *American Journal of Political Science* 44 (January 2000): 35–50.

22. With instant-runoff voting, people rank the different candidates in order of preference, and votes are assigned to the candidates listed first. If no candidate reaches the minimum needed for election, the lowest ranked candidate is eliminated, and that person's ballots are reassigned to the voters' second choices. By successively eliminating the least popular candidates, election officials can identify a winner (or winners). Poundstone, *Gaming the Vote, supra* note 20, 164–67.

23. Lijphart, "Presidentialism," *supra* note 1, 98.

24. Davis v. Bandemer, 478 U.S. 109, 132–33 (1986). This concern about persistent denial of influence in the political process provides a key reason for courts to invoke the Equal Protection Clause to protect people against discrimination. Geoffrey R. Stone et al., *Constitutional Law*, 6th ed. (New York: Aspen, 2009), 524.

25. The text for each of the Federalist Papers can be found at the website of the Library of Congress, http://thomas.loc.gov/home/histdox/fedpapers.html; Leon D. Epstein, *Political Parties in the American Mold* (Madison: University of Wisconsin Press, 1986), 80–81; B. Dan Wood, *The Myth of Presidential Representation* (Cambridge: Cambridge University Press, 2009), 6–7 (Washington quote on 6).

26. Wood, *Myth of Presidential Representation, supra* note 25, 19, 110, 117–19; Barbara Sinclair, *Party Wars: Polarization and the Politics of National Policy Making* (Norman: University of Oklahoma Press, 2006), 349–50.

27. Bruce Ackerman, *We the People: Foundations* (Cambridge: Belknap Press of Harvard University Press, 1991), 67–69; Stone et al., *Constitutional Law, supra* note 24, 21. To be sure, the framers created a House that initially had fewer members than most

state legislatures so they could ensure election of the elite in society. Gordon S. Wood, *Representation in the American Revolution*, rev. ed. (Charlottesville: University of Virginia Press, 2008), 56–57. See also Gordon S. Wood, *The Creation of the American Republic, 1776–1787* (Chapel Hill: University of North Carolina Press, 1969), 506–18. The 17th Amendment now provides for direct election of senators, and the Electoral College may not serve the screening function that the framers expected.

28. Wood, *Representation, supra* note 27, 22–24; Samuel E. Morison, Henry S. Commager, and William E. Leuchtenburg, *The Growth of the American Republic*, 7th ed. (New York: Oxford University Press, 1980), vol. 1, 253. Similarly, Federalist 63 cited the virtues of a Senate composed of "temperate and respectable" citizens who could protect the nation from a public that might act at times against it true interests.

29. Wood, *Representation, supra* note 27, 54–68; Wood, *Creation, supra* note 27, 547–53.

30. Gary L. Gregg II, *The Presidential Republic: Executive Representation and Deliberative Democracy* (Lanham, MD: Rowman & Littlefield, 1997), 8. Andrew Jackson and other presidents also have taken this position. Ibid., 4–5; Robert A. Dahl, "Myth of the Presidential Moderate," *Political Science Quarterly* 105 (Autumn 1990): 355–72, 356–57, 360–61; Dana D. Nelson, *Bad for Democracy: How the Presidency Undermines the Power of the People* (Minneapolis: University of Minnesota Press, 2008), 82–83.

31. Lijphart, "Presidentialism," *supra* note 1, 103.

32. Daryl L. Levinson and Richard H. Pildes, "Separation of Parties, Not Powers," *Harvard Law Review* 119 (June 2006): 2311–86, 2370–75.

33. Mary Ann Glendon, *The New Family and the New Property* (Toronto: Butterworths, 1981), 12–14; Lawrence Stone, *The Family, Sex and Marriage in England, 1500–1800* (New York: Harper and Row, 1977), 85–86 (both also noting that family before 1500 could include neighbors and other nonrelatives). Economics drove much of the change in family dynamics. When wealth was determined by ownership of land, property passed along blood lines through the generations. Indeed, the laws of intestacy gave priority to even distant cousins over the spouse of a deceased landowner. As the industrial economy began to develop and capital began to supplant land as the primary source of wealth, the marital household became the primary source of a person's social and economic status. Glendon, *New Family, supra*, 12, 15–16. There were other influences as well in the shift to the patriarchal, nuclear family. Stone, *Family, supra*, 658–66 (discussing urbanization, the American spirit of individualism, and other influences).

34. Leslie J. Harris, Lee E. Teitelbaum, and June Carbone, *Family Law*, 3rd ed. (New York: Aspen, 2005), 32, 35–37; Martha Minow, "'Forming Underneath Everything That Grows:' Toward a History of Family Law," *Wisconsin Law Review* 1985 (July–August): 819–98, 827–28; Lenore J. Weitzman, "Legal Regulation of Marriage: Tradition and Change," *California Law Review* 62 (July–September 1974): 1169–1288, 1172. To be sure, actual practices did not conform strictly to the letter of the law, but single women enjoyed greater legal rights than did married women, though still less than those enjoyed by men. Minow, "Forming Underneath," *supra*, 852–57; Lee E. Teitelbaum, "Family History and Family Law," *Wisconsin Law Review* 1985 (September–October): 1135–81, 1140.

35. Glendon, *New Family, supra* note 33, at 12–13

36. In re Doe, 418 S.E.2d 3, 7 (Ga. 1992).

37. Donald Oken, "What to Tell Cancer Patients: A Study of Medical Attitudes," *Journal of the American Medical Association* 175 (April 1, 1961): 1120–28, 1123; Dennis H. Novack et al., "Changes in Physicians' Attitudes toward Telling the Cancer Patient," *Journal of American Medical Association* 241 (March 2, 1979): 897–900, 898, table 1 (using the same survey questions as in the 1961 study).

38. Christine Laine and Frank Davidoff, "Patient-Centered Medicine: A Professional Evolution," *Journal of the American Medical Association* 275 (January 10, 1996): 152–56, 152 (Hippocrates quote); Peter H. Schuck, "Rethinking Informed Consent," *Yale Law Journal* 103 (January 1994): 899–959, 900.

39. Jaime S. King and Benjamin W. Moulton, "Rethinking Informed Consent: The Case for Shared Medical Decision-Making," *American Journal of Law and Medicine* 32, no. 4 (2006): 429–501, 431.

40. Laine and Davidoff, "Patient-Centered Medicine," *supra* note 38, 152.

41. King and Moulton, "Rethinking Informed Consent," *supra* note 39, 468–70; David S. Brody et al., "Patient Perception of Involvement in Medical Care: Relationship to Illness Attitudes and Outcomes," *Journal of General Internal Medicine* 4 (November 1989): 506–11, 509–10; Sarah L. Clever et al., "Primary Care Patients' Involvement in Decision-Making Is Associated with Improvement in Depression," *Medical Care* 44 (May 2006): 398–405; Mary Catherine Beach, Patrick S. Duggan, and Richard D. Moore, "Is Patients' Preferred Involvement in Health Decisions Related to Outcomes for Patients with HIV?," *Journal of General Internal Medicine* 22 (August 2007): 1119–24, 1122. Recall also the point from chapter 3 that involving patients as a co-decision-maker supplies an effective check on physicians who might provide treatments that are expensive and not likely to result in any benefit.

42. Clever et al., "Primary Care Patients' Involvement," *supra* note 41, 403; David Orentlicher, "The Influence of a Professional Organization on Physician Behavior," *Albany Law Review* 57 (Summer 1994): 583–605, 585–86.

43. Gregg, *Presidential Republic, supra* note 30, 91 (discussing George Mason's proposal for a three-person executive); Herman Finer, *The Presidency: Crisis and Regeneration: An Essay in Possibilities* (Chicago: University of Chicago Press, 1960), 303–6.

Notes to Chapter 7

1. To be precise, public polarization was greater for Obama during his first three years than for other presidents during their first three years. The public became more polarized in year four of the George W. Bush administration.

2. In April 2011, House Republicans unveiled a Medicare-voucher proposal that would have given Medicare recipients a tax credit to offset the costs of purchasing private health care insurance. Robert Pear, "G.O.P. Blueprint Would Remake Health Policy," *New York Times*, April 5, 2011. Public opposition to the proposal led the Democratic-led Senate to force a vote and put Republicans on record as supporting an idea that was going nowhere. Jennifer Steinhauer, "Democrats Force a Medicare Vote, Pressuring G.O.P.," *New York Times*, May 26, 2011.

3. Elizabeth Bumiller, "U.S. Sees Washington as Mad, and the Capital Doesn't Argue," *New York Times*, July 31, 2011; Jeffrey M. Jones, "Congressional Approval

Recovers Slightly, Now 17%," *Gallup Politics*, April 19, 2012, http://www.gallup.com/poll/153968/Congressional-Approval-Recovers-Slightly.aspx (accessed November 8, 2012). For approval ratings back to 1974, see Jeffrey M. Jones, "Congress' Job Approval Rating Worst in Gallup History," *Gallup Politics*, December 15, 2010, http://www.gallup.com/poll/145238/Congress-Job-Approval-Rating-Worst-Gallup-History.aspx (accessed November 8, 2012).

4. Michael Dobbs, "Obama and Health Care," *Fact Checker* (blog), *Washington Post*, January 24, 2008, http://voices.washingtonpost.com/fact-checker/2008/01/obama_and_health_care.html (accessed November 8, 2012).

5. To some extent, it makes sense when a committed minority blocks a policy that has majority support. Majorities can exploit their power unfairly. In addition, legislators appropriately consider both the level of support and the intensity of support for policy proposals. If the support for a policy is lukewarm among the majority while there is strong opposition among the minority, then the minority's more intense feelings may compensate for its smaller numbers.

6. Arend Lijphart, *Patterns of Democracy: Government Forms and Performance in Thirty-Six Countries* (New Haven: Yale University Press, 1999), 259–60.

7. When oversight committees investigate executive branch conduct because of its problematic nature, the committees can deter repetition of the conduct. Brian D. Feinstein, "Oversight as a Means of Congressional Control over Administration" (Working Paper, September 1, 2012), http://papers.ssrn.com/sol3/papers.cfm?abstract_id=2137149 (finding that "infractions" are 22 percent less likely to recur when they are the subject of oversight hearings; accessed November 8, 2012).

8. Daryl L. Levinson and Richard H. Pildes, "Separation of Parties, Not Powers," *Harvard Law Review* 119 (June 2006): 2311–86, 2370–71.

9. Bernie Becker and Vicki Needham, "Senate Republicans Vow to Hold Up Nominees to Force Action on Trade Deals," *On the Money* (blog), *The Hill*, March 14, 2011, http://thehill.com/blogs/on-the-money/1005–trade/149381-senate-republicans-vow-to-hold-up-presidential-nominees-to-force-action-on-trade-deals (accessed November 8, 2012); Binyamin Appelbaum and Jennifer Steinhauer, "Trade Deals Pass Congress, Ending 5-Year Standoff," *New York Times*, October 13, 2011.

10. Barbara Sinclair, *Party Wars: Polarization and the Politics of National Policy Making* (Norman: University of Oklahoma Press, 2006), 354; Jim Angle, "GOP Vows to Ramp Up Investigations of Obama Administration If It Wins House," *Fox News*, September 4, 2010, http://www.foxnews.com/politics/2010/09/04/gop-vows-ramp-investigations-obama-administration-wins-house/ (accessed November 8, 2012); Eric Schmitt, "Top Investigator for House Panel Leaves under Fire," *New York Times*, May 7, 1998.

11. Evan Bayh, "Why I'm Leaving the Senate," *New York Times*, February 21, 2010; Jennifer Steinhauer, "Snowe Opts Not to Seek Re-election in Maine," *New York Times*, February 29, 2012.

12. I have chosen the 50 percent and 100 percent figures for illustrative purposes. It is not important that they be 50 percent and 100 percent but only that they have a ratio of 1 to 2. Changing the percentages to 5 percent and 10 percent would not affect the analysis.

13. George A. Quattrone and Amos Tversky, "Contrasting Rational and Psycho-

logical Analyses of Political Choice," *American Political Science Review* 82 (September 1988): 719–36, 721 (1988).

14. Marjorie Randon Hershey, *Party Politics in America*, 13th ed. (New York: Pearson Longman, 2009), 282–83; Lee Sigelman, Paul J. Wahlbeck, and Emmett H. Buell, Jr., "Vote Choice and the Preference for Divided Government: Lessons of 1992," *American Journal of Political Science* 41 (July 1997): 879–94, 879. In contrast, presidents rarely had to deal with an opposition majority in either house of Congress between 1897 and 1954. In that fifty-eight-year stretch, the country experienced a national government divided by party during only eight of the years. Prior to 1897, one-party control of the executive and legislative branches was almost guaranteed by the use of party-printed ballots that voters used to cast their vote. By the 1888 election, the United States was using government-printed secret ballots. James L. Sundquist, "Needed: A Political Theory for the New Era of Coalition Government in the United States," *Political Science Quarterly* 103 (Winter 1989): 613–35, 613, 617.

15. Michael Lewis-Beck and Richard Nadeau, "Split-Ticket Voting: The Effects of Cognitive Madisonianism," *Journal of Politics* 66 (February 2004): 97–112, 107–8. See also Thomas M. Carsey and Geoffrey C. Layman, "Policy Balancing and Preferences for Party Control of Government," *Political Research Quarterly* 57 (December 2004): 541–50, 544–45 (finding support for divided government among 17 percent of voters in an Illinois survey). The name "cognitive Madisonianism" comes from the analogy of dividing power between the parties with Madison's division of power among the three branches of the national government. Everett C. Ladd, "Public Opinion and the 'Congress Problem,'" *Public Interest* 100 (Summer 1990): 57–67, 66–67.

Some scholars observe that split-ticket voting occurs when the legislative candidate and the presidential candidate share similar ideological views even though they come from different parties. Paul Frymer, "Ideological Consensus within Divided Party Government," *Political Science Quarterly* 109 (Summer 1994): 287–311; Bernard Grofman, William Koetzle, Michael P. McDonald, and Thomas L. Brunell, "A New Look at Split-Ticket Outcomes for House and President: The Comparative Midpoints Model," *Journal of Politics* 62 (February 2000): 34–50. Other scholars believe that voters look for different qualities in their presidential and congressional candidates. Gary C. Jacobson, *The Electoral Origins of Divided Government: Competition in U.S. House Elections, 1946–1988* (Boulder, CO: Westview, 1990), 105–37. See also Sigelman et al., "Vote Choice," *supra* note 14, 890 (finding that split-ticket voting in 1992 reflected preferences for particular candidates, allegiance to incumbents, and party identification).

16. One also could spin out more complicated scenarios predicting opposition to a two-person presidency. For example, even if Democrats and Republicans believed they had a roughly 50 percent chance of winning the presidency, they could be risk seekers and prefer the 50 percent odds of winning all of the executive power to the certainty of winning 50 percent of the executive power.

17. There also could be support for a two-person presidency if Democrats and Republicans both believed they had a 50 percent chance of winning the presidency. One side might be risk averse and prefer the 100 percent chance of winning half of the presidential power. Adding the cognitive Madisonians could again yield a majority.

18. I include as independents people who identified themselves as independent

Democrats, independent Republicans, or independent independents in the American National Election Studies. In these studies, people were asked, "Generally speaking, do you usually think of yourself as a Republican, a Democrat, an Independent, or what?" If they answered "Independent or Other," they were asked if they thought of themselves as "closer to the Republican or Democratic party?" The data are reported at American National Election Studies, "Party Identification 7-Point Scale (Revised in 2008)," http://electionstudies.org/nesguide/toptable/tab2a_1.htm (accessed November 8, 2012), and also at Michael S. Beck, *The American Voter Revisited* (Ann Arbor: University of Michigan Press, 2008), 114.

19. Robert Elgie, e-mail message to author, November 14, 2011. And the public may have voted for cohabitation not because it desired bipartisan governance but because it was displeased with the current president and wanted to cabin his influence until the next presidential election. Robert Elgie, "'Cohabitation': Divided Government French-Style," in *Divided Government in Comparative Perspective*, ed. Robert Elgie (Oxford: Oxford University Press, 2001), 117–18. Other sources for this paragraph include ibid., 116–17; Andrew Knapp and Vincent Wright, *The Government and Politics of France*, 5th ed. (New York: Routledge, 2006), 128.

20. Robert Elgie, *Political Institutions in Contemporary France* (Oxford: Oxford University Press, 2003), 103.

21. Peter Shane, *Madison's Nightmare: How Executive Power Threatens American Democracy* (Chicago: University of Chicago Press, 2009), 32–37, 143–45.

22. Steven G. Calabresi and Christopher S. Yoo, *The Unitary Executive: Presidential Power from Washington to Bush* (New Haven: Yale University Press), 2008, 14–15.

23. Neal Devins and David E. Lewis, "Not-So-Independent Agencies," *Boston University Law Review* 88 (April 2008): 459–98; Free Enterprise Fund v. Public Company Accounting Oversight Board, 130 S. Ct. 3138 (2010).

Notes to Chapter 8

1. Paul Krugman, "Pass the Bill," *New York Times*, December 18, 2009 (writing that "it's time to revise the rules" to take away the filibuster); Thomas Geoghegan, "Mr. Smith Rewrites the Constitution," *New York Times*, January 11, 2010 (arguing that the filibuster is unconstitutional); Howard H. Baker, Jr., "Rule XXII: Don't Kill It!," *Washington Post*, April 27, 1993 (defending the filibuster).

Bibliography

Abramowitz, Alan. *The Disappearing Center: Engaged Citizens, Polarization, and American Democracy*. New Haven: Yale University Press, 2010.

———. "Partisan Polarization and the Rise of the Tea Party Movement." Paper presented at the annual meeting of the American Political Science Association, Seattle, Washington, September 1–4, 2011. http://papers.ssrn.com/sol3/papers.cfm?abstract_id=1903153 (accessed November 8, 2012).

Abramson, Paul R., John H. Aldrich, Phil Paolino, and David W. Rohde. "Third Party and Independent Candidates in American Politics: Wallace, Anderson, and Perot." *Political Science Quarterly* 110 (Autumn 1995): 349–67.

Ackerman, Bruce. "The Emergency Constitution." *Yale Law Journal* 113 (March 2004): 1029–91.

———. "The New Separation of Powers." *Harvard Law Review* 113 (January 2000): 633–729.

———. *We the People: Foundations*. Cambridge: Belknap Press of Harvard University Press, 1991.

Ackerman, Bruce, and David Golove. *Is NAFTA Constitutional?* Cambridge: Harvard University Press, 1995.

Adler, David Gray. "Clinton, the Constitution, and the War Power." In Adler and Genovese, *The Presidency and the Law*, 19–57.

———. "Court, Constitution, and Foreign Affairs." In Adler and George, *The Constitution and the Conduct of American Foreign Policy*, 19–56.

———. "The President's Recognition Power." In Adler and George, *The Constitution and the Conduct of American Foreign Policy*, 133–57.

Adler, David Gray, and Michael A. Genovese, eds. *The Presidency and the Law: The Clinton Legacy*. Lawrence: University Press of Kansas, 2002.

Adler, David Gray, and Larry N. George, eds. *The Constitution and the Conduct of American Foreign Policy*. Lawrence: University Press of Kansas, 1996.

———. Introduction to Adler and George, *The Constitution and the Conduct of American Foreign Policy*, 1–16.

Aldrich, John H. *Why Parties? The Origin and Transformation of Political Parties in America*. Chicago: University of Chicago Press, 1995.

Aliprantis, Charalambos C., and Subir K. Chakrabarti. *Games and Decision Making*. 2nd ed. New York: Oxford University Press, 2011.

Alter, Jonathan. *The Promise: President Obama, Year One*. New York: Simon and Schuster, 2010.

Altshuler, Fred H. "Comparing the Nixon and Clinton Impeachments." *Hastings Law Journal* 51 (April 2000): 745–52.

Amar, Akhil. *America's Unwritten Constitution: The Precedents and Principles We Live By*. New York: Basic Books, 2012.

Amy, Douglas J. *Real Choices/New Voices: How Proportional Representation Elections Could Revitalize American Democracy*. 2nd ed. New York: Columbia University Press, 2002.

Andersen, William R. *Mastering Administrative Law*. Durham: Carolina Academic Press, 2010.

Aranson, Peter H., Ernest Gellhorn, and Glen O. Robinson. "A Theory of Legislative Delegation." *Cornell Law Review* 68 (November 1982): 1–67.

Ashworth, Tony. *Trench Warfare, 1914–1918: The Live and Let Live System*. New York: Holmes and Meier, 1980.

Axelrod, Robert M. *The Evolution of Cooperation*. New York: Basic Books, 1984.

Aycock, Marlyn, Mercer Cross, and Elder Witt. *Watergate: Chronology of a Crisis*. Washington, DC: Congressional Quarterly, 1975.

Bagley, Nicholas, and Richard L. Revesz. "Centralized Oversight of the Regulatory State." *Columbia Law Review* 106 (October 2006): 1260–1329.

Barron, David J., and Martin S. Lederman. "The Commander in Chief at the Lowest Ebb—A Constitutional History." *Harvard Law Review* 121 (February 2008): 941–1112.

Bartels, Larry M. "Partisanship and Voting Behavior, 1952–1996." *American Journal of Political Science* 44 (January 2000): 35–50.

Batlle y Ordóñez, José. "A Collegial Executive for Uruguay." In *Parliamentary versus Presidential Government*, edited by Arend Lijphart, 175–77. New York: Oxford University Press, 1992.

Beach, Mary Catherine, Patrick S. Duggan, and Richard D. Moore. "Is Patients' Preferred Involvement in Health Decisions Related to Outcomes for Patients with HIV?" *Journal of General Internal Medicine* 22 (August 2007): 1119–24.

Beck, Michael S. *The American Voter Revisited*. Ann Arbor: University of Michigan Press, 2008.

Bejesky, Robert. "Undermining Egalitarian Principles of Federalism? A Cross-National Comparison of India, Mexico, and the United States." *Temple International and Comparative Law Journal* 14 (Fall 2000): 363–400.

Berry, Christopher R., Barry C. Burden, and William G. Howell, "The President and the Distribution of Federal Spending." *American Political Science Review* 104 (November 2010): 783–99.

Berry, Christopher R., and Jacob E. Gersen. "The Unbundled Executive." *University of Chicago Law Review* 75 (Fall 2008): 1385–1434.

Binder, Sarah A. "The Dynamics of Legislative Gridlock, 1947–96." *American Political Science Review* 93 (September 1999): 519–33.

Bisnow, Mark. *Diary of a Dark Horse: The 1980 Anderson Presidential Campaign.* Carbondale: Southern Illinois University Press, 1983.

Blinder, Alan S. *The Quiet Revolution: Central Banking Goes Modern.* New Haven: Yale University Press, 2004.

Blinder, Alan S., and John Morgan. "Are Two Heads Better than One? Monetary Policy by Committee." *Journal of Money, Credit and Banking* 37 (October 2005): 789–811.

Blumberg, Herbert H. "Group Decision Making and Choice Shift." In *Small Group Research: A Handbook,* edited by A. Paul Hare, Herbert H. Blumberg, Martin F. Davies, and M. Valerie Kent, 195–210. Norwood, NJ: Ablex, 1994.

Boatwright, Mary T., Daniel J. Gargola, and Richard J. A. Talbert. *The Romans: From Village to Empire.* New York: Oxford University Press, 2004.

Bogle, John C., and David F. Swensen. *Common Sense on Mutual Funds: New Imperatives for the Intelligent Investor.* 10th ed. Hoboken, NJ: Wiley, 2010.

Bornstein, Gary, and Ilan Yaniv. "Individual and Group Behavior in the Ultimatum Game: Are Groups More 'Rational' Players?" *Experimental Economics* 1 (June 1998): 101–8.

Bowman, Frank O., III, and Stephen L. Sepinuck. "'High Crimes & Misdemeanors': Defining the Constitutional Limits on Presidential Impeachment." *Southern California Law Review* 72 (September 1999): 1517–98.

Bradley, Curtis A., and Martin S. Flaherty. "Executive Power Essentialism and Foreign Affairs." *Michigan Law Review* 102 (February 2004): 545–688.

Bradley, Curtis A., and Eric A. Posner. "Presidential Signing Statements and Executive Power." *Constitutional Commentary* 23 (Winter 2006): 307–64.

Brandon, Mark E. *Free in the World: American Slavery and Constitutional Failure.* Princeton: Princeton University Press, 1998.

Bressman, Lisa Schultz, and Michael P. Vandenbergh. "Inside the Administrative State: A Critical Look at Presidential Control." *Michigan Law Review* 105 (October 2006): 47–99.

Brewer, Marilynn B., and Rupert J. Brown. "Intergroup Relations." In Gilbert, Fiske, and Lindzey, *Handbook of Social Psychology,* vol. 2, 554–94.

Brewer, Mark D., Mack D. Mariani, and Jeffrey M. Stonecash. "Northern Democrats and Party Polarization in the U.S. House." *Legislative Studies Quarterly* 27 (August 2002): 423–44.

Brody, David S., Suzanne M. Miller, Caryn E. Lerman, David G. Smith, and G. Craig Caputo. "Patient Perception of Involvement in Medical Care: Relationship to Illness Attitudes and Outcomes." *Journal of General Internal Medicine* 4 (November 1989): 506–11.

Brown, Ellyn L. "The Hill-Burton Act, 1946–1980: Asynchrony in the Delivery of Health Care to the Poor." *Maryland Law Review* 39, no. 2 (1979): 316–75.

Brownstein, Ronald. *The Second Civil War: How Extreme Partisanship Has Paralyzed Washington and Polarized America.* New York: Penguin, 2007.

Burke, Peter J. "Interaction in Small Groups." In *Handbook of Social Psychology,* edited by John Delamater, 363–87. New York: Springer, 2006.

Calabresi, Steven G. "Political Parties as Mediating Institutions." *University of Chicago Law Review* 61 (Fall 1994): 1479–1533.

Calabresi, Steven G., and Kevin H. Rhodes. "The Structural Constitution: Unitary Executive, Plural Judiciary." *Harvard Law Review* 105 (April 1992): 1153–1216.

Calabresi, Steven G., and Christopher S. Yoo. *The Unitary Executive: Presidential Power from Washington to Bush.* New Haven: Yale University Press, 2008.

Callaway, Michael R., Richard G. Marriott, and James K. Esser. "Effects of Dominance on Group Decision Making: Toward a Stress Reduction Explanation of Groupthink." *Journal of Personality and Social Psychology* 49 (October 1985): 949–52.

Canes-Wrone, Brandice, William G. Howell, and David E. Lewis. "Toward a Broader Understanding of Presidential Power: A Reevaluation of the Two Presidencies Thesis." *Journal of Politics* 70 (January 2008): 1–16.

Caro, Robert A. *The Years of Lyndon Johnson: The Passage of Power.* New York: Knopf, 2012.

Carothers, Thomas. "The End of the Transition Paradigm." *Journal of Democracy* 13 (January 2002): 5–21.

Carsey, Thomas M., and Geoffrey C. Layman. "Policy Balancing and Preferences for Party Control of Government." *Political Research Quarterly* 57 (December 2004): 541–50.

Chalos, Peter, and Sue Pickard. "Information Choice and Cue Use: An Experiment in Group Information Processing." *Journal of Applied Psychology* 70 (November 1985): 634–41.

Chemerinsky, Erwin. *Constitutional Law: Principles and Policies.* 4th ed. New York: Wolters Kluwer, 2011.

———. "The Question's Not Clear, but Party Government Is Not the Answer." *William and Mary Law Review* 30 (Winter 1989): 411–23.

Chen, Chia-Wei, J. Barry Lin, and Bingsheng Yi. "CEO Duality and Firm Performance—An Endogenous Issue." *Corporate Ownership & Control* 6 (Fall 2008): 58–65.

Clark, Terry Nichols. "The Swiss Communal Ethic." In *Commonwealth: The Other Road to Democracy—The Swiss Model of Democratic Self-Governance,* edited by Daniel J. Elazar, 137–152. Lanham, MD: Lexington Books, 2001.

Clever, Sarah L., Daniel E. Ford, Lisa V. Rubenstein, et al. "Primary Care Patients' Involvement in Decision-Making Is Associated with Improvement in Depression." *Medical Care* 44 (May 2006): 398–405.

Coleman, John J. "United Government, Divided Government, and Party Responsiveness." *American Political Science Review* 93 (December 1999): 821–35.

Coleman, John J., and David C. W. Parker. "The Consequences of Divided Government." In *The Oxford Handbook of the American Presidency,* edited by George C. Edwards III and William G. Howell, 383–402. New York: Oxford University Press, 2009.

Collins, James C., and Morten T. Hansen. *Great by Choice: Uncertainty, Chaos, and Luck? Why Some Thrive Despite Them All.* New York: HarperCollins, 2011.

Cooper, David J., and John H. Kagel. "Are Two Heads Better than One? Team versus Individual Play in Signaling Games." *American Economic Review* 95 (June 2005): 477–509.

Cooper, Phillip J. *By Order of the President: The Use and Abuse of Executive Direct Action*. Lawrence: University Press of Kansas, 2002.

———. "George W. Bush, Edgar Allan Poe, and the Use and Abuse of Presidential Signing Statements." *Presidential Studies Quarterly* 35 (September 2005): 515–32.

Corwin, Edward S. *The President, Office and Powers, 1787–1957; History and Analysis of Practice and Opinion*. 4th rev. ed. New York: NYU Press, 1957.

———. "The Steel Seizure Case: A Judicial Brick without Straw." *Columbia Law Review* 53 (January 1953): 53–66.

Cronin, Thomas E. *The State of the Presidency*. 2nd ed. Boston: Little, Brown, 1980.

Cutler, Lloyd N. "Now Is the Time for All Good Men." *William and Mary Law Review* 30 (Winter 1989): 387–402.

Dahl, Robert A. "Myth of the Presidential Moderate." *Political Science Quarterly* 105 (Autumn 1990): 355–72.

Dahya, Jay, and Nickolaos G. Travlos. "Does the One Man Show Pay? Theory and Evidence on the Dual CEO Revisited." *European Financial Management* 6 (March 2000): 85–98.

Dalton, Dan R., Michael A. Hitt, S. Trevis Certo, and Catherine M. Dalton. "The Fundamental Agency Problem and Its Mitigation: Independence, Equity, and the Market for Corporate Control." *Academy of Management Annals* 1, no. 1 (2007): 1–64.

Davis, Colin. *Scenes of Love and Murder: Renoir, Film and Philosophy*. London: Wallflower, 2009.

Davis, James H. "Some Compelling Intuitions about Group Consensus Decisions, Theoretical and Empirical Research, and Interpersonal Aggregation Phenomena: Selected Examples, 1950–1990." *Organizational Behavior and Human Decision Processes* 52 (June 1992): 3–38.

Devins, Neal. "Signing Statements and Divided Government." *William & Mary Bill of Rights Journal* 16 (October 2007): 63–79.

Devins, Neal, and David E. Lewis. "Not-So-Independent Agencies." *Boston University Law Review* 88 (April 2008): 459–98.

Dovidio, John F., and Samuel L. Gaertner. "Intergroup Bias." In Fiske, Gilbert, and Lindzey, *Handbook of Social Psychology*, vol. 2, 1084–1121.

Duverger, Maurice. *Political Parties: Their Organization and Activity in the Modern State*. 3rd ed. London: Methuen, 1964.

Edwards, George C., III, Andrew Barrett, and Jeffrey Peake. "The Legislative Impact of Divided Government." *American Journal of Political Science* 41 (April 1997): 545–63.

Edwards, Mickey. *The Parties versus the People: How to Turn Republicans and Democrats into Americans*. New Haven: Yale University Press, 2012.

Elgie, Robert. "'Cohabitation': Divided Government French-Style." In *Divided Government in Comparative Perspective*, edited by Robert Elgie, 106–26. Oxford: Oxford University Press, 2001.

———. *Political Institutions in Contemporary France*. Oxford: Oxford University Press, 2003.

Ellis, Donald G., and B. Aubrey Fisher. *Small Group Decision Making: Communication and the Group Process.* 4th ed. New York: McGraw-Hill, 1994.

Ely, John Hart. *War and Responsibility: Constitutional Lessons of Vietnam and Its Aftermath.* Princeton: Princeton University Press, 1993.

Epstein, David, and Sharyn O'Halloran. *Delegating Powers: A Transaction Cost Politics Approach to Policy Making under Separate Powers.* New York: Cambridge University Press, 1999.

Epstein, Lee, and Jeffrey A. Segal. *Advice and Consent: The Politics of Judicial Appointments.* New York: Oxford University Press, 2005.

Epstein, Leon D. *Political Parties in the American Mold.* Madison: University of Wisconsin Press, 1986.

Farber, Daniel A. *Lincoln's Constitution.* Chicago: University of Chicago Press, 2003.

Feinstein, Brian D. "Oversight as a Means of Congressional Control over Administration." Working Paper, September 1, 2012. http://papers.ssrn.com/sol3/papers.cfm?abstract_id=2137149 (accessed November 8, 2012).

Finer, Herman. *The Presidency: Crisis and Regeneration: An Essay in Possibilities.* Chicago: University of Chicago Press, 1960.

Finkelman, Paul. "The Cost of Compromise and the Covenant with Death." In "Compromise and Constitutionalism," special issue, *Pepperdine Law Review* 38 (2011): 845–88.

Fiorina, Morris P. "Legislative Choice of Regulatory Forms: Legal Process or Administrative Process?" *Public Choice* 39 (January 1982): 33–66.

Fiorina, Morris P., Samuel J. Abrams, and Jeremy C. Pope. *Culture War? The Myth of a Polarized America.* 3rd ed. Boston: Longman, 2011.

Fisher, Louis. *Presidential War Power.* Lawrence: University Press of Kansas, 1995.

———. "Unchecked Presidential Wars." *University of Pennsylvania Law Review* 148 (May 2000): 1637–72.

Fisk, Catherine, and Erwin Chemerinsky. "The Filibuster." *Stanford Law Review* 49 (January 1997): 181–254.

Fiske, Susan T., Daniel T. Gilbert, and Gardner Lindzey, eds. *Handbook of Social Psychology.* 2 vols. 5th ed. Hoboken, NJ: Wiley, 2010.

Fitts, Michael A. "The Legalization of the Presidency: A Twenty-Five Year Watergate Retrospective." *St. Louis University Law Journal* 43 (Summer 1999): 725–40.

———. "The Paradox of Power in the Modern State: Why a Unitary, Centralized Presidency May Not Exhibit Effective or Legitimate Leadership." *University of Pennsylvania Law Review* 144 (January 1996): 827–902.

Flaherty, Martin S. "The Most Dangerous Branch." *Yale Law Journal* 105 (May 1996): 1725–1839.

Fleishman, Joel L., and Arthur H. Aufses. "Law and Orders: The Problem of Presidential Legislation." *Law and Contemporary Problems* 40 (Summer 1976): 1–45.

Foner, Eric. *Give Me Liberty! An American History.* 3rd ed. New York: Norton, 2011.

Frank, Robert H., and Philip J. Cook. *The Winner-Take-All Society: How More and More Americans Compete for Ever Fewer and Bigger Prizes, Encouraging Economic Waste, Income Inequality, and an Impoverished Cultural Life.* New York: Free Press, 1995.

Frankel, Jeffrey A., and Peter R. Orszag. Introduction to *American Economic Policy in the 1990s*, edited by Jeffrey A. Frankel and Peter R. Orszag, 1–16. Cambridge: MIT Press, 2002.

Frymer, Paul. "Ideological Consensus within Divided Party Government." *Political Science Quarterly* 109 (Summer 1994): 287–311.

———. *Uneasy Alliances: Race and Party Competition in America*. Princeton: Princeton University Press, 1999.

Frymer, Paul, and Albert Yoon. "Political Parties, Representation, and Federal Safeguards." *Northwestern University Law Review* 96 (Spring 2002): 977–1026.

Garber, Marc N., and Kurt A. Wimmer. "Presidential Signing Statements as Interpretations of Legislative Intent: An Executive Aggrandizement of Power." *Harvard Journal on Legislation* 24 (Summer 1987): 363–95.

Gardner, James A. "Can Party Politics Be Virtuous?" *Columbia Law Review* 100 (April 2000): 667–701.

———. "Deliberation or Tabulation? The Self-Undermining Constitutional Architecture of Election Campaigns." *Buffalo Law Review* 54 (April 2007): 1413–82.

———. "Madison's Hope: Virtue, Self-Interest, and the Design of Electoral Systems." *Iowa Law Review* 86 (October 2000): 87–172.

Gilbert, Daniel T., Susan T. Fiske, and Gardner Lindzey, eds. *The Handbook of Social Psychology*. 2 vols. 4th ed. New York: McGraw-Hill, 1998.

Gilboa, Itzhak. *Rational Choice*. Cambridge: MIT Press, 2010.

Gladwell, Malcolm. *Outliers: The Story of Success*. Boston: Little, Brown, 2008.

Glendon, Mary Ann. *The New Family and the New Property*. Toronto: Butterworths, 1981.

Goldsmith, Jack L. *The Terror Presidency: Law and Judgment inside the Bush Administration*. New York: Norton, 2007.

González, Luis Eduardo, and Charles Guy Gillespie. "Presidentialism and Democratic Stability in Uruguay." In Linz and Valenzuela, *The Failure of Presidential Democracy*, 225–52.

Goodwin, James S., and Jean M. Goodwin. "The Tomato Effect: Rejection of Highly Efficacious Therapies." *Journal of the American Medical Association* 251 (May 11, 1984): 2387–90.

Gordon, Sanford C. "Politicizing Agency Spending Authority: Lessons from a Bush-Era Scandal." *American Political Science Review* 105 (November 2011): 717–34.

Graham, Hugh Davis. "Richard Nixon and Civil Rights: Explaining an Enigma." *Presidential Studies Quarterly* 26 (Winter 1996): 93–106.

Greenberg, Edward S., and Benjamin I. Page. *The Struggle for Democracy*. 7th ed. New York: Pearson Longman, 2005.

Greenberg, Stanley B. *Middle Class Dreams: The Politics and Power of the New American Majority*. New York: Times Books, 1995.

Greene, Abner S. "Checks and Balances in an Era of Presidential Lawmaking." *University of Chicago Law Review* 61 (Winter 1994): 123–96.

Gregg, Gary L., II. *The Presidential Republic: Executive Representation and Deliberative Democracy*. Lanham, MD: Rowman & Littlefield, 1997.

Grofman, Bernard, William Koetzle, Michael P. McDonald, and Thomas L. Brunell. "A New Look at Split-Ticket Outcomes for House and President: The Comparative Midpoints Model." *Journal of Politics* 62 (February 2000): 34–50.

Guinier, Lani. "No Two Seats: The Elusive Quest for Political Equality." *Virginia Law Review* 77 (November 1991): 1413–1514.

Gutmann, Amy, and Dennis Thompson. *The Spirit of Compromise: Why Governing Demands It and Campaigning Undermines It.* Princeton: Princeton University Press, 2012.

Hacker, J. David. "A Census-Based Count of the Civil War Dead." *Civil War History* 57 (December 2011): 307–48.

Hacker, Jacob S., and Paul Pierson. *Winner-Take-All Politics: How Washington Made the Rich Richer—and Turned Its Back on the Middle Class.* New York: Simon and Schuster, 2010.

Hackman, J. Richard, and Nancy Katz. "Group Behavior and Performance." In Fiske, Gilbert, and Lindzey, *Handbook of Social Psychology*, vol. 2, 1208–51.

Harris, Leslie J., Lee E. Teitelbaum, and June Carbone. *Family Law.* 3rd ed. New York: Aspen, 2005.

Hasen, Richard L. "Entrenching the Duopoly: Why the Supreme Court Should Not Allow the States to Protect the Democrats and Republican from Political Competition." *Supreme Court Review*, 1997, 331–71.

Hathaway, Oona A. "Presidential Power over International Law: Restoring the Balance." *Yale Law Journal* 119 (November 2009): 140–268.

Hebe, William. "Executive Orders and the Development of Presidential Power." *Villanova Law Review* 17 (March 1972): 688–712.

Heichelheim, Fritz M., Cedric A. Yeo, and Allen Mason Ward. *A History of the Roman People.* 2nd ed. Englewood Cliffs, NJ: Prentice-Hall, 1984.

Henkin, Louis. *Foreign Affairs and the United States Constitution.* 2nd ed. New York: Oxford University Press, 1996.

Hershey, Marjorie Randon. *Party Politics in America.* 13th ed. New York: Pearson Longman, 2009.

Hitchner, R. Bruce. "From Dayton to Brussels: The Story behind the Constitutional and Governmental Reform Process in Bosnia and Herzegovina." *Fletcher Forum of World Affairs* 30 (Winter 2006): 125–36.

Hofstadter, Richard. *The Idea of a Party System: The Rise of Legitimate Opposition in the United States, 1780–1840.* Berkeley: University of California Press, 1969.

Hong, Lu, and Scott E. Page. "Groups of Diverse Problem Solvers Can Outperform Groups of High-Ability Problem Solvers." *Proceedings of the National Academy of Sciences* 101 (November 16, 2004): 16385–89.

Hovenkamp, Herbert, and Phillip E. Areeda. *Antitrust Law: An Analysis of Antitrust Principles and Their Application.* 14 vols. 2nd ed. New York: Aspen, 2005.

Howell, William G. *Power without Persuasion: The Politics of Direct Presidential Action.* Princeton: Princeton University Press, 2003.

Howell, William G., and Jon C. Pevehouse. *While Dangers Gather: Congressional Checks on Presidential War Powers.* Princeton: Princeton University Press, 2007.

Issacharoff, Samuel. "Democracy and Collective Decision Making." *International Journal of Constitutional Law* (April 2008): 231–66.

———. "Introduction: The Structures of Democratic Politics." *Columbia Law Review* 100 (April 2000): 593–97.

Issacharoff, Samuel, Pamela S. Karlan, and Richard H. Pildes. *The Law of Democracy: Legal Structure of the Political Process.* 3rd ed. New York: Foundation, 2007.

Issacharoff, Samuel, and Richard H. Pildes. "Politics as Markets: Partisan Lockups of the Democratic Process." *Stanford Law Review* 50 (February 1998): 643–717.

Jacobson, Gary C. *The Electoral Origins of Divided Government: Competition in U.S. House Elections, 1946–1988.* Boulder, CO: Westview, 1990.

Janis, Irving L. *Groupthink: Psychological Studies of Policy Decisions and Fiascoes.* 2nd ed. Boston: Houghton Mifflin, 1982.

Johanssen, Robert W. "Stephen A. Douglas' New England Campaign, 1860." *New England Quarterly* 35 (June 1962): 162–86.

Johnsen, Dawn E. "What's a President to Do? Interpreting the Constitution in the Wake of Bush Administration Abuses." *Boston University Law Review* 88 (April 2008): 395–419.

Joseph, Edward P., and R. Bruce Hitchner. *Making Bosnia Work: Why EU Accession Is Not Enough.* Washington, DC: United States Institute of Peace, 2008. http://www .usip.org/files/resources/1_7.PDF (accessed November 8, 2012).

Kagan, Elena. "Presidential Administration." *Harvard Law Review* 114 (June 2001): 2245–2385.

Kang, Michael S. "Sore Loser Laws and Democratic Contestation." *Georgetown Law Journal* 99 (April 2011): 1013–75.

Kassop, Nancy. "Expansion and Contraction: Clinton's Impact on the Scope of Presidential Power." In Adler and Genovese, *The Presidency and the Law*, 1–18.

Katyal, Neal Kumar. "Internal Separation of Powers: Checking Today's Most Dangerous Branch from Within." *Yale Law Journal* 115, no. 9 (2006): 2314–49.

Kelly, Sean Q. "Divided We Govern: A Reassessment." *Polity* 25 (Spring 1993): 475–84.

Kenyon, Cecelia M. "Men of Little Faith: The Anti-Federalists on the Nature of Representative Government." *William and Mary Quarterly* 12 (January 1955): 3–43.

Ketcham, Jonathan D., Laurence C. Baker, and Donna MacIsaac. "Physician Practice Size and Variations in Treatment and Outcomes: Evidence from Medicare Patients with AMI." *Health Affairs* 26 (January 2007): 195–205.

Khurana, Rakesh. *Searching for a Corporate Savior: The Irrational Quest for Charismatic CEOs.* Princeton: Princeton University Press, 2002.

King, Anthony. "Ministerial Autonomy in Britain." In Laver and Shepsle, *Cabinet Ministers*, 203–25.

King, Jaime S., and Benjamin W. Moulton. "Rethinking Informed Consent: The Case for Shared Medical Decision-Making." *American Journal of Law and Medicine* 32, no. 4 (2006): 429–501.

Kitrosser, Heidi. "Secrecy and Separated Powers: Executive Privilege Revisited." *Iowa Law Review* 92 (February 2007): 489–543.

Klarman, Michael. "*Bush v. Gore* through the Lens of Constitutional History." *California Law Review* 89 (December 2001): 1721–65.

Kleinerman, Benjamin A. *The Discretionary President: The Promise and Peril of Executive Power.* Lawrence: University Press of Kansas, 2009.

Kline, Dee Ann. "Intuitive Team Decision Making." In *How Professionals Make Deci-*

sions, edited by Henry Montgomery, Raanan Lipshitz, and Berndt Brehmer, 171–82. Mahwah, NJ: Erlbaum, 2005.

Klöti, Ulrich. "The Government." In *Handbook of Swiss Politics,* 2nd ed., edited by Ulrich Klöti, Peter Knoepfel, Hanspeter Kriesi, Wolf Linder, Yannis Papadopoulos, and Pascal Sciarini, 145–69. Zürich: Neue Zürcher Zeitung, 2007.

Knapp, Andrew, and Vincent Wright. *The Government and Politics of France.* 5th ed. New York: Routledge, 2006.

Kocher, Martin G., and Matthias Sutter. "The Decision Maker Matters: Individual versus Group Behavior in Experimental Beauty-Contest Games." *Economic Journal* 115 (January 2005): 200–223.

Koh, Harold H. *The National Security Constitution: Sharing Power after the Iran-Contra Affair.* New Haven: Yale University Press, 1990.

———. "Why the President Almost Always Wins in Foreign Affairs." In Adler and George, *The Constitution and the Conduct of American Foreign Policy,* 158–80.

Kommers, Donald P. *The Constitutional Jurisprudence of the Federal Republic of Germany.* 2nd ed. Durham: Duke University Press, 1997.

Kotz, Nick. *Judgment Days: Lyndon Baines Johnson, Martin Luther King, Jr., and the Laws That Changed America.* Boston: Houghton Mifflin, 2005.

Kramer, Larry D. "Putting the Politics Back into the Political Safeguards of Federalism." *Columbia Law Review* 100 (January 2000): 215–93.

Krause, George A., and David B. Cohen. "Presidential Use of Executive Orders, 1953–1994." *American Politics Quarterly* 25 (October 1997): 458–81.

Krehbiel, Keith. "Institutional and Partisan Sources of Gridlock: A Theory of Divided and Unified Government." *Journal of Theoretical Politics* 8 (January 1996): 7–40.

———. *Pivotal Politics: A Theory of U.S. Lawmaking.* Chicago: University of Chicago Press, 1998.

Kriesi, Hanspeter, and Alexandre H. Trechsel. *The Politics of Switzerland: Continuity and Change in a Consensus Democracy.* Cambridge: Cambridge University Press, 2008.

Kurland, Philip B., and Ralph Lerner, eds. *The Founders' Constitution.* 5 vols. Chicago: University of Chicago Press, 1987.

Ladd, Everett C. "Public Opinion and the 'Congress Problem.'" *Public Interest* 100 (Summer 1990): 57–67.

Laine, Christine, and Frank Davidoff. "Patient-Centered Medicine: A Professional Evolution." *Journal of the American Medical Association* 275 (January 10, 1996): 152–56.

Lakhani, Karim R., Lars Bo Jeppesen, Peter A. Lohse, and Jill A. Panetta, "The Value of Openness in Scientific Problem Solving." Working paper, October 2006. http://www.hbs.edu/research/pdf/07-050.pdf (accessed November 8, 2012).

Langbein, John H. "The Uniform Prudent Investor Act and the Future of Trust Investing." *Iowa Law Review* 81 (March 1996): 641–69.

Laver, Michael, and Kenneth A. Shepsle. "Cabinet Government in Theoretical Perspective." In Laver and Shepsle, *Cabinet Ministers,* 298–99.

———. "Cabinet Ministers and Government Formation in Parliamentary Democracies." In Laver and Shepsle, *Cabinet Ministers,* 3–12.

———, eds. *Cabinet Ministers and Parliamentary Government*. Cambridge: Cambridge University Press, 1994.

Lawson, Gary. "Delegation and Original Meaning." *Virginia Law Review* 88 (April 2002): 327–404.

———. "The Rise and Rise of the Administrative State." *Harvard Law Review* 107 (April 1994): 1231–54.

———. "What Lurks Beneath: NSA Surveillance and Executive Power." *Boston University Law Review* 88 (April 2008): 375–93.

Lee, Gia B. "The President's Secrets." *George Washington Law Review* 76 (February 2008): 197–261.

Leonard, Gerald. *The Invention of Party Politics: Federalism, Popular Sovereignty, and Constitutional Development in Jacksonian Illinois*. Chapel Hill: University of North Carolina Press, 2002.

Lessig, Lawrence, and Cass R. Sunstein. "The President and the Administration." *Columbia Law Review* 94 (January 1994): 1–119.

Levine, John M., and Richard L. Moreland. "Small Groups." In Gilbert, Fiske, and Lindzey, *The Handbook of Social Psychology*, vol. 2, 415–69.

Levinson, Daryl J. "Empire-Building Government in Constitutional Law." *Harvard Law Review* 118 (January 2005): 915–72.

Levinson, Daryl L., and Richard H. Pildes. "Separation of Parties, Not Powers." *Harvard Law Review* 119 (June 2006): 2311–86.

Levinson, Sanford. "Compromise and Constitutionalism." In "Compromise and Constitutionalism," special issue, *Pepperdine Law Review* 38 (2011): 821–43.

———. *Our Undemocratic Constitution: Where the Constitution Goes Wrong (and How We the People Can Correct It)*. New York: Oxford University Press, 2006.

Levinson, Sanford, and Ernest A. Young. "Who's Afraid of the Twelfth Amendment?" In *Bush v. Gore* issue, *Florida State University Law Review* 29 (2001): 925–73.

Lewis-Beck, Michael, and Richard Nadeau. "Split-Ticket Voting: The Effects of Cognitive Madisonianism." *Journal of Politics* 66 (February 2004): 97–112.

Liberman, Lee S. "*Morrison v. Olson*: A Formalistic Perspective on Why the Court Was Wrong." *American University Law Review* 38 (Winter 1989): 313–58.

Lijphart, Arend. Introduction to *Parliamentary versus Presidential Government*, edited by Arend Lijphart, 1–27. Oxford: Oxford University Press, 1992.

———. *Patterns of Democracy: Government Forms and Performance in Thirty-Six Countries*. New Haven: Yale University Press, 1999.

———. "Presidentialism and Majoritarian Democracy: Theoretical Observations." In Linz and Valenzuela, *The Failure of Presidential Democracy*, 91–105.

———. *Thinking about Democracy: Power Sharing and Majority Rule in Theory and Practice*. London: Routledge, 2008.

Lijphart, Arend, Ronald Rogowski, and R. Kent Weaver. "Separation of Powers and Cleavage Management." In *Do Institutions Matter? Government Capabilities in the United States and Abroad*, edited by R. Kent Weaver and Bert A. Rockman (Washington, DC: Brookings Institution, 1993).

Linder, Wolf. *Swiss Democracy: Possible Solutions to Conflict in Multicultural Societies*. 3rd ed. Houndmills, UK: Palgrave Macmillan, 2010.

Linz, Juan J. "The Perils of Presidentialism." *Journal of Democracy* 1 (Winter 1990): 51–69.

———. "Presidential or Parliamentary Democracy: Does It Make a Difference?" In Linz and Valenzuela, *The Failure of Presidential Democracy*, 3–87.

Linz, Juan J., and Arturo Valenzuela, eds. *The Failure of Presidential Democracy*. Baltimore: Johns Hopkins University Press, 1994.

Lobel, Jules. "Conflicts between the Commander in Chief and Congress: Concurrent Power over the Conduct of War." *Ohio State Law Journal* 69, no. 3 (2008): 391–467.

Lofgren, Charles A. "*United States v. Curtiss-Wright Export Corporation*: A Historical Reassessment." *Yale Law Journal* 83 (November 1973): 1–32.

Madison, James. *The Debates in the Federal Convention of 1787 Which Framed the Constitution of the United States of America*. Edited by Gaillard Hunt and James Brown Scott. Amherst, NY: Prometheus Books, 1987.

Mainwaring, Scott. "Presidentialism, Multipartism, and Democracy: The Difficult Combination." *Comparative Political Studies* 26 (July 1993): 198–228.

Mainwaring, Scott, and Timothy R. Scully. "Democratic Governance in Latin America: Eleven Lessons from Recent Experience." In *Democratic Governance in Latin America*, edited by Scott Mainwaring and Timothy R. Scully, 365–97. Stanford: Stanford University Press, 2010.

Mann, Thomas E., and Norman J. Ornstein. *It's Even Worse than It Looks: How the American Constitutional System Collided with the New Politics of Extremism*. New York: Basic Books, 2012.

Marshall, William P. "Break Up the Presidency? Governors, State Attorneys General, and Lessons from the Divided Executive." *Yale Law Review* 115, no. 9 (2006): 2446–79.

———. "Eleven Reasons Why Presidential Power Inevitably Expands and Why It Matters." *Boston University Law Review* 88 (April 2008): 505–22.

Martin, Justin. *Nader: Crusader, Spoiler, Icon*. New York: Basic Books, 2002.

Mason, Jim. *No Holding Back: The 1980 John B. Anderson Presidential Campaign*. Lanham, MD: University Press of America, 2011

Matthews, Donald R. *U.S. Senators and Their World*. Chapel Hill: University of North Carolina Press, 1960.

Mayer, Kenneth. *With the Stroke of a Pen: Executive Orders and Presidential Power*. Princeton: Princeton University Press, 2001.

Mayhew, David R. *Divided We Govern: Party Control, Lawmaking and Investigations, 1946–2002*. 2nd ed. New Haven: Yale University Press, 2005.

McCarty, Nolan M., Keith T. Poole, and Howard Rosenthal. *Polarized America: The Dance of Ideology and Unequal Riches*. Cambridge: MIT Press, 2006.

McCauley, Clark. "The Nature of Social Influence in Groupthink: Compliance and Internalization." *Journal of Personality and Social Psychology* 57 (August 1989): 250–60.

McCormick, Richard P. *The Second American Party System: Party Formation in the Jacksonian Era*. Chapel Hill: University of North Carolina Press, 1966.

McCullough, David G. *John Adams*. New York: Simon and Schuster, 2001.

McDowell, Gary L. "Bork Was the Beginning: Constitutional Moralism and the

Politics of Federal Judicial Selection." *University of Richmond Law Review* 39 (March 2005): 809–18.

McRae, Kenneth D. *Conflict and Compromise in Multilingual Societies: Switzerland.* Waterloo, ON: Wilfrid Laurier University Press, 1983.

Meindl, James R., Sanford B. Ehrlich, and Janet M. Dukerich. "The Romance of Leadership." *Administrative Science Quarterly* 30 (March 1985): 78–102.

Mello, Michael. *Against the Death Penalty: The Relentless Dissents of Justices Brennan and Marshall.* Boston: Northeastern University Press, 1996.

Mendell, David. *Obama: From Promise to Power.* New York: Amistad, 2007.

Mill, John Stuart. "Considerations on Representative Government." In *On Liberty and Other Essays*, edited by John Gray, 203–467. New York: Oxford University Press, 2008.

Minow, Martha. "'Forming Underneath Everything That Grows': Toward a History of Family Law." *Wisconsin Law Review* 1985 (July–August): 819–98.

Moe, Terry M. "Presidents, Institutions, and Theory." In *Researching the Presidency: Vital Questions, New Approaches*, edited by George C. Edwards III, John H. Kessel, and Bert A. Rockman, 337–85. Pittsburgh: University of Pittsburgh Press, 1993.

Moe, Terry M., and William G. Howell. "The Presidential Power of Unilateral Action." *Journal of Law, Economics & Organization* 15 (April 1999): 132–79.

Monks, Robert A. G., and Nell Minow. *Corporate Governance.* 4th ed. West Sussex, UK: Wiley, 2008.

Morison, Samuel E., Henry S. Commager, and William E. Leuchtenburg. *The Growth of the American Republic.* 2 vols. 7th ed. New York: Oxford University Press, 1980.

Moss, Kenneth B. *Undeclared War and the Future of U.S. Foreign Policy.* Washington, DC: Woodrow Wilson International Center for Scholars, 2008.

Müller, Wolfgang C. "Models of Government and the Austrian Cabinet." In Laver and Shepsle, *Cabinet Ministers*, 15–34.

Müller-Rommel, Ferdinand. "The Role of German Ministers in Cabinet Decision Making." In Laver and Shepsle, *Cabinet Ministers*, 150–68.

Nelson, Dana D. *Bad for Democracy: How the Presidency Undermines the Power of the People.* Minneapolis: University of Minnesota Press, 2008.

Nelson, Ronald L. "The U.S. Supreme Court and the Institutional Role of Political Parties in the Political Process: What Tradition?" *Widener Law Journal* 15, no. 1 (2005): 85–108.

Nemeth, Charlan J., and Margaret Ormiston, "Creative Idea Generation: Harmony versus Stimulation," *European Journal of Social Psychology* 37 (May–June 2007): 524–35.

Nemeth, Charlan J., Bernard Personnaz, Marie Personnaz, and Jack A. Goncalo. "The Liberating Role of Conflict in Group Creativity: A Study in Two Countries." *European Journal of Social Psychology* 34 (July–August 2004): 365–74.

Neustadt, Richard E. *Presidential Power and the Modern Presidents: The Politics of Leadership from Roosevelt to Reagan.* New York: Free Press, 1990.

Novack, Dennis H., Robin Plumer, Raymond L. Smith, Herbert Ochitill, Gary R. Morrow, and John M. Bennett. "Changes in Physicians' Attitudes toward Telling the Cancer Patient." *Journal of American Medical Association* 241 (March 2, 1979): 897–900.

Nowak, Martin, and Karl Sigmund. "A Strategy of Win-Stay, Lose-Shift That Outperforms Tit-for-Tat in the Prisoner's Dilemma Game." *Nature* 364 (July 1, 1993): 56–58.

Nzelibe, Jide O., and Matthew C. Stephenson. "Complementary Constraints: Separation of Powers, Rational Voting and Constitutional Design." *Harvard Law Review* 123 (January 2010): 617–53.

Oberlander, Jonathan. *The Political Life of Medicare*. Chicago: University of Chicago Press, 2003.

Oken, Donald. "What to Tell Cancer Patients: A Study of Medical Attitudes." *Journal of the American Medical Association* 175 (April 1, 1961): 1120–28.

Olson, Theodore B. "The Impetuous Vortex: Congressional Erosion of Presidential Authority." In *The Fettered Presidency: Legal Constraints on the Executive Branch*, edited by L. Gordon Crovitz and Jeremy A. Rabkin, 225–44. Washington, DC: American Enterprise Institute, 1989.

O'Malley, Michael. *The Wisdom of Bees: What the Hive Can Teach Business about Leadership, Efficiency, and Growth*. New York: Portfolio, 2010.

Orentlicher, David. "Conflicts of Interest and the Constitution." *Washington and Lee Law Review* 59 (Summer 2002): 713–66.

———. "The Influence of a Professional Organization on Physician Behavior." *Albany Law Review* 57 (Summer 1994): 583–605.

———. "Paying Physicians More to Do Less: Financial Incentives to Limit Care." *University of Richmond Law Review* 30 (January 1996): 155–97.

———. "Rationing Health Care: It's a Matter of the Health Care System's Structure." *Annals of Health Law* 19 (Summer 2010): 449–64.

Ortiz, Daniel R. "Duopoly versus Autonomy: How the Two-Party System Harms the Major Parties." *Columbia Law Review* 100 (April 2000): 753–74.

O'Toole, James, Jay Galbraith, and Edward E. Lawler III. "The Promise and Pitfalls of Shared Leadership: When Two (or More) Heads Are Better than One." In Pearce and Conger, *Shared Leadership*, 250–67.

Owens, John E. "Presidential Power and Congressional Acquiescence in the 'War' on Terrorism: A New Constitutional Equilibrium?" *Politics & Policy* 34 (June 2006): 258–303.

Page, Scott E. *The Difference: How the Power of Diversity Creates Better Groups, Firms, Schools, and Societies*. Princeton: Princeton University Press, 2007.

———. *Diversity and Complexity*. Princeton: Princeton University Press, 2011.

Palmer, Matthew S. R. "Collective Cabinet Decision Making in New Zealand." in Laver and Shepsle, *Cabinet Ministers*, 226–50.

Pearce, Craig L., and Jay A. Conger. "All Those Years Ago: The Historical Underpinnings of Shared Leadership." In Pearce and Conger, *Shared Leadership*, 1–18.

———, eds. *Shared Leadership: Reframing the Hows and Whys of Leadership*. Thousand Oaks, CA: Sage, 2003.

Percival, Robert V. "Presidential Management of the Administrative State: The Not-So-Unitary Executive." *Duke Law Journal* 51 (December 2001): 963–1013.

Perkins, Anne G. "Negotiations: Are Two Heads Better than One?" *Harvard Business Review* 71 (November–December 1993): 13–14.

Persily, Nathaniel. "Toward a Functional Defense of Political Party Autonomy." *New York University Law Review* 76 (June 2001): 750–824.

Pierce, Roy. "The Executive Divided against Itself: Cohabitation in France, 1986–1988." *Governance* 4 (July 1991): 270–94.

Pildes, Richard H. "Why the Center Does Not Hold: The Causes of Hyperpolarized Democracy in America." *California Law Review* 99 (April 2011): 273–333.

Pildes, Richard H., and Cass R. Sunstein. "Reinventing the Regulatory State." *University of Chicago Law Review* 62 (Winter 1995): 1–129.

Posner, Eric. "The Constitution of the Roman Republic: A Political Economy Perspective." University of Chicago, Public Law & Legal Theory Working Paper, October 31, 2010. http://papers.ssrn.com/sol3/papers.cfm?abstract_id=1701981 (accessed November 8, 2012).

Posner, Eric A., and Adrian Vermeule. *The Executive Unbound: After the Madisonian Republic.* New York: Oxford University Press, 2010.

———. "Interring the Nondelegation Doctrine." *University of Chicago Law Review* 69 (Fall 2002): 1721–62.

Post, Jerrold M. "Narcissism and the Charismatic Leader-Follower Relationship." *Political Psychology* 7 (December 1986): 675–88.

Poundstone, William. *Gaming the Vote: Why Elections Aren't Fair (and What We Can Do about It).* New York: Hill and Wang, 2008.

Prakash, Saikrishna B., and Michael D. Ramsey. "The Executive Power over Foreign Affairs." *Yale Law Journal* 111 (November 2001): 231–356.

Quattrone, George A., and Amos Tversky. "Contrasting Rational and Psychological Analyses of Political Choice." *American Political Science Review* 82 (September 1988): 719–36.

Raiffa, Howard, John Richardson, and David Metcalfe. *Negotiation Analysis: The Science and Art of Collaborative Decision Making.* Cambridge: Belknap Press of Harvard University Press, 2002.

Ramirez, Jorge A. "Iraq War: Anticipatory Self-Defense or Unlawful Unilateralism?" *California Western International Law Journal* 4 (Fall 2003): 1–28.

Ramsey, Michael D. *The Constitution's Text in Foreign Affairs.* Cambridge: Harvard University Press, 2007.

Rapoport, Ronald, and Walter J. Stone. *Three's a Crowd: The Dynamic of Third Parties, Ross Perot, and Republican Resurgence.* Ann Arbor: University of Michigan Press, 2005.

Rappaport, Michael B. "The Selective Nondelegation Doctrine and the Line Item Veto: A New Approach to the Nondelegation Doctrine and Its Implications for *Clinton v. City of New York.*" *Tulane Law Review* 76 (December 2001): 265–372.

Rhinow, René, and Annemarie Huber-Hotz. "The Future of the Political System." In *The New Switzerland: Problems and Policies,* edited by Rolf Kieser and Kurt R. Spillmann, 16–31. Palo Alto, CA: Society for the Promotion of Science and Scholarship, 1996.

Roberts, Jason M., and Steven S. Smith. "Procedural Contexts, Party Strategy, and Conditional Party Voting in the U.S. House of Representatives, 1971–2000." *American Journal of Political Science* 47 (April 2003): 305–17.

Robinson, Greg. *By Order of the President: FDR and the Internment of Japanese Americans.* Cambridge: Harvard University Press, 2001.

Rockenbach, Bettina, Abdolkarim Sadrieh, and Barbara Mathauschek. "Teams Take the Better Risks." *Journal of Economic Behavior and Organization* 63 (July 2007): 412–22.

Rosenberg, Gerald N. *The Hollow Hope: Can Courts Bring about Social Change?* 2nd ed. Chicago: University of Chicago Press, 2008.

Rosenblum, Nancy L. *On the Side of the Angels: An Appreciation of Parties and Partisanship.* Princeton: Princeton University Press, 2008.

Rosenstone, Steven J., Roy L. Behr, Edward H. Lazarus. *Third Parties in America: Citizen Response to Major Party Failure.* 2nd ed. Princeton: Princeton University Press, 1996.

Rozell, Mark J. *Executive Privilege: Presidential Power, Secrecy, and Accountability.* 2nd ed. Lawrence: University Press of Kansas, 2002.

———. "Executive Privilege Revived? Secrecy and Conflict during the Bush Presidency." *Duke Law Journal* 52 (November 2002): 403–21.

Rushefsky, Mark E. *Public Policy in the United States: At the Dawn of the Twenty-First Century.* 3rd ed. Armonk, NY: M. E. Sharpe, 2002.

Ryden, David K. *Representation in Crisis: The Constitution, Interest Groups, and Political Parties.* Albany: SUNY Press, 1996.

Samaha, Adam M. "Government Secrets, Constitutional Law, and Platforms for Judicial Intervention." *UCLA Law Review* 53 (April 2006): 909–76.

Samuels, David J. "Presidentialized Parties: The Separation of Powers and Party Organization and Behavior." *Comparative Political Studies* 35 (May 2002): 461–83.

Samuels, David J., and Matthew S. Shugart. *Presidents, Parties, and Prime Ministers: How the Separation of Powers Affects Party Organization and Behavior.* Cambridge: Cambridge University Press, 2010.

Sargentich, Thomas O. "The Limits of the Parliamentary Critique of the Separation of Powers." *William and Mary Law Review* 34 (Spring 1993): 679–739.

Sartori, Giovanni. "Neither Presidentialism nor Parliamentarism." In Linz and Valenzuela, *The Failure of Presidential Democracy*, 106–18.

Savage, Charlie. *Takeover: The Return of the Imperial Presidency and the Subversion of American Democracy.* Boston: Little, Brown, 2007.

Schattschneider, E. E. *The Struggle for Party Government.* College Park: University of Maryland Program in American Civilization, 1948. Reprinted in *The Party Battle* (New York: Arno, 1974).

Scheuerman, William E. *Liberal Democracy and the Social Acceleration of Time.* Baltimore: Johns Hopkins University Press, 2004.

———. *The Realist Case for Global Reform.* Cambridge, UK: Polity, 2011.

Schlesinger, Arthur M., Jr., ed. *History of U.S. Political Parties.* 5 vols. New York: Chelsea House, 1973.

———. *The Imperial Presidency.* Boston: Houghton Mifflin, 1973. Reprinted with a new epilogue, 1989.

Schoenbrod, David. *Power without Responsibility: How Congress Abuses the People through Delegation.* New Haven: Yale University Press, 1993.

Schuck, Peter H. "Rethinking Informed Consent." *Yale Law Journal* 103 (January 1994): 899–959.

Schwarz, Frederick A. O., and Aziz Z. Huq. *Unchecked and Unbalanced: Presidential Power in a Time of Terror.* New York: New Press, 2007.

Scott, Janny. *A Singular Woman: The Untold Story of Barack Obama's Mother.* New York: Riverhead Books, 2011.

Shafer, Byron E., and Richard Johnston. *End of Southern Exceptionalism: Class, Race, and Partisan Change in the Postwar South.* Cambridge: Harvard University Press, 2006.

Shane, Peter M. *Madison's Nightmare: How Executive Power Threatens American Democracy.* Chicago: University of Chicago Press, 2009.

Shane, Peter M., and Harold H. Bruff. *Separation of Powers Law: Cases and Materials.* Durham: Carolina Academic Press, 1996.

Shugart, Matthew Soberg, and John M. Carey. *Presidents and Assemblies: Constitutional Design and Electoral Dynamics.* Cambridge: Cambridge University Press, 1992.

Sigelman, Lee, Paul J. Wahlbeck, and Emmett H. Buell, Jr. "Vote Choice and the Preference for Divided Government: Lessons of 1992." *American Journal of Political Science* 41 (July 1997): 879–94.

Silverstein, Gordon. *Imbalance of Powers: Constitutional Interpretation and the Making of American Foreign Policy.* New York: Oxford University Press, 1997.

Sinclair, Barbara. *Party Wars: Polarization and the Politics of National Policy Making.* Norman: University of Oklahoma Press, 2006.

Sloane, Robert D. "The Scope of Executive Power in the Twenty-First Century: An Introduction." *Boston University Law Review* 88 (April 2008): 341–51.

Stewart, Richard B. "The Reformation of American Administrative Law." *Harvard Law Review* 88 (May 1975): 1667–1813.

Stone, Geoffrey R., Louis M. Seidman, Cass R. Sunstein, Mark Tushnet, and Pamela S. Karlan. *Constitutional Law.* 6th ed. New York: Aspen, 2009.

Stone, Lawrence. *The Family, Sex and Marriage in England, 1500–1800.* New York: Harper & Row, 1977.

Straus, Susan G., Andrew M. Parker, James M. Bruce, and Jacob W. Dembosky. *The Group Matters: A Review of the Effects of Group Dynamics on Processes and Outcomes in Analytic Teams.* Santa Monica, CA: RAND, 2009. http://www.rand.org/pubs/working_papers/WR580 (accessed November 8, 2012).

Strauss, Peter L. "The Place of Agencies in Government: Separation of Powers and the Fourth Branch." *Columbia Law Review* 84 (April 1984): 573–669.

———. "Presidential Rulemaking." *Chicago-Kent Law Review* 72, no. 4 (1995): 965–86.

Strøm, Kaare. "Delegation and Accountability in Parliamentary Democracies." *European Journal of Political Research* 37 (May 2000): 261–89.

Sundquist, James L. *Constitutional Reform and Effective Government.* Rev. ed. Washington, DC: Brookings Institution, 1992.

———. *Dynamics of the Party System.* Washington, DC: Brookings Institution, 1983.

———. "Needed: A Political Theory for the New Era of Coalition Government in the United States." *Political Science Quarterly* 103 (Winter 1989): 613–35.

Sunstein, Cass. "Order without Law." *University of Chicago Law Review* 68 (Summer 2001): 757–73.

Surowiecki, James. *The Wisdom of Crowds: Why the Many Are Smarter than the Few and How Collective Wisdom Shapes Business, Economies, Societies, and Nations*. New York: Doubleday, 2004.

Tansill, Charles C., ed. *Documents Illustrative of the Formation of the Union of the American States*. Washington, DC: Government Printing Office, 1927.

Teitelbaum, Lee L. "Family History and Family Law." *Wisconsin Law Review* 1985 (September–October): 1135–81.

Thompson, Leigh, Erika Peterson, and Susan E. Brodt. "Team Negotiation: An Examination of Integrative and Distributive Bargaining." *Journal of Personality and Social Psychology* 70 (January 1996): 66–78.

Tribe, Laurence H. *American Constitutional Law*. Vol. 1. 3rd ed. New York: Foundation, 2000.

———. "The Unbearable Wrongness of *Bush v. Gore*." *Constitutional Commentary* 19 (Winter 2002): 571–607.

Verney, Douglas V. *The Analysis of Political Systems*. London: Routledge and Kegan Paul, 1959.

Vladeck, Stephen I. "The Passive-Aggressive Virtues." *Columbia Law Review Sidebar* 111 (October 20, 2001): 122–41.

Vo, Thuy-Nga T. "To Be or Not to Be Both CEO and Board Chair." *Brooklyn Law Review* 76 (Fall 2010): 65–129.

Wade, William, and Christopher Forsyth. *Administrative Law*. 10th ed. Oxford: Oxford University Press, 2009.

Waller, Christopher J. "A Bargaining Model of Partisan Appointments to the Central Bank." *Journal of Monetary Economics* 29 (June 1992): 411–28.

Washington, George. "Farewell Address." In *A Compilation of the Messages and Papers of the Presidents*, vol. 1, 205–16, edited by James D. Richardson. New York: Bureau of National Literature, 1897.

Weitzman, Lenore J. "Legal Regulation of Marriage: Tradition and Change." *California Law Review* 62 (July–September 1974): 1169–1277.

Willner, Ann Ruth. *The Spellbinders: Charismatic Political Leadership*. New Haven: Yale University Press, 1984.

Wills, Garry. *Bomb Power: The Modern Presidency and the National Security State*. New York: Penguin, 2010.

Wilson, James Q., and John J. DiIulio. *American Government: Institutions and Policies*. 11th ed. Boston: Houghton Mifflin, 2008.

Wilson, Woodrow. "Constitutional Government in the United States." In *The Papers of Woodrow Wilson: Volume 18, 1908–1909*, edited by Arthur S. Link, David W. Hirst, John E. Little, John M. Mulder, Sylvia Elvin Fontijn, and M. Halsey Thomas, 69–216. Princeton: Princeton University Press, 1974.

———. *The New Freedom: A Call for the Emancipation of the Generous Energies of a People*. Englewood Cliffs, NJ: Prentice-Hall, 1961.

Wing, Kenneth. "The Community Service Obligation of Hill-Burton Health Facilities." *Boston College Law Review* 23 (May 1982): 577–90.

Wood, B. Dan. *The Myth of Presidential Representation*. Cambridge: Cambridge University Press, 2009.

Wood, Gordon S. *The American Revolution: A History*. New York: Modern Library, 2002.

———. *The Creation of the American Republic, 1776–1787*. Chapel Hill: University of North Carolina Press, 1969.

———. *Representation in the American Revolution*. Rev. ed. Charlottesville: University of Virginia Press, 2008.

Woodward, C. Vann. *Tom Watson: Agrarian Rebel*. New York: Oxford University Press, 1963.

Yoo, John C. "The Continuation of Politics by Other Means: The Original Understanding of War Powers." *California Law Review* 84 (March 1996): 167–305.

———. "Kosovo, War Powers, and the Multilateral Failure." *University of Pennsylvania Law Review* 148 (May 2000): 1673–1731.

Zeng, Ming, and Xiao-Ping Chen. "Achieving Cooperation in Multiparty Alliances: A Social Dilemma Approach to Partnership Management." *Academy of Management Review* 28 (October 2003): 587–605.

Index

About the Author

David Orentlicher is Samuel R. Rosen Professor at the Indiana University Robert H. McKinney School of Law. A scholar of constitutional law and a former state representative, Orentlicher also has taught at Princeton University and the University of Chicago Law School. He earned degrees in law and medicine at Harvard and specializes as well in health care law and ethics.